THE WOMAN QUESTION

THE WOMAN QUESTION
Society and Literature in Britain and America, 1837–1883

Volume 2: Social Issues

Elizabeth K. Helsinger
Robin Lauterbach Sheets
William Veeder

THE UNIVERSITY OF CHICAGO PRESS
Chicago & London

The University of Chicago Press, Chicago 60637
The University of Chicago Press, Ltd., London

University of Chicago Press edition 1989
Printed in the United States of America
98 97 96 95 94 93 92 91 90 89   5 4 3 2 1

Library of Congress Cataloging in Publication Data

Helsinger, Elizabeth K., 1943–
  The woman question.

  Originally published: New York : Garland, 1983.
  Bibliography: p.
  Includes index.
  Contents: v. 1. Defining voices—v. 2. Social issues
—v. 3. Literary issues.
    1. Women—England—History—19th century.   2. Women—
United States—History—19th century.   3. Women in lit-
erature.   4. Feminism—England—History—19th century.
5. Feminism—United States—History—19th century.
I. Sheets, Robin Ann.   II. Veeder, William R.   III. Title.
HQ1599.E5H44   1989   305.4'0942   88-27796
ISBN 0-226-32666-7 (pbk.; v. 1)
        0-226-32667-5 (pbk.; v. 2)
        0-226-32668-3 (pbk.; v. 3)

⊗ The paper in this publication meets the minimum requirements
of the American National Standard for Information Sciences—
Permanence of Paper for Printed Library Materials,
ANSI Z39.48-1984.

Acknowledgments

In the eight years since this project was conceived we have accumulated many debts. In particular we would like to thank Nina Auerbach, Edy Cobey, Donald W. Dayton, Michael P. Ditchkofsky, T.J. Edelstein, Clarissa Erwin, Mary Anne Ferguson, Robert Ferguson, Dan Gottlieb, John S. and Robin Haller, Sally Hoffheimer, Randolph Woods Ivy, Robin Jacoby, Elizabeth Janeway, U.C. Knoepflmacher, Margaret Lourie, Ann Matthews, Katharine Rogers, Sue Sayne, Joanne Schlichter, Kitty Von Pabst, George Worth, John Wright, Bonnie Zimmerman, the Humanities Division of the University of Chicago, the Taft Foundation, and the University of Cincinnati Research Council.

We are grateful to the following for permission to reproduce works in their collections: Forbes Magazine Collection (illustration 1, Volume I; illustration 2, Volume II); The Tate Gallery, London (illustration 5, Volume III); The Metropolitan Museum of Art, Rogers Fund, 1908 (illustration 7, Volume III). For permission to reprint material from previously published works we wish to thank: Harvard University Press and Manchester University Press for excerpts from The Letters of Elizabeth Gaskell, edited by J.A.V. Chapple and Arthur Pollard; University of California Press for a passage quoted in Christina Rossetti, by Lona M. Packer; Yale University Library and Yale University Press for a Barbara Bodichon letter included in The George Eliot Letters, edited by Gordon Haight. We have made every effort to identify the owners of copyrighted material; we would appreciate having any oversights called to our attention.

Finally, to our spouses, Howard and Jim and Mary, to the three children who have grown up with this project, Aaron and

Sarah and Maisie, and to the three children who were born while it was underway, the two Alex's and Willy, we owe thanks for their respective patience or joyful obliviousness to our long and often perplexed encounter with the Victorian Woman Question.

Contents

Illustrations

Introduction

Discoveries about Victorian women have within the last decade raised serious doubts about our modern understanding of the nineteenth century. What really were the culture's attitudes toward men and women? The question is much less easy to answer now than it once seemed to be. Close study of public opinion between 1837 and 1883 suggests that the traditional model of "a" Victorian attitude—patriarchal domination, expressed publicly as "woman worship"—is inadequate. The predominant form of Victorian writing about women is not pronouncement but debate. Moreover, the arguments in this debate were both more complex and more fluid than the model of a single dominant cultural myth would indicate. For Victorians of "the articulate classes,"[1] the Woman Question, as they themselves called it, really was a question.

Almost any public statement bearing on the Woman Question —whether an essay, a review, a novel, a poem, a lecture, a cartoon, or a painting—was likely to generate a chain of responses, and to be read as a response to prior statements in an ongoing public discussion. To view any of these statements out of context, which as modern readers we often do when we study a novel or a painting, may properly emphasize the integrity of imaginative creation but can only distort our perception of Victorian thinking about women. Charlotte Brontë, Elizabeth Cady Stanton, and John Stuart Mill were not isolated dissenters from a chorus praising one womanly ideal. The controversies in which Brontë, Stanton, and Mill participated form the context for prescriptive writers like Sarah Ellis and Anthony Comstock. Until we understand how these voices of protest and prescription relate to the larger contemporary discussion, the old concept of a single public Victorian attitude toward women will remain largely intact.

For the present study, we have reconstructed the debate which surrounds prescriptive pronouncements, protests, and imaginative literature about women. Though many of the voices are no longer familiar, most were regular or momentarily prominent contributors to the public discourse of their time. Some are close to the centers of a literate, governing, and opinion-shaping class; others are more eccentric. All, however, were responding to one another in public forums—in books and pamphlets, from pulpits and lecterns, and above all, through the periodicals. For the most part, these exchanges did not take place on a high theoretical plane; they were precipitated by particular political, economic, scientific, religious, or cultural events, and they focused on specific and limited problems. Should married women be granted property rights? What can be done about the high infant mortality rate among mothers working in the mills? What do physiological studies of evolutionary man indicate about women's mental capacities? Does the popularity of sensation novels reveal suppressed anti-social impulses among female readers? Nearly every contemporary topic provoked controversy over women, but the diversity of opinions and issues should not obscure the crucial point: for literate Anglo-American Victorians, woman's nature and place were called into question.

To convey the special qualities of the Victorian debate we have departed in several ways from both the normal format (the anthology or collection of documents) and the prevailing approaches of recent work on the Woman Question. We wish to preserve the polemical immediacy of public controversy by letting the Victorians speak for themselves in the give-and-take of the original debate. At the same time, however, particular voices and controversies need to be placed within their social and cultural context. Our book is thus a critical history of controversies presented directly through Victorian speakers. We have varied the proportions of text and analysis from chapter to chapter. Where the intrinsic interest of the texts is great, especially if they are unfamiliar today, we have quoted generously; in other cases we have excerpted more sparingly and expanded our historical and critical commentary. To include some forgotten writers important in their own day we have omitted sustained analysis of others, like Mary Wollstonecraft, whose work is better known and more accessible today.

We have also departed from prevailing practice by considering British and American discussions together as parts of a single debate. On some issues, of course, the discussions are simply parallel, while others diverge to follow national or local concerns. Nonetheless, Victorian Britain and America formed a single community of letters, within which national variations in the treatment of women provided yet another subject for common discussion. Our writers constantly refer to, quote, and directly respond to statements of conditions from across the Atlantic. Though we have not attempted a comprehensive comparison of British and American views, we have included numerous instances of cross-Atlantic exchanges, and noted parallels and divergences of opinion in particular controversies. Where it became necessary to choose between British and American versions of a debate, we have given the one less familiar today, usually the British—except where the American controversy was notably more heated (as in the case of most religious issues). Our Anglo-American perspective affirms for the Woman Question as a whole what Mary Macarthur observed of the womens' trade union leagues: that the British movement was both the grandmother and the granddaughter of the American.[2]

Finally, our treatment of the Woman Question departs from much recent practice by focusing on middle-class opinions and including male as well as female voices. These choices reflect the nature of the public debate: it was a largely middle-class discussion in which both men and women participated. We have not set out to uncover new examples of the lost views of working class or female sub-cultures. We have, however, made extensive use of the work of feminist critics and social historians who have explored these hidden strains of behavior and opinion. As far as possible, we have tried to indicate the distance between those perceptions of women which shaped the public debate, and evidence which suggests a different Victorian reality. Our aim is to study the nature of that distance and, wherever possible, to examine the reasons for it: personal, social, and cultural. However, this should not suggest that public perception was always at odds with private practice and belief. Conflicting opinions and competing mythologies did find expression within the public debate. Moreover, those who defended "woman's place" and those who sympathized with women's rights were often far more closely linked than we had suspected.

It is, indeed, often difficult to predict where the "conservative" and "dissenting" positions will lie in any particular controversy—or to predict just which assumptions about woman's nature conservatives or dissenters will employ in their arguments. Relatively few Victorians maintained rigidly consistent theoretical positions. Many of the most outspoken, like Elizabeth Cady Stanton, could appeal—with equal conviction and in the same speech—to conflicting cultural myths about women. And even those who were theoretically consistent might still disagree over practical applications: whether, for example, women should be doctors. Conversely, defenders of women doctors might make different assumptions about women's intellectual abilities, rights to professional training, or special feminine characteristics (like patience and solicitude) which fitted them for medicine. Such diversity of both argument and conclusion makes any strict definition of feminist or anti-feminist positions very difficult. We can speak more accurately not of positions but of a set of competing, though not mutually exclusive, myths or models for woman's place in society. Controversialists used these myths to argue for opposing solutions to contemporary problems.

Among such myths we have found four which are especially pervasive. First, the familiar Angel in the House—the wife and mother described in Sarah Ellis' conduct manuals, praised in Felicia Heman's poetry, and embodied in the Agnes Wickfield of Dickens' *David Copperfield*. Her nature is loving and self-sacrificing; her responsibilities, domestic and maternal. Although she is a delicate creature worshipped and protected by husbands and sons, she not only works hard at home but also provides continuity and moral strength in a rapidly changing society. Second, the model of complete equality—women as equal contracting partners with men, legally, sexually, and economically free agents in both domestic and professional matters. Though this model had some famous and articulate advocates—Mill, William Thompson, George Drysdale, Susan B. Anthony—it was so disconcertingly radical and so much at odds with the widespread interest in woman's "special" nature and duties that it seems to have played a smaller role in the public debate than two other competitors to the angelic ideal. One of these might be called the Angel out of the House. Although this model for woman's behavior accepted fundamental differences between men and women, it extended the wife's sphere beyond her home and family. The Angel out of the House did not challenge the leadership of men, but she did define her own distinctive tasks, ministering to the needs of the world at large through philanthropy or social service. The incarnation of this freed Angel, in the popular view, was Florence Nightingale. Finally, there is a radical version of the angelic ideal which combines a belief in woman's distinctive nature with claims for a leadership role in the world—a female saviour leading the way to a fuller humanity and ushering in a new era of community and love. This vision of woman's unique role, which might best be described as apocalyptic feminism, attracted both eccentrics like Eliza Farnham and, to some extent, even staunch conservatives like Sara Josepha Hale, editor of *Godey's Lady's Magazine*. For some, like Farnham, it amounted to an absolute claim to female superiority; for others, like Margaret Fuller, a temporary claim for woman's special role within an overall vision of human equality. Though this view of woman, like the egalitarian view, was held by a minority, it affected surprisingly large numbers of women, especially in America. In the last third of the century it helped fuel the campaigns to abolish contagious diseases acts, hold men to a single sexual standard, promote temperance, improve prisons, and reform corrupt municipal governments. The distinctions between the Angel in the House, the Angel out of the House, and the Female Saviour are often particularly difficult to draw. One or more of these three related but competing myths of woman underlie most of the arguments brought forward in the Woman Question.

These alternative views of woman have, of course, relatives and antecedents before 1837. The Victorian Woman Question is only one chapter in the history of that debate. Both the advocates of an angelic ideal and, particularly, the advocates of equality have important predecessors among late eighteenth and early nineteenth-century writers. Many of the particular issues debated by Victorians had also been discussed before. Yet Victorians themselves, beyond a rare reference to blue stockings or Mary Wollstonecraft, or to early female preachers and writers, did not often trace their views back to the immediate past. To some extent they were right: distinctive emphases, particular myths, even a common set of terms—"woman's mission," "woman's sphere," "woman's influence"—unite the varied controversies between the 1830s and the 1880s.

We have begun our history with six chapters which illustrate the particularly Victorian qualities of the debate. Volume I: *Defining Voices* is exemplary rather than historical; it focuses on representative texts, figures, and controversies for what they reveal about the general character of the Woman Question rather than for their historical connections with earlier and later phases of the debate. The second and third volumes of our study reconstruct and analyze the debate in society and literature as it evolved across the half century from Victoria's accession to the mid-1880s. Volume II: *Social Issues* traces the progress of controversy in law, science, work, and religion. Chapter 1 examines the major legal questions of custody, married women's property rights, divorce, and suffrage, contrasting the generally sympathetic response to protective legislation with the hostility provoked by attempts to establish woman's separate legal identity in marriage and the body politic. Chapter 2 follows changing arguments in three basic areas of scientific controversy: woman's sexual capacity, her intellectual capability, and her developmental potential. The debates over women's work, as presented in Chapter 3, address the central question of whether women ought ideally to work or to stay home; the immediate issues are women's factory work, the single woman problem, and prostitution. Chapter 4 analyzes the religious controversies generated by the Genesis stories of the creation and fall, the question of female ministry, and the larger issue of Christianity's effects upon women. Volume III: *Literary Issues* follows literary debates over the same period, dealing first with public discussion of the woman writer and second with the debate over a variety of literary heroines.

One last word. The authors of this history have sometimes found themselves in no more agreement than their Victorian subjects. On most matters our discussions have led to consensus, but we realize that our individual perceptions and myths—like those of the Victorians—run deep, and will be reflected in the selection of voices as well as in the commentary on them. The structure, the format, and the emphases on common themes and arguments are our joint decisions, but each chapter is the work of a single author. Some differences in attitude between them we have not attempted to resolve. Many of the questions debated in the nineteenth century are still very much alive. We can only offer our own differences as testimony to the continuing vitality of the debate.

Notes

[1]So named by G.M. Young, *Victorian England: Portrait of an Age* (London: Oxford Univ. Press, 1936), p. 6.

[2]At the 1919 Convention of the National Women's Trade Union League of America, quoted by Gladys Boone in *The Women's Trade Union League in Great Britain and the United States of America* (New York: Columbia Univ. Press, 1942), p. 20.

The Woman Question
SOCIAL ISSUES

MILL'S LOGIC; OR, FRANCHISE FOR FEMALES
'PRAY CLEAR THE WAY, THERE, FOR THESE-A-PERSONS.'
30.3.1867

1. Mill's Logic; or, Franchise for Females
Punch, 1867

1

LAW

The social myths about Victorian womanhood were inconsistent with legal reality.[1] Parents and clergymen taught that marriage was the purpose of life, but law regarded it as the end of a woman's autonomous existence. Although conduct manuals encouraged the wife to transform her home into a sacred shelter from the world's cares, courts allowed it to become a prison where she could be forcibly confined by her husband. Poets and painters celebrated the young mother's beauty, but judges could not give her custody of her children. While moralists praised woman's ennobling influence on others, the politicians who denied her a vote made certain that she had no power over legislation affecting her own life.

By mid-century, women such as Caroline Norton, Barbara Bodichon, Elizabeth Cady Stanton, and Caroline Dall were writing detailed appraisals of the common law upon which both English and American jurisprudence rested. "To understand the laws under which I must live," said Dall, "no recondite learning, no broad scholarship, no professional study, can be fitly required. It is a woman's judgment in matters that concern women that the world demands, before any radical change can be made."[2] Like Bodichon, the writers might have begun with the assumption that "the mere statement of what the law is might almost seem to

3

supply sufficient reason why it should be altered."[3] But analysis quickly gave way to argument and to organized political activity as the women encountered opposition from the government, the press, and the public.

Caroline Dall was one of the few critics to decry the legal condition of single women. In economic terms, a single woman, or *feme sole*, held many of the same rights as a man: she could acquire property, assume responsibilities for her debts, enter into a contract, make a will, sue and be sued. Yet Dall objected:

1. To the withholding of the elective franchise.
2. To the law's preference of males, and the issue of males, in the division of estates.
3. We object to the estimate of woman which the law sustains, which shuts her out from all public employment, for many branches of which she is better fitted than man.
4. We object to that estimate of woman's chastity, which makes its existence or nonexistence of importance only as it affects the comfort or income of man.

No single woman, having been seduced, has any remedy at common law; neither has her mother nor next friend. If her father can prove *service* rendered, he may sue for loss of service. . . . In the eye of this law, female chastity is only valuable for the work it can do. (46, 43–44)

However, until suffrage became a key issue in the mid-1860s, protest centered on laws affecting married women. According to English common law, a woman forfeited power over herself and her property when she entered wedlock. "The law immediately steps in," said Bodichon, "and she finds herself legislated for, and her condition of life suddenly and entirely changed."[4] The most famous definition of a married woman's legal status was provided in 1765 by the English jurist William Blackstone:

By marriage, the very being or legal existence of a woman is suspended, or at least incorporated or consolidated into that of the husband, under whose wing, protection, or cover she performs everything, and she is therefore called in our law a *feme covert*.[5]

American women also experienced the practical and psychological consequences of coverture because much of their legal system was based on English common law which was, according to Dall, "the basis of all that is objectionable in our legislation."[6] Behind the doctrine of coverture were tradition, the argument of expediency, and the theory of common conjugal interest that had already been attacked by William Thompson [see Volume I, Chapter 2]. Under coverture, the wife was not liable for her debts. Nor was she prosecuted for most crimes committed in her husband's presence: the law assumed that she acted under her husband's coercion. But if her responsibilities were limited, so were her rights. A married woman could not sign a lease, initiate a lawsuit, or make a will. The home may have been her sphere, but the husband had complete control of the family finances. Her personal property, her earnings, and even her children belonged entirely to her husband. If he mistreated her, separation and divorce were extremely difficult to obtain. Moreover, even when a husband abandoned his wife, he retained control of her property. As far as the law was concerned, the two were still one and that one was the husband.

Although the outrages accommodated under the law were serious enough in themselves, the effects were not limited to wives who suffered from actual abuse. According to historian J.W. Kaye, coverture exerted a subtle but pervasive influence on the aspirations and education of *all* women. Writing for the *North British Review* in 1855, Kaye says:

> The larger and more important section of the women of England must be legal nonentities. That the effect of this is to limit the aspirations, to paralyze the energies, and to demoralize the characters of women, is not to be denied. They are born and educated as it were, for total absorption. . . . We make women what they are—we reduce them to dependence, and then taunt them with being incapable of independent action. Partly by our system of education—partly by our wise laws—we reduce them to the lowest possible level, keep them there, and revile them for not mounting higher. . . .
>
> This theory of the non-existence of women pursues its victims from the school-room to the grave. Trained from the first to be dependent upon men, they pass through different stages of dependence, and at the last find that they cannot bequeath to another man the ring on their finger, which they may have worn from their earliest girlhood, or the Bible in which they first learnt to spell. To attain and preserve a condition of independence, it is necessary that they should abide in a state of singleness, which is, more or less, a state of reproach. Single women are legally capable of independent action, but they are seldom or never educated for it. It

cannot be said that they are educated for the proper discharge of the duties of wife and mother; but they are educated for the non-existence which that condition involves. And it is often the perception of this which drives women into matrimony without any assurance, sometimes scarcely even with a hope, of domestic happiness. What else are they to do? If they continue in their singleness, having been educated for non-existence, they are incapable of acting for themselves. They are fit, indeed, only to be absorbed.[7]

In contrast, journalist Margaret Oliphant insists that the wife's lack of a separate legal existence expresses "an infallible truth" about marriage. For the 1856 *Blackwood's*, she adopts a male persona to argue that "marrying is like dying—as distinct, as irrevocable, as complete."

We have small faith, for our own part, in what is called class legislation, and smallest faith of all in that species of class legislation which could make the man an intentional and voluntary oppressor of the woman. This idea, that the two portions of human kind are natural antagonists to each other, is, to our thinking, at the very outset, a monstrous and unnatural idea. . . . There is no man in existence so utterly separated from one-half of his fellow-creatures as to be able to legislate against them in the interests of his own sex. . . . It is possible that the poor may legislate against the rich, or the rich against the poor, but to make such an antagonism between men and women is against all reason and all nature. . . .

No law of human origin can reach every possible development of human temper and organisation; injured wives and unhappy husbands are accidents uncurable by law; and it would be almost as wise to legislate for the race, on the supposition that every member of it had a broken leg, as on the more injurious hypothesis that tryanny, oppression, and injustice, rankled within the heart of every home.

. . . It is a mere trick of words to say that the woman loses her existence, and is absorbed in her husband. Were it so in reality—and were it indeed true, "that the poor rivulet loseth her name, is carried and recarried with her new associate, beareth no sway, possesseth nothing"—then would the question of female inferiority be fairly proved and settled once for all. Mightly indeed must be the Titanic current of that soul which could receive one whole human being, full of thoughts, affections, and emotions, into its tide, and yet remain uncoloured and unchanged. There is no such monster of a man, and no such nonentity of a woman, in ordinary life. Which of us does not carry our wife's thoughts in our brain, and our wife's likings in our heart, with the most innocent unconsciousness that they are not our own original property? . . . The only true rule of Marriage remains unimpugnable; and if it is either a legal or a poetic fiction to call man and wife one person, then all sacredness, purity, and noble sentiment, departs from the bond between them.[8]

Oliphant was willing to overlook "those desperate exceptional cases which occur now and then to prove barbarism and injustice in every law," but other Victorians believed that a reformed legal system would encourage widespread social change; that it was the function of law to protect the injured party, no matter how "exceptional" the case; and that instances of abuse were more common than public records would indicate. Early reforms were based on the need to defend wives from their husbands' mistreatment. Although the campaign for protective legislation threatened the sentimental faith in male chivalry, women made important gains with laws that allowed the courts to acknowledge the mother's custody rights, to safeguard the earnings of some married women, and to grant separation on more favorable terms. Women's advocates encountered more opposition when they moved beyond these pleas for the court's protection and asked instead for a separate legal existence, first in marriage and then in the body politic. To own property or win the vote would represent a serious alteration in status. The beginning of legal existence, or the end of coverture, came with the extension of property rights to married women, the area in which British and American women achieved their greatest success. However, at the end of the century, two matters remained unresolved: women did not have equal access to absolute divorce and they were specifically excluded from the franchise. Freedom still eluded them—in the most private area of their lives *and* in the most political.

The arguments for changing the legal status of women were similar in both countries, but the history of that change is much more complicated in America because each state made its own provisions for marriage, divorce, child custody, and property rights. Reform generally came earlier in America, but sometimes quite haltingly: a state might liberalize its property laws, but wait decades to remove divorce restrictions. Because the legal treatment of American women varied enormously from region to region and was within individual states often inconsistent, this chapter concentrates on England. With issues debated at the national level and laws made by one legislative body, the controversy there can be seen with greater clarity. The major legal questions are presented here in the order they captured public attention: custody, married women's property rights, divorce, and suffrage.

I

When a prominent Massachusetts woman who had been banished from her home by an unfaithful and abusive husband asked that her daughter be allowed to join her in a new residence, her own brother warned that such efforts were useless. "The child belongs by law to the father," he said, "and it is your place to submit." The woman defied the law, ran away with her daughter, and turned to Susan B. Anthony for assistance. A year later when the father seized the child on her way home from school, the mother had no remedy in court. In 1861, common law still gave the father complete control over the children.[9]

In England, if the father failed to support the children or harmed them, the Court of Chancery did have the power to intervene to protect the children, but in practice the court did not interfere unless the children had property. The mother's wishes were never considered, and the court did not have the right to grant her access to the children. After the father's death, the mother might still be denied her children: in his will the father could designate anyone he chose as their guardian, even his mistress. American courts moved more quickly to protect the children, but gave little recognition to the mother's rights. At the end of the century, only nine states granted equal guardianship; in all the others, the father had sole custody and control of the persons, education, earnings, and estates of minor children. Custody rights came gradually in America as various states reworked their divorce laws, but in England one woman's assault on the law created a national sensation and provided the impetus for the Infants and Child Custody Bill of 1839.

Popular poet, novelist, and one of London's most acclaimed beauties, Caroline Norton turned to the law in desperation after her husband sent their three sons to an unknown destination and refused to allow her to see them.[10] By leaving his home and returning to her family, Caroline escaped injury, but she had no way of seeing her children—unless she could change the law.

Caroline Norton accepted women's inferiority, but she did not countenance their oppression. Seeking protection rather than equality, she presented her personal dilemma to Parliament and the English public.

In an 1836 pamphlet, Caroline Norton asked that the custody of children under the age of seven be given to the mother and that the custody of older children be determined by the court. Early in 1837 she sent privately printed copies of the essay to a few acquaintances, including Thomas Talfourd. As a barrister, Talfourd regretted that he had been obligated to uphold the custody laws; as a recently elected member of Parliament, he was ready to reform them by introducing a bill based on the provisions of Norton's pamphlet. Opposing the bill in the House of Commons, Sir Edward Sugden argued that "a wise legislature . . . would seek to bind married persons by a common interest. . . . The great tie which prevents the separation of married persons is their common children. . . . Now this Bill, by providing the wife with the means of always commanding access to her children, removed many of the obstacles which stood at present in the way of separation." In the House of Lords, Lord Brougham compared the existing custody law with other discriminatory laws and concluded that the law was "not more oppressive to the wife in this than in other cases."[11]

Outside Parliament, John Kemble denounced the proposed legislation as an unprecedented attempt "to overthrow the foundation of society." Although Kemble's attack—published first in *British and Foreign Quarterly Review* and then as a booklet distributed to the peers—revealed a general hostility toward women, much of his anger was directed against Caroline Norton herself. This "she-devil" and "she-beast" was, Kemble believed, the author of a recent article on women's rights, Talfourd's mistress, and the originator of his bill. Kemble charged that the Infants and Child Custody Bill would destroy marriage, corrupt the state, and undermine Christianity.

> If this last and strongest and only effectual prevention still existing against separation, (viz. the certain assurance in the mind of every wife, that, if she will desert her husband's house, the sphere of her duties, and, be it ever remembered, the only proper home of his children, she does ipso facto lose the right of access to them,)—if this prevention be once taken away, it is as certain as anything in the whole world of direct cause and effect, that

separations will increase! You cannot diminish the checks to licentiousness without increasing the chances of their occurrence! You cannot take away the least of the safeguards of domestic virtue without an injury to public morality. What madness then and atrocious wickedness it would be to take away, not merely the least, not merely one out of a number, but the greatest, the last, the only remaining bar against the outbreak of ever-tempting lusts, and then hope that they will afterwards restrain themselves on account of your impotent good wishes, and unheeded sermons and vain regrets! As well might you expect, when you have un-barred the cages of so many wild beasts, that they will remain quietly in them at the wish of their keepers! . . .

What is manifest, as to the operation of the Bill, is this; that it directly violates the great fundamental law of society, the law of paternity; it directly annuls the father's right to have *sole* command in his own house, and over his own legitimate children, whilst the same responsibility for their conduct is thrown on him as ever; and this we affirm to be grossly unjust, and therefore grossly im-moral. . . .

A man when he marries is sure only of one blessing, and that is, that however his wife may ultimately prove herself, at all events, if he has children by her, he will have the satisfaction, through the power secured to him at present by the law, of bringing them up as sons worthy of himself, as virtuous moral beings. Else why should a man take the trouble to bind himself by an indissoluble bond, unless it were in this hope and with this assurance? He hopes and trusts that at some future day, when he is growing old and about to depart, his sons will repay all his care and kindness by their love and honour, and transmit his name unsullied to posterity. But if you take away the paternal right, what advantage has a legitimate father over the illegitimate?

. . . This sole and absolute power over the children, to the exclusion of every one else, is a fundamental right vested in the man, as man and father, from the beginning. The paternal power is the oldest and most sacred right belonging to a man—the right that ought to be most religiously guarded. Such being the doctrine deducible from the authority of the Christian Scriptures, Serjeant Talfourd's Custody of Infants' Bill, that proposes to destroy this right, is therefore directly antichristian.[12]

When the bill was discussed again in 1839, Caroline Norton urged its passage in a pamphlet which she sent to all members of Parliament. *A Plain Letter to the Lord Chancellor on the Infant Custody Bill* appeared under a male pseudonym because she feared that "if they knew it was a woman's writing it would have less weight." Posing as "Pearce Stevenson, Esquire,"Norton responds to Sugden, Brougham, and Kemble.

That check cannot be said to be *removed* which never existed. . . . Till the painful disclosures consequent on the discussion of this Bill, were made; it never was publicly known or understood that the father had a right to deprive his wife of her infant children at any moment, and for any cause; it never was publicly known or understood, that infidelity and brutality on the part of the husband, and blamelessness on the part of the wife, made no difference in the decisions of courts of justice: it never was publicly known or understood, that in this free country, a man could take his innocent legitimate child from his wife, and give it to the woman with whom he was living, and that the English law, the law which boasts "a remedy for every wrong,"—the law of the country which piques itself on the protection of the oppressed—gave that mother no redress, but left her child in the custody of its father's mistress. . . .

A woman may bear cheerfully the poverty which anomalies in the laws of property may entail upon her; and she may struggle patiently through such an unjust ordeal of shame as Lord Brougham described; but against the inflicted and unmerited loss of her children she *cannot* bear up; that she has not deserved *that* blow, only adds to its bitterness: it is the master feeling of her life; the strong root of all the affections of her heart; and, in spite of the enumeration of every real or fancied grievance incidental to her position, she will still hold *that* injustice to stand foremost, distinct, and paramount above them all. . . .

His [Kemble's] great argument is the inferiority of woman. . . . To him the word *woman* signifies a bad woman; he cannot conceive any other case. . . . Where was the *mother* of this man?—in her grave, or on this earth, when he undertook to speak of the whole female sex, as of animals who required caging and chaining? —of English wives and mothers as if they all desired to forsake their homes—as if they all hated and rebelled against their husbands—as if they only waited for some revolting watch-word of liberty to give loose to every wild and profligate feeling that stains our commingled nature? Did this author never see that very usual and customary sight, a modest and affectionate wife? Did he never see a woman watching the cradle of her sick child? . . .

We are apt to treat with contempt and surprise the customs of other nations in the matter of marriage and laws for women; we consider it an infringement of natural rights, that a young girl should be given away by her parents or superiors to a man she never saw, without liberty of choice or refusal; we protest against the doctrines of the Turks, that women have no souls and are but the toys of passion. Yet what a ludicrous contradiction our own law implies, when it gives the young girl a power of choice, and considers the *mother* a cypher. The condition of mother is far more important than that of a young unmarried girl. She is under God responsible for the souls and bodies of the new generation confided to her care; and the woman who is mother to the children of a profligate and tyrannical husband, is bound by her *duty*, even if she were not moved by the strong instinct of her own heart, to struggle against the seizure of her infants. It is not *her* happiness alone that is involved, *theirs* is also at stake; their comfort, their well-being, perhaps the tenor of their whole future lives, depend on their not being legally permitted to be made the innocent victims of their father's caprice. To refuse the protection which would enable a blameless wife to continue her care of infants in such a case, merely on the plea that the law will not interfere with the husband, what is it but to deny the position of the woman as a rational and accountable creature? What is it but to adopt in a degree the Turkish creed, and consider her merely as the toy of an hour? What is it but to say, "In the bloom of your beauty you were given to belong to this man; his satiated fancy has wandered from you to another; there is no help for it; you are nothing of yourself; the children borne by you while his attachment lasted, are of course his; the law does not acknowledge your separate claim or share in them; they neither belong to you, nor you to them."[13]

The plea reached a sympathetic audience. The *Law Review* commended "Mr. Stevenson" for his "able and eloquent pamphlet" and *Fraser's* called it a "very valuable document" which should be "in the hands of all members of parliament, and of every woman."[14] Both reviewers found Kemble's attack reprehensible and hastened to defend Caroline Norton as a woman who had been doubly wronged, first by a mean and irresponsible husband, then by a malicious press. The responses to her case reveal the contradictory attitudes toward Victorian women: for Kemble's *British and Foreign Quarterly* Caroline Norton was an adulterous "she-beast"; in *Fraser's* she was an English mother who had been "injured, oppressed, and bereaved." By asking for her children, Caroline Norton challenged patriarchal prerogatives, but her emphasis on maternal love was perfectly consistent with the new ideology articulated by Sarah Lewis and others [see Volume I, Chapter 1].

In its final version, the Infants and Child Custody Bill of 1839 granted much less than Norton and Talfourd had asked. It provided only that women against whom adultery had not been proved might *ask* the court to have custody of children under seven years of age and to have access to older children at stated intervals; in practice, judges continued to favor the fathers. The Custody Act of 1873 extended the mother's rights somewhat further: first, by empowering the court to give her custody of children up to the age of sixteen; second, by removing the restrictions which barred women convicted of adultery from seeking custody. In 1886 the Custody of Infants Act gave the mother guardianship in the event of the father's death, but as long as the father lived, he retained the authority to decide upon the religion, education, and upbringing of the children. Equal rights and responsibilities for both parents were not established until the Guardianship of Infants Act in 1925.

The Infants and Child Custody Bill of 1839 provided no relief for Norton herself because George took the children out of the country to escape the court's jurisdiction. In 1842, when he realized that his own carelessness had caused the death of their youngest son, George relented and allowed the other two boys to rejoin their mother. Although Caroline Norton's reconciliation with her children did not result from the bill she helped to write, Harriet Martineau perceived its larger historical significance: the Infants and Child Custody Bill of 1839 was "the first blow struck at the oppression of English legislation in relation to women."[15]

II

At mid-century, attention centered on married women's property rights. Although reform began earlier in America, the 1850s were crucial in the much-studied state of New York and in England.[16] Elizabeth Cady Stanton addressed the New York Legislature in 1854 and 1860, while in England Caroline Norton and Barbara Bodichon influenced the parliamentary debates of 1857. Unlike suffrage and divorce, the campaign for property rights did not arouse strong opposition among women themselves. While women gave strong support to the cause, legislative resistance was intense. The struggle to extend property rights lasted about a quarter of a century: from 1836 to 1860 in New York, and from 1856 to 1882 in England.

Under English common law, the marriage contract transferred to the husband all the wife's personal property, including that which she might subsequently acquire by inheritance or by her own exertions, and gave him administration of her landed estates. The inability to own property subjected the married woman to other legal disabilities and left her financially dependent on her husband's good will. Although the husband was expected to maintain and support his wife, his obligation was difficult to enforce. Parents in the middle and upper classes recognized the precariousness of the woman's position. In England families traditionally settled separate property on their daughters, and in New York the passage of the Married Women's Property Act of 1848 had assured the prosperous Dutch landowners that their female children could retain title to their inherited property. The rich could escape the injustices of the common law, while the poor had neither the money to provide a settlement nor the political influence to change the law.

Barbara Bodichon explained the inequities of the property laws in an 1854 pamphlet that had "an immediate and wide sale."[17] *A Brief Summary, in Plain Language, of the Most Important Laws concerning Women* led to discussion within the Law Amendment Society, an organized campaign among feminists, public meetings, and an 1856 parliamentary petition signed by more than twenty-six thousand women, including Elizabeth Barrett Browning, Jane Carlyle, Eliza Fox, Elizabeth Gaskell, Anna Jameson, Geraldine Jewsbury, Harriet Martineau, and Bessie Rayner Parkes. They declared:

> That in rendering the husband responsible for the entire maintenance of his family, the law expresses the necessity of an age, when the man was the only money-getting agent; but that, since the custom of the country has greatly changed in this respect the position of the female sex, the law of maintenance no longer meets the whole case. That since modern civilisation, in definitely extending the sphere of occupation for women, has in some measure broken down their pecuniary dependence upon men, it is time that legal protection be thrown over the produce of their labour, and that in entering the state of marriage, they no longer pass from freedom into the condition of a slave, all whose earnings belong to his master and not to himself.[18]

As a result of Bodichon's work, in 1857 Sir Thomas Perry introduced a bill that would give married women the right to hold real and personal property, to sign contracts, and to make wills. Such a proposal threatened to undermine the doctrine of

coverture and to redistribute much of England's wealth. As one
M.P. said, the bill would "involve a material change in the social
and political institutions of a nation," and would place women
"in a 'strong-minded and independent position.'"[19]

At the same time, Caroline Norton was also asking for
improved property rights. For Bodichon, whose father had provided her with an independent income, reform represented a
remedy for injustice and a logical accommodation to the economic conditions of modern life; for Norton it was a matter of
personal survival. Caroline Norton left her husband after he
failed in his scandalous attempt to divorce her in 1836, but she
could not force him to pay the allowance owed her; nor could she
gain control of her property and earnings. *A Letter to the Queen*,
which she published under her own name in 1855, describes her
plight and asks for the court's assistance.

> The natural position of woman is inferiority to man. Amen!
> That is a thing of God's appointing, not of man's devising. I believe it
> sincerely, as a part of my religion: and I accept it as a matter proved
> to my reason. I never pretended to the wild and ridiculous doctrine
> of equality. I will even hold that (as one coming under the general
> rule that the wife must be inferior to the husband), *I* occupy that
> position. *Uxor fulget radiis Mariti*; I am Mr. Norton's inferior; I am the
> clouded moon of that sun. Put me then—(my ambition extends no
> further)—in the same position as all his other inferiors! In that of
> his housekeeper, whom he could not libel with impunity, and
> without possible defence; of an apprentice whom he could not
> maltreat lawlessly, even if the boy "condoned" original ill-usage; of
> a scullion, whose wages he could not refuse on the plea that she is
> legally "non-existent"; of the day-labourer, with whom he would
> not argue that his signature to a contract is "worthless." Put me
> under *some* law of protection; and do not leave me to the mercy of
> one who has never shewn me mercy. . . .
>
> From the date of my mother's death, [Mr. Norton] has with-
> held entirely, and with perfect impunity, my income as his wife. I
> do not receive, and have not received for the last three years, a
> single farthing from him. He retains, and always has retained,
> property that was left in my home—gifts made to me by my own
> family on my marriage, and to my mother by your Majesty's aunt,
> H.R.H. the Duchess of York. . . . He receives from my trustees
> the interest of the portion bequeathed me by my father, who died
> in the public service. . . . If my father lived, it is to be presumed
> there is no man he would see with greater abhorrence than Mr.
> Norton. . . .

I have also (as Mr. Norton impressed on me, by subpoenaing my publishers) the power of earning, by literature,—which fund (though it be the grant of Heaven, and not the legacy of earth) is no more legally mine than my family property. . . . The "existent" husband subpoenaed my bankers; compelled them to produce their books, and sent his attorney to make extracts at their bank, of all sums entered in my private account. He also subpoenaed my publishers; to compel them to declare what were the copyrights they held of me, and what sums they had paid me: for, (amazing to say,) the copyrights of my work are *his*, by law: my very soul and brains are not my own! . . .

When Mr. Norton allowed me, I say, to be publicly subpoenaed in court, to defend himself by a quibble from a just debt, and subpoenaed my publishers to meet me there, he taught me what my gift of writing was worth. Since he would not leave even *that* source tranquil and free in my destiny, let him have the triumph of being able at once to embitter and to turn its former current. He has made me dream that it was meant for a higher and stronger purpose,—that gift which came not from man, but from God. It was meant to enable me to rouse the hearts of others to examine into all the gross injustice of these laws,—to ask the "nation of gallant gentlemen," whose countrywoman I am, for once to hear a woman's pleading on the subject. . . .

For *this*, I believe, God gave me the power of writing. To this I devote that power. I abjure all other writing, till I see these laws altered. I care not what ridicule or abuse may be the result of that declaration. They who cannot bear ridicule and abuse, are unfit and unable to advance *any* cause: and once more I deny that this is my personal cause; it is the cause of all the women of England. If *I* could be justified and happy to-morrow, I would still strive and labour in it; and if I were to die to-morrow, it would still be a satisfaction to me that I had so striven. Meanwhile, my husband has a legal lien (as he has publicly proved), on the copyright of my works. Let him claim the copyright of THIS![20]

Caroline Norton elicited endorsements from a wide range of writers on the Woman Question. In America Wendell Phillips concluded a suffrage speech by insisting that Norton be given the "right to her brain, to her hands, to her toil, to her ballot." Eliza Lynn Linton rebuked "Public Functionists" who wanted women to vote and to hold office, but she joined her country-woman's crusade to end the oppressive marriage laws.[21] In Parliament Lord Lyndhurst read passages from *A Letter to the Queen* during the continuing debates over the Matrimonial Causes Act and proposed amendments based on her case. When the Act was passed in 1857, the court was empowered to order payment of separate maintenance to a wife or to her trustee. A separated or divorced wife recovered her rights to inherit or bequeath her own property, to enter into contracts, and to sue or be sued as if she were single. Moreover, a wife deserted by her husband could protect her earnings against his claim.

Hailed by the *Englishwoman's Journal* as the first law to recognize the rights and responsibilities of women as breadwinners,[22] the Matrimonial Causes Act was nonetheless something of a disappointment. It assisted women in "extraordinary circumstances"—i.e., women who had been separated, divorced, or deserted without cause—but unlike Perry's proposal, it did not alter the status of women within marriage. After its passage, conservatives maintained that the law need not concern itself with married women: their property was already "protected" by their husbands. Politicians had deliberately used one women's bill against another. According to Lord St. Leonards, the amendments to the Matrimonial Causes Act were intended to "prevent a greater evil"—the passage of Perry's "most mischievous" bill, which would "place the whole marriage law . . . on a different footing and give a wife all the distinct rights of citizenship."[23] Thus Parliament extended protection to vulnerable women without granting equality to all.

The maneuver did not end the argument: between 1857 and 1882 eighteen related bills were introduced in Parliament. When supporters cited the liberalized property laws in the northeastern United States, they were accused of trying to "Americanize" English institutions. While some opponents declared that law should not intrude upon the privacy of marriage, others insisted that the husband should make all financial decisions if he were to exercise the authority vested in him by scripture, custom, and common law. Many predicted that extending property rights would have a detrimental effect on the home; with economic independence, women would be more assertive, slower to marry and quicker to divorce.

These and other objections were met in 1868 by Frances Power Cobbe. Writing for *Fraser's*, she rejects the three basic defenses of existing laws: justice, expediency, and sentiment. A skilled rhetorician who flattered Englishmen for their "generous hearts and chivalrous natures," Cobbe is particularly adept at using her adversaries' assumptions against them.

First, the grounds of Justice.

Man is the natural bread-winner. Woman lives by the bread which man has earned. Ergo, it is fit and right that the man who wins should have absolute disposal, not only of his winnings, but of every other small morsel or fraction of earnings or property she may possess. It is a fair return to him for his labour in the joint interests of both. He supports her, pays any debts she has incurred before or after marriage, and provides for the children which are hers as well as his. For all this, it is but just he should receive whatever she has to give. . . .

Then for Expediency. . . . Somebody must rule in a household, or everything will go to rack and ruin; and disputes will be endless. If somebody is to rule it can only be the husband, who is wiser, stronger, knows more of the world, and in any case has not the slightest intention of yielding his natural predominance. But to give a man such rule he must be allowed to keep the purse. Nothing but the power of the purse—in default of the stick—can permanently and thoroughly secure authority. Besides, for the good of the whole family, for the children and the wife herself, it is far more expedient that all the resources of the family should be directed by a single hand, and that hand the one that can best transact business of all kinds. . . .

Lastly, for the sentimental view. . . . We are rarely allowed in debating it to examine accurately the theory of conjugal justice. We are called upon rather to contemplate the beautiful ideal of absolute union of heart, life, and purse which the law has provided for, and which alone it deigns to recognise. . . . How painful is the notion of a wife holding back her money from him who is every day toiling for her support! How fair is the ideal picture of absolute concession on her part of all she possesses of this world's dross to the man to whom she gives her heart and life! . . .

What, in the first place, of the Justice of giving all a woman's property to her husband? The argument is, that the wife gets an ample *quid pro quo. Does* she get it under the existing law? That is the simple question.

In the first place, many husbands are unable, from fault or from misfortune, to maintain their wives. Of this the law takes no note, proceeding on reasoning which may be reduced to the syllogism:

A man who supports his wife ought to have all her property;
Most men support their wives;
Therefore, all men ought to have all the property of their wives. . . .

When all that a woman possesses in the present and future is handed over unreservedly by the law to her husband, is there the smallest attempt at obtaining security that he on his part *can* fulfil that obligation which is always paraded as the equivalent, namely, the obligation to support her for the rest of her life? . . .

But waiving the point of the *inability* of many husbands to fulfil their side of the understood engagement, one thing, at all events, it must behove the law to do. Having enforced her part on the woman, it is bound to enforce his part on the man, *to the utmost of his ability.* The legal act by which a man puts his hand in his wife's pocket, or draws her money out of the savings' bank, is perfectly clear, easy, inexpensive. The corresponding process by which the wife can obtain food and clothing from her husband when he neglects to provide it—what may it be? Where is it described? . . . What is the actual fact? Simply that the woman's remedy for her husband's neglect to provide her with food, has been practically found unattainable. The law which has robbed her so straightforwardly, has somehow forgotten altogether to secure for her the supposed compensation. . . .

So much for the Justice of the Common Law. What now shall we say to its Expediency? . . . The law *when the husband is really wise and good* is a dead letter. But for the opposite cases, exceptions though they be, yet alas! too numerous, where the husband is a fool, a gambler, a drunkard, and where the wife is sensible, frugal, devoted to the interests of the children,—is it indeed expedient that the whole and sole power should be lodged in the husband's hands; the power not only over all they already have in common, but the power over all she can ever earn in future? . . .

But it is the alleged *helplessness* of married women which, it is said, makes it indispensable to give all the support of the law, *not* to them, but to the stronger persons with whom they are unequally yoked. 'Woman is physically, mentally, and morally inferior to man.' Therefore it follows—what?—that the law should give to her bodily weakness, her intellectual dulness, her tottering morality, all the support and protection which it is possible to interpose between so poor a creature and the strong being always standing over her? By no means. Quite the contrary of course. The husband being already physically, mentally, and morally his wife's superior must in justice receive from the law additional strength by being constituted absolute master of her property. . . .

But the great and overwhelming argument against the Expediency of the Common Law in this matter is the simple fact that no parent or guardian possessed of means sufficient to evade it by a marriage settlement ever dreams of permitting his daughter or ward to undergo its (supposed) beneficial action. The parent who neglected to demand such a settlement from a man before he gave him his daughter, would be thought to have failed in the performance of one of his most obvious and imperative duties. Even the law itself in its highest form in the realm (that of the Court of Chancery) invariably requires settlements for its wards. How then can it be argued that the same rule is generally considered expedient, yet invariably evaded by all who have means to evade it? . . . The only persons for whom the existing law is expedient are fortune-hunters, who, if they can befool young women of property so far as to induce them to elope, are enabled thereby to grasp all their inheritance. . . .

But, as we have said already, there is an argument which has more force in determining legislation about marriage than either considerations of Justice or of Expediency. It is the sentiment entertained by the majority of men on the subject; the ideal they have formed of wedlock, the poetical vision in their minds of a wife's true relation to her husband. Legislators talk in Parliament with a certain conviction that the principles of fairness and policy are the only ones to be referred to *there*. But whenever the subject is freely discussed, in private or in a newspaper, there is sure to burst out sooner or later the real feeling at bottom. . . . Let us try to fathom this sentiment, for till we understand it we are but fighting our battles in the dark. Is it not this—that a woman's whole life and being, her soul, body, time, property, thought, and care, ought to be given to her husband; that nothing short of such absorption in him and his interests makes her a true wife; and that when she is thus absorbed even a very mediocre character and inferior intellect can make a man happy in a sense no splendour of endowments can otherwise do? Truly I believe this is the feeling at the bottom of nearly all men's hearts, and of the hearts of thousands of women also. . . . [The typical man] is impatient at the notion of a marriage in which this conception of absolute absorption of his wife's interests in his own shall not be fulfilled; and, so far as legislation can create such an ideal, he is resolved that it shall do so.

So far all is plain and natural, but the question is this: Supposing such marriages to be the most desirable, do men set the right way about securing them, by making such laws as the Common Law of England? Is perfect love to be called out by perfect dependence? Does an empty purse necessarily imply a full heart? Is a generous-natured woman likely to be won or rather to be alienated and galled by being made to feel she has no choice but submission? Surely there is great fallacy in this direction. The idea which we are all agreed ought to be realised in marriage is that of the highest possible Union. But what *is* that most perfect Union? Have we not taken it in a most gross commercial sense, as if even here we were a nation of shopkeepers? . . .

The union of two human beings may, as preachers say, be considered three ways. Firstly, there is the sort of union between any friends who are greatly attached to one another; a union oftenest seen, perhaps, between two sisters, who each have full liberty to come and go, and dispose of their separate resources, but who yet manage commonly to live in harmony and affection, and not unfrequently to bring up a whole batch of little nephews and nieces in their common abode. . . .

Secondly, there is the Union of the celebrated Siamese twins, who are tied together—not by Mother Church but by Mother Nature—so effectually that Sir William Fergusson and Sir William Wilde are equally powerless to release them. Each of them has, however, the satisfaction of dragging about his brother as much as he is dragged himself; and if either have a pocket, that other must needs have every facility of access thereto.

Lastly, for the most absolute type of Union of all, we must seek an example in the Tarantula Spider. As most persons are aware, when one of these delightful creatures is placed under a glass with a companion of his own species a little smaller than himself, he forthwith gobbles him up; making him thus, in a very literal manner, 'bone of his bone' (supposing tarantulas to have any bones) 'and flesh of his flesh.' The operation being completed, the victorious spider visibly acquires double bulk, and thenceforth may be understood to 'represent the family' in the most perfect manner conceivable.

Now, of these three types of union, it is singular that the only one which seems to have approved itself, in a pecuniary point of view, to the legislative wisdom of England should be that of the Tarantula. Unless a man be allowed to eat up the whole of a woman's fortune, there is apparently no union possible between their interests. Partnerships, limited liabilities, and all other devices for amalgamation of property are here considered inadmissible. The way in which brothers and sisters settle their affairs when they reside under the same roof would never suffice, it seems, to keep things straight between those who hold a yet more tender and trustful relationship.[24]

The Married Women's Property Act which was passed in 1870 was fraught with compromise and contradiction: it allowed women to keep possession only of their earnings and to inherit personal property and small sums of money; everything else, whether acquired before marriage or after, belonged to the husband. The most important changes came in 1882 when another act provided that a married woman might keep all real and personal property that was hers at the time of marriage or acquired later. Although the wife's status was not exactly that of a man or a *feme sole*, she was able to dispose of her separate property in a will or convey it to her husband. She acquired the right to contract and sue along with the corresponding liability for her debts; she also gained full rights and liabilities with regard to torts committed by or against her during marriage. The Married Women's Property Act of 1882 had a number of peculiarities, including the provision for "restraint against anticipation," which was a way to prevent a wife from freely alienating her property or from anticipating future rents and profits. It was, nonetheless, the most important piece of new legislation affecting Englishwomen. If working women earned about £16 million a year and women of the middle and upper classes held about £16 million in property, then the property acts did indeed carry through one of the great reallocations of property in English history.[25] Moreover, the Married Women's Property Act of 1882 demanded an end to the old doctrine of the legal unity of husband and wife. Hereafter the courts were obligated to recognize two distinct entities—in theory if not always in practice. With new laws also carrying in many American states, Victorian women made their greatest legal advance in their increased rights to own and control property.

III

In 1832, John Stuart Mill wrote, "The indissolubility of marriage is the keystone of a woman's present lot. . . . And the truth is, that this question of marriage cannot properly be considered by itself alone. The question is not what marriage ought to be, but a far wider question, what woman ought to be."[26] The marriage relation could call woman's role into question more directly—and more explosively—than any other area of the Victorian debate. Much opposition to child custody and property rights resulted from uncertainty about the future of marriage: many Victorians feared that women would reject marriage if they were given the prospect of their children's company or financial independence without it. Throughout the period, attempts to alter the marriage laws by political campaign and by individual protest continued to increase the anxiety.

In England and America lawyers worked to simplify complex and inconsistent procedures relating to marriage and divorce. Outside the courts and legislatures, such prominent couples as

Harriet Taylor and John Stuart Mill, Robert Dale Owen and Mary Jane Robinson, and Lucy Stone and Henry Blackwell pledged that their marriages would not be based on laws which gave one party power over the other.[27] English and American socialists promulgated and, in some instances, acted upon more extreme ideas: the Saint-Simonians preached that marriage was morally based on affection and that it should be dissolved without publicity, without expense, and without dishonor if that affection ceased to exist; Robert Owen and his followers wanted a cheap system of divorce to be available in the communities they founded; the Perfectionists developed a plan for "complex marriage" that made divorce unnecessary; and the Fourierists sought to abolish marriage altogether.[28] However, because divorce was a controversial and extremely disturbing issue, the majority of feminists avoided it, insisting that the political and educational changes they sought would contribute to the stability of marriage and the happiness of the home. Only the most radical—or the most desperate—espoused the cause. The women's argument for reform and the legislators' response to it are illustrated by two controversies: the Matrimonial Causes Act of 1857 and the New York Marriage Debate of 1860.

In England the marriage and divorce laws were administered by ecclesiastical courts, and divorce was granted on extremely limited terms. For cases of cruelty and adultery, the Church of England allowed a rough equivalent of a judicial separation called *divorce a mensa et thoro* (divorced from bed and board). This process did not actually dissolve a marriage: neither spouse was free to remarry and the husband retained control of the wife's property. A true divorce, or *divorce a vinculo*, could be granted only by private act of Parliament; this method was available to the very rich and used almost exclusively by men.[29] A parliamentary divorce, like the marriage settlement, allowed the wealthy to circumvent the restraints of common law while leaving everyone else helpless.

To obtain an absolute divorce, a husband had to file suit against his wife's alleged lover. The charge, called "criminal conversation," was based on the assumption that the wife was a chattel, the value of which had been damaged by the defendant. The wife's character and economic interests were at stake, but she was not allowed to appear in court to defend herself. The husband was then obligated to take the case to the ecclesiastical courts, and finally to Parliament. The expense, the inefficiency, and the irregularities in admitting evidence made this process the subject of much concern. The Royal Commission on Divorce, which was appointed in 1850, censured the high cost of divorce proceedings, but remained more interested in simplifying the court system and improving the administration of law than in assisting women.

Caroline Norton discovered the injustice of the English divorce laws in 1836 when her husband accused her of adultery. Driven by anger, financial need, and political expediency, George Norton charged Lord Melbourne, Caroline's friend, his patron, and the Whig Prime Minister, with criminal conversation, and sued him for £10,000 in damages. The evidence against Melbourne was so slight that the jury voted for acquittal without leaving the box. Caroline Norton was declared innocent, but she was legally bound to a man she despised: George could not divorce her because she had not committed adultery; she could not divorce him because she had once condoned his cruelty by returning to his home.

During the unhappy years after the trial, Caroline Norton gave careful attention to the government's attempts to reform the divorce laws. Dismayed by the irrelevant quarrels and repeated delays which characterized the parliamentary debates of the mid-1850s and by the inadequacy of the bill under consideration, she published *A Letter to the Queen on Lord Chancellor Cranworth's Marriage and Divorce Bill* so that men might hear "a woman's pleading on the subject." *A Letter to the Queen* argues for economic protection, but the 1855 pamphlet also attacks the double standard that Lord Cranworth wanted to sanction with his marriage bill. Unlike such a radical feminist as Harriet Taylor, Caroline Norton does not demand that divorce "be attained by any *without any reason* assigned and at a small expense."[30] She asks only that husbands and wives be subject to the same standards. She is outraged that the bickering men in the House of Lords will not consider using the Scottish law as a model for reform.

In one thing only they generally agreed, they congratulated Lord Cranworth upon that portion of his plan which provided that Justice should have her scales ready weighted in favour of the stronger party—viz., that women should not be discouraged from forgiving their husbands, by making adultery in the male sex a ground of divorce—"*as in Scotland.*"

Now, what is meant by this implied slur on the social condition of our sister country? What is meant by this dread of the assimilation of the Marriage laws north and south of the Tweed?

Oh! is it not a sad and marvellous thing, that professional prejudice and the prejudice of sex, can so warp and bend high and honourable minds, that a man like Lord Cranworth, in Lord Cranworth's position,—the most responsible for justice in England; —should take the view Lord Cranworth took—and use the arguments Lord Cranworth used—in support of what? In support of a measure to *legalise* a special indulgence to the animal passions of men.

Lord Campbell, when some doubt is expressed whether divorce ought to be permitted at all, to either sex, rises and says divorce of the wife is "in accordance with Scripture." In what portion of Holy Writ does he find it in "accordance with Scripture" that adultery is no sin in a man? Are not men warned not only against sin, but even against wandering desires? . . . Are we to have one religion for women and another for men, as we have already one law for women and another for men,—ecclesiastical law for the woman, and common law for the man? . . .

Either let men renounce the privilege of divorce, and the assertion that marriage is a dissoluble contract,—or allow the weaker party that refuge from intolerable wrong, which they claim as a matter of necessity for themselves. The Ecclesiastical law, which denies the dissolubility of marriages, is intelligible, (though not so intelligible how, that being the case, ecclesiastics re-marry persons divorced by parliament). And the Scotch law, which reverses the ecclesiastical law, and makes marriage dissoluble for both sexes and all classes, is intelligible. But the Lord Chancellor's Bill, which denies to the poor what it gives to the rich—and grants to the husband what it refuses to the wife—is *not* intelligible on any principle of justice. (22-23, 59)

The peers had religious, social, and economic arguments for supporting the double standard: they cited the scriptural verses that allowed a man to punish his wife for adultery; they said that a man's transgression did not ruin his family's reputation as a woman's did; and they warned that illegitimate children would interfere with the correct line of descent. With the Lord Chancellor insisting that he was unwilling to open up "the whole question of the marriage relationship," Parliament did not confront the complicated issues raised in the New York Marriage Debate of 1860. Although Lyndhurst and several others used Caroline Norton's pamphlet to argue that the wife should have the right to petition for divorce in case of the husband's adultery, Cranworth disagreed.

> THE LORD CHANCELLOR said, there was an appearance of great justice about the proposal . . . that the same privilege should be accorded to the one sex as to the other. . . . Their Lordships had not, however, to consider whether the sin was as great in the one case as in the other, but they were required to adopt such legislation as might be most expedient for this country. . . . Without entering into any discussion of the question upon moral or religious grounds, every man must feel that the injury was not the same. A wife might, without any loss of caste, and possibly with reference to the interests of her children, or even of her husband, condone an act of adultery on the part of the husband; but a husband could not condone a similar act on the part of a wife. No one would venture to suggest that a husband could possibly do so, and for this, among other reasons which had been pointed out by jurists—that the adultery of the wife might be the means of palming spurious offspring upon the husband, while the adultery of the husband could have no such effect with regard to the wife.[31]

American feminist Caroline Dall rejected Cranworth's reasoning in *Women's Rights Under the Law.*

> If a man cannot bring a false representative into *his own family,* he can carry it into his neighbor's, when his profligate life violates the social compact; and, as to his own family, his vices may injure it far more than the infidelity of his wife. At the worst, her misconduct will only bring into the shelter of his home a child who grows up protected socially by her fraud; but, if *he* choose to "spend his substance in riotous living," his wife and children may, while the law gives him exclusive right to their common property, be deserted, or driven from their homes, to make room for those who are the companions of his guilt. (75-76)

Unfortunately, such protests had little effect. The law that was finally passed in England did make divorce and separation simpler and more accessible: it created new courts and lowered the costs somewhat. The Matrimonial Causes Act of 1857 helped women by suppressing the action for criminal conversation and by allowing separation on more beneficial terms. But it also sustained the double standard, thereby denying women equal rights to an absolute divorce. Although the new law permitted the husband to divorce his wife for adultery, it required that she prove adultery *and* an additional offense, such as incest, cruelty, bigamy, rape, bestiality, or desertion for more than two years. Some improvement was made with the Matrimonial Causes Act of 1884—a wife deserted by an adulterous husband could petition for divorce immediately instead of waiting two years, and the court could no longer imprison a wife for noncompliance with an order for restitution of conjugal rights—but the double standard retained the force of law until the 1920s, in America as well as in England. During the first quarter of the twentieth century, at least three states—Texas, North Carolina, and Kentucky—still allowed a husband to divorce his wife if he could prove that she had committed a single act of adultery, while denying a wife a divorce under similar circumstances.

In America, Theodore Dwight Woolsey, the conservative president of Yale, gave reluctant approval to the Matrimonial Causes Act of 1857 and prayed that the door would "never open wider in England for the more censurable kinds of divorce."[32] But in 1867 when his influential essays began appearing, most Americans realized that they were already living with a more complicated situation: a bewildering range of laws and an increasing divorce rate. State, county, and even city legislation made American marriage a decidedly local option. The South was generally strict—South Carolina recognized no cause whatever for divorce—while in New England the dissenting tradition fostered more liberal laws. By 1849, for example, Connecticut granted divorce for adultery, fraudulent contract, willful desertion, habitual drunkenness, intolerable cruelty, and "any such misconduct as permanently destroys the happiness of the petitioner and defeats the purpose of the marriage relationship." New "western" states were very permissive. Indiana maintained a long list of causes, including an 1824 omnibus clause granting full divorce "on petition of the injured person 'in all cases where the court in its discretion' shall deem the same 'just and reasonable.'" At mid-century, divorce was a frequent subject of discussion because most states were enlarging the causes of divorce and transferring jurisdiction from the legislatures to the courts.[33]

One state remained particularly tangled and balky. Although New York recognized annulment and separation, it granted absolute divorce only in cases of adultery. Repeatedly the Albany legislature refused to extend the grounds for divorce beyond adultery to desertion, cruelty, and drunkenness. The New York law was not at all typical, but the controversy it generated reflects the spectrum of national opinion on divorce.

Horace Greeley, editor of the *New York Tribune*, insists upon maintaining the current law; Robert Dale Owen, the influential Indiana politician, advocates reform.³⁴ As a warning to New York, Greeley points to Indiana, "the paradise of free lovers," and attacks Owen as the author of a law "which enables men or women to get unmarried nearly at pleasure" (571). Owen declares, "It is in New York and New England, refusing reasonable divorce, that free-love prevails, not in Indiana" (574). Greeley invokes divine authority, arguing that Christ permitted divorce only in cases of adultery (Matt. 19:9). Owen suggests that Christ had broader intentions. The injunction against looking at women with lust (Matt. 5:28) demonstrates "that the proper cause for divorce is, not the mere physical act of infidelity, but that adultery of the heart which quenches conjugal love" (585); by mitigating the harshness of the Old Testament (esp. Deut. 24: 1), Jesus proves that "divorce laws may properly vary, in different stages of civilization" (586). When Greeley defines marriage as "union for life" (587), Owen asks, "Why, in its vice-fostering perversion, should a life of bickering be dragged on, till death, at last, brings separation and peace? . . . Is it in order that the intangible generality called SOCIETY may be propitiated and appeased?" (600). Greeley answers:

> The vice of our age, the main source of its aberrations, is a morbid Egotism, which overrides the gravest social necessities in its mad pursuit of individual, personal ends. Your fling at that "intangible generality called SOCIETY" is directly in point. You are concerned chiefly for those who, having married unfortunately, if not viciously, seek relief from their bonds; I am anxious rather to prevent, or at least to render infrequent, immoral, and unfit sexual unions hereafter. The miseries of the unfitly mated may be deplorable; but to make divorce easy is in effect to invite the sensual and selfish to profane the sanctions of Marriage whenever appetite and temptation may prompt. . . . To the libertine, the egotist, the selfish, sensual seeker of personal and present enjoyment at whatever cost to others, the Indissolubility of Marriage is an obstacle, a restraint, a terror; and God forbid that it should ever cease to be! Thousands would take a wife as readily, as thoughtlessly, as heartlessly, as they don a new coat or sport a new cravat, if it were understood that they might unmarry themselves whenever satiety, or disgust, or mutual dislike, should prompt to that step. . . .

You think the difference between us to be simply this: I allow Divorce for a single cause (Adultery), you for several causes; and you would thus reduce it, from a question of principle, to one of details. But you cannot deny that my one ground of Divorce is that expressly affirmed to be such by Jesus Christ, to the exclusion and negation of all others. Nor can you fail to see that if, as I hold, the paramount (not sole) Divine end of Marriage is Parentage, or the perpetuation and increase, under fit auspices, of the Human Race, then that crime which vitiates and confuses parentage may logically be deemed the sole sufficient reason for annulling a marriage. To my mind, therefore, our difference is clearly and emphatically one of principle.

As spokesman for the orthodox point of view, Greeley was very much on the mind of Elizabeth Cady Stanton when she called leading feminists to New York City for the Tenth National Women's Rights Convention. In an 1853 letter to Susan B. Anthony, Stanton had written, "It is vain to look for the elevation of woman so long as she is degraded in marriage. . . . The right idea of marriage is at the foundation of all reforms."[35] By 1860, Stanton and Anthony believed feminists at least were ready to consider the marriage question, but the debate on May 10-11 shows how easily it could sunder alliances within the movement. Is marriage a divine sacrament, a legal and social contract, or a private union of equal parties? If a husband is cruel or irresponsible, should a wife work for his redemption or seek happiness elsewhere? Can divorce destroy the most fundamental human relationship, or will it finally make possible "true marriage"? Feminists are themselves divided. The New York Marriage Debate did not hasten reform— indeed, additional grounds for absolute divorce were not added until 1966—but the Americans go far beyond the English in questioning the relationship between marriage and woman's identity.

ELIZABETH CADY STANTON: Mrs. President—I repudiate the popular idea of man's degradation and total depravity. I place man above all governments, all institutions—ecclesiastical and civil—all constitutions and laws. (Applause). It is a mistaken idea, that the same law that oppresses the individual can promote the highest good of society. The best interests of a community never can require the sacrifice of one innocent being—of one sacred right. In the settlement, then, of any question, we must simply consider the highest good of the individual. It is the inalienable right of all to be happy. . . .

For years, there has been before the Legislature of this State a variety of bills, asking for divorce in cases of drunkenness, insanity, desertion, cruel and brutal treatment, endangering life. My attention was called to this question very early in life, by the sufferings of a friend of my girlhood, a victim of one of those unfortunate unions, called marriage. What my great love for that young girl, and my holy intuitions, then decided to be right, has not been changed by years of experience, observation, and reason. I have pondered well these things in my heart, and ever felt the deepest interest in all that has been written and said upon the subject, and the most profound respect and loving sympathy for those heroic women, who, in the face of law and public sentiment, have dared to sunder the unholy ties of a joyless, loveless union.

If marriage is a human institution, about which man may legislate, it seems but just that he should treat this branch of his legislation with the same common-sense that he applies to all others. If it is a mere legal contract, then should it be subject to the restraints and privileges of all other contracts. A contract, to be valid in law, must be formed between parties of mature age, with an honest intention in said parties to do what they agree. The least concealment, fraud, or deception, if proved, annuls the contract. A boy can not contract for an acre of land, or a horse, until he is twenty-one, but he may contract for a wife at fourteen. If a man sell a horse, and the purchaser find in him great incompatibility of temper—a disposition to stand still when the owner is in haste to go—the sale is null and void, and the man and his horse part company. But in marriage, no matter how much fraud and deception are practiced, nor how cruelly one or both parties have been misled; no matter how young, inexperienced, or thoughtless the parties, nor how unequal their condition and position in life, the contract can not be annulled. . . .

Where two beings are drawn together, by the natural laws of likeness and affinity, union and happiness are the result. Such marriages might be Divine. But how is it now? You all know our marriage is, in many cases, a mere outward tie, impelled by custom, policy, interest, necessity; founded not even in friendship, to say nothing of love; with every possible inequality of condition and development. In these heterogeneous unions, we find youth and old age, beauty and deformity, refinement and vulgarity, virtue and vice, the educated and the ignorant, angels of grace and goodness, with devils of malice and malignity: and the sum of all this is human wretchedness and despair; cold fathers, sad mothers, and hapless children, who shiver at the hearthstone, where the fires of love have all gone out. . . . Now, who shall say that it is right to take two beings, so unlike, and anchor them right side by side, fast bound—to stay all time, until God shall summon one away?

Do wise, Christian legislators need any arguments to convince them that the sacredness of the family relation should be protected at all hazards? . . . Can there be anything sacred at that family altar, where the chief-priest who ministers makes sacrifice of human beings, of the weak and the innocent? where the incense offered up is not to the God of justice and mercy, but to those heathen divinities, who best may represent the lost man in all his grossness and deformity? Call that sacred, where woman, the mother of the race—of a Jesus of Nazareth—unconscious of the true dignity of her nature, of her high and holy destiny, consents to live in legalized prostitution!—her whole soul revolting at such gross association!—her flesh shivering at the cold contamination of that embrace, held there by no tie but the iron chain of the law, and a false and most unnatural public sentiment? . . .

Men and brethren, look into your asylums for the blind, the deaf and dumb, the idiot, the imbecile, the deformed, the insane; go out into the by-lanes and dens of this vast metropolis, and contemplate that reeking mass of depravity; pause before the terrible revelations made by statistics, of the rapid increase of all this moral and physical impotency, and learn how fearful a thing it is to violate the immutable laws of the beneficent Ruler of the universe; and there behold the terrible retributions of your violence on woman! Learn how false and cruel are those institutions, which, with a coarse materialism, set aside those holy instincts of the woman to bear no children but those of love! In the best condition of marriage, as we now have it, to woman comes all the penalties and sacrifices. A man, in the full tide of business or pleasure, can marry and not change his life one iota; he can be husband, father, and everything beside; but in marriage, woman gives up all. Home is her sphere, her realm. Well, be it so. If here you will make us all-supreme, take to yourselves the universe beside; explore the North Pole; and, in your airy car, all space; in your Northern homes and cloud-capt towers, go feast on walrus flesh and air, and lay you down to sleep your six months' night away, and leave us to make these laws that govern the inner sanctuary of our own homes, and faithful satellites we will ever be to the dinner-pot, the cradle, and the old arm-chair. (Applause). . . .

But, say you, does not separation cover all . . . difficulties? No one objects to separation when the parties are so disposed. But, to separation there are two very serious objections. First, so long as you insist on marriage as a divine institution, as an indissoluble tie, so long as you maintain your present laws against divorce, you make separation, even, so odious, that the most noble, virtuous, and sensitive men and women choose a life of concealed misery, rather than a partial, disgraceful release. Secondly, those who, in their impetuosity and despair, do, in spite of public sentiment, separate, find themselves in their new position beset with many temptations to lead a false, unreal life. This isolation bears especially hard on woman. Marriage is not all of life to man. His resources for amusement and occupation are boundless. He has the whole world for his home. His business, his politics, his club, his friendships with either sex, can help to fill up the void made by an unfortunate union or separation. But to woman, marriage is all and everything; her sole object in life—that for which she is educated—the subject of all her sleeping and her waking dreams. Now, if a noble, generous girl of eighteen marries, and is unfortunate, because the cruelty of her husband compels separation, in her dreary isolation, would you drive her to a nunnery; and shall she be a nun indeed? Her solitude is nothing less, as, in the present undeveloped condition of woman, it is only through our fathers, brothers, husbands, sons, that we feel the pulsations of the great outer world.

. . . This question of divorce, they tell us, is hedged about with difficulties; that it can not be approached with the ordinary rules of logic and common-sense. It is too holy, too sacred to be discussed, and few seem disposed to touch it. From man's standpoint, this may be all true, as to him they say belong reason, and the power of ratiocination. Fortunately, I belong to that class endowed with mere intuitions, a kind of moral instinct, by which we feel out right and wrong. In presenting to you, therefore, my views of divorce, you will of course give them the weight only of the woman's intuitions. But inasmuch as that is all God saw fit to give us, it is evident we need nothing more. Hence, what we do perccive of truth must be as reliable as what man grinds out by the longer process of reason, authority, and speculation.

Horace Greeley, in his recent discussion with Robert Dale Owen, said, this whole question has been tried, in all its varieties and conditions, from indissoluble monogamic marriage down to free love; that the ground has been all gone over and explored. Let me assure him that but just one-half of the ground has been surveyed, and that half but by one of the parties, and that party certainly not the most interested in the matter. Moreover, there is one kind of marriage that has not been tried, and that is, a contract made by equal parties to live an equal life, with equal restraints and privileges on either side. Thus far, we have had the man marriage, and nothing more.

. . . We can not take our gauge of womanhood from the past, but from the solemn convictions of our own souls, in the higher development of the race. No parchments, however venerable with the mould of ages, no human institutions, can bound the immortal wants of the royal sons and daughters of the great I Am,—rightful heirs of the joys of time, and joint heirs of the glories of eternity.

If in marriage either party claims the right to stand supreme, to woman, the mother of the race, belongs the scepter and the crown. Her life is one long sacrifice for man. You tell us that among all womankind there is no Moses, Christ, or Paul,—no Michael Angelo, Beethoven, or Shakspeare,—no Columbus, or Galileo,—no Locke or Bacon. Behold those mighty minds attuned to music and the arts, so great, so grand, so comprehensive,— these are our great works of which we boast! Into you, O sons of earth, go all of us that is immortal. In you center our very life-thoughts, our hopes, our intensest love. For you we gladly pour out our heart's blood and die, knowing that from our suffering comes forth a new and more glorious resurrection of thought and life. (Loud applause).

REV. ANTOINETTE BROWN BLACKWELL followed, and prefaced her remarks by saying: "Ours has always been a free platform. We have believed in the fullest freedom of thought and in the free expression of individual opinion. I propose to speak upon the subject discussed by our friend, Mrs. Stanton. It is often said that there are two sides to every question; but there are three sides, many sides, to every question. Let Mrs. Stanton take hers; let Horace Greeley take his; I only ask the privilege of stating mine. (Applause).

I believe that the highest laws of life are those which we find written within our being; that the first moral laws which we are to obey are the laws which God's own finger has traced upon our own souls. Therefore, our first duty is to ourselves, and we may never, under any circumstances, yield this to any other. I say we are first responsible to ourselves, and to the God who has laid the obligation upon us, to make ourselves the grandest we may. Marriage grows out of the relations of parties. The law of our development comes wholly from within; but the relation of marriage supposes two persons as being united to each other, and from this relation originates the law. Mrs. Stanton calls marriage a "tie." No, marriage is a *relation*; and, once formed, that relation continues as long as the parties continue with the natures which they now essentially have. Let, then, the two parties deliberately, voluntarily consent to enter into this relation. It is one which, from its very nature, must be permanent. Can the mother ever destroy the relation which exists between herself and her child? Can the father annul the relation which exists between himself and his child? Then, can the father and mother annul the relation which exists between themselves, the parents of the child? It can not be. The interests of marriage are such that they can not be destroyed, and the only question must be, "Has there been a marriage in this case or not?" If there has, then the social law, the obligations growing out of the relation, must be life-long.

But I assert that every woman, in the present state of society, is bound to maintain her own independence and her own integrity of character; to assert herself, earnestly and firmly, as the equal of man, who is only her peer. This is her first right, her first duty; and if she lives in a country where the law supposes that she is to be subjected to her husband, and she consents to this subjection, I do insist that she consents to degradation; that this is sin, and it is impossible to make it other than sin. True, in this State, and in nearly all the States, the idea of marriage is that of subjection, in all respects, of the wife to the husband—personal subjection, subjection in the rights over their children and over their property; but this is a false relation. Marriage is a union of equals—equal interests being involved, equal duties at stake; and if any woman has been married to a man who chooses to take advantage of the laws as they now stand, who chooses to subject her, ignobly, to his will, against her own, to take from her the earnings which belong to the family, and to take from her the children which belong to the family, I hold that that woman, if she can not, by her influence, change this state of things, is solemnly obligated to go to some State where she can be legally divorced; and then she would be as solemnly bound to return again, and, standing for herself and her children, regard herself, in the sight of God, as being bound still to the father of those children, to work for his best interests, while she still maintains her own sovereignty. Of course, she must be governed by the circumstances of the case. She may be obliged, for the protection of the family, to live on one continent while her husband is on the other: but she is never to forget that in the sight of God and her own soul, she is his wife, and that she owes to him the wife's loyalty; that to work for his redemption is her highest social obligation, and that to teach her children to do the same is her first motherly duty. . . .

No grown-up human being ought to rush blindly into this most intimate, most important, most enduring of human relations. . . . Let the young girl be instructed that, above her personal interests, her home, and social life, she is to have a great life purpose, as broad as the rights and interests of humanity. . . . Let her be taught that she ought not to be married in her teens. Let her wait, as a young man does, if he is sensible, until she is twenty-five or thirty. (Applause). She will then know how to choose properly, and probably she will not be deceived in her estimate of character; she will have had a certain life-discipline, which will enable her to control her household matters with wise judgment, so that, while she is looking after her family, she may still keep her great life purpose, for which she was educated, and to which she has given her best energies, steadily in view. She need not absorb herself in her home, and God never intended that she should; and then, if she has lived according to the laws of physiology, and according to the laws of common-sense, she ought to be, at the age of fifty years, just where man is, just where our great men are, in the very prime of life! When her young children have gone out of her home, then let her enter in earnest upon the great work of life outside of home and its relations. (Applause). . . .

ERNESTINE L. ROSE said:—Mrs. President—The question of a Divorce law seems to me one of the greatest importance to all parties, but I presume that the very advocacy of divorce will be called "Free Love." For my part (and I wish distinctly to define my position), I do not know what others understand by that term; to me, in its truest significance, love must be free, or it ceases to be love. In its low and degrading sense, it is not love at all, and I have as little to do with its name as its reality.

The Rev. Mrs. Blackwell gave us quite a sermon on what woman ought to be, what she ought to do, and what marriage ought to be; an excellent sermon in its proper place, but not when the important question of a Divorce law is under consideration. She treats woman as some ethereal being. It is very well to be ethereal to some extent, but I tell you, my friends, it is quite requisite to be a little material, also. At all events, we are so, and, being so, it proves a law of our nature. (Applause). . . .

Mrs. Blackwell told us that, marriage being based on the perfect equality of husband and wife, it can not be destroyed. But is it so? Where? Where and when have the sexes yet been equal in physical or mental education, in position, or in law? When and where have they yet been recognized by society, or by themselves, as equals? "Equal in rights," says Mrs. B. But are they equal in rights? If they were, we would need no conventions to claim our rights. "She can assert her equality." Yes, she can assert it, but does that assertion constitute a true marriage? And when the husband holds the iron heel of legal oppression on the subjugated neck of the wife until every spark of womanhood is crushed out, will it heal the wounded heart, the lacerated spirit, the destroyed hope, to assert her equality? And shall she still continue the wife? Is that a marriage which must not be dissolved? (Applause). . . .

Mr. Greeley tells us, that, marriage being a Divine institution, nothing but death should ever separate the parties; but when he was asked, "Would you have a being who, innocent and inexperienced, in the youth and ardor of affection, in the fond hope that the sentiment was reciprocated, united herself to one she loved and cherished, and then found (no matter from what cause) that his profession was false, his heart hollow, his acts cruel, that she was degraded by his vice, despised for his crimes, cursed by his very presence, and treated with every conceivable ignominy—would you have her drag out a miserable existence as his wife?" "No, no," says he; "in that case, they ought to separate." Separate? But what becomes of the union divinely instituted, which death only should part? (Applause).

The papers have of late been filled with the heart-sickening accounts of wife-poisoning. Whence come these terrible crimes? From the want of a Divorce law. Could the Hardings be legally separated, they would not be driven to the commission of murder to be free from each other; and which is preferable, a Divorce law, to dissolve an unholy union, which all parties agree is no true marriage, or a murder of one, and an execution (legal murder) of the other party? But had the unfortunate woman, just before the poisoned cup was presented to her lips, pleaded for a divorce, Mrs. Blackwell would have read her a sermon equal to St. Paul's "Wives, be obedient to your husbands," only she would have added, "You must assert your equality," but "you must keep with your husband and work for his redemption, as I would do for my husband"; and Mr. Greeley would say, "As you chose to marry him, it is your own fault; you must abide the consequences, for it is a 'divine institution, a union for life, which nothing but death can end.'" (Applause). . . .

But what is marriage? A human institution, called out by the needs of social, affectional human nature, for human purposes, its objects are, first, the happiness of the parties immediately concerned, and, secondly, the welfare of society. Define it as you please, these are only its objects; and therefore if, from well-ascertained facts, it is demonstrated that the real objects are frustrated, that instead of union and happiness, there are only discord and misery to themselves, and vice and crime to society, I ask, in the name of individual happiness and social morality and well-being, why such a marriage should be binding for life?—why one human being should be chained for life to the dead body of another? . . .

I therefore, ask for a Divorce law. Divorce is now granted for some crimes; I ask it for others also. It is granted for a State's prison offense. I ask that personal cruelty to a wife, whom he swore to "love, cherish, and protect," may be made a heinous crime—a perjury and a State's prison offense, for which divorce shall be granted. Willful desertion for one year should be a sufficient cause for divorce, for the willful deserter forfeits the sacred title of husband or wife. Habitual intemperance, or any other vice which makes the husband or wife intolerable and abhorrent to the other, ought to be sufficient cause for divorce. I asked for a law of Divorce, so as to secure the real objects and blessings of married life, to prevent the crimes and immoralities now practiced, to prevent "Free Love," in its most hideous form, such as is now carried on but too often under the very name of marriage, where hypocrisy is added to the crime of legalized prostitution. "Free Love," in its degraded sense, asks for no Divorce law. It acknowledges no marriage, and therefore requires no divorce. I believe in true marriages; and therefore I ask for a law to free men and women from false ones. (Applause). . . .

WENDELL PHILLIPS then said: . . . This Convention is no Marriage Convention—if it were, the subject would be in order; but this Convention, if I understand it, assembles to discuss the laws that rest unequally upon women, not those that rest equally upon men and women. . . . We have nothing to do with a question which affects both sexes equally. Therefore, it seems to me we have nothing to do with the theory of marriage, which is the basis, as Mrs. Rose has very clearly shown, of divorce. . . .

MRS. BLACKWELL: . . . It must come upon this platform, for at present it is a relation which legally and socially bears unequally upon women. We must have temporary redress for the wife. The whole subject must be incidentally opened for discussion. The only question is one of present fitness. Was it best, under all the circumstances, to introduce it now? I have not taken the responsibility of answering in the affirmative. But it must come here and be settled, sooner or later, because its interests are everywhere, and all human relations center in this one marriage relation. (Applause). . . .

SUSAN B. ANTHONY: . . . As to the point that this question does not belong to this platform,—from that I totally dissent. Marriage has ever been a one-sided matter, resting most unequally upon the sexes. By it, man gains all—woman loses all; tyrant law and lust reign supreme with him—meek submission and ready obedience alone befit her. Woman has never been consulted; her wish has never been taken into consideration as regards the terms of the marriage compact. By law, public sentiment and religion, from the time of Moses down to the present day, woman has never been thought of other than as a piece of property, to be disposed of at the will and pleasure of man. And this very hour, by our statute-books, by our (so called) enlightened Christian civilization, she has no voice whatever in saying what shall be the basis of the relation. She must accept marriage as man proffers it, or not at all.

And then again, on Mr. Phillips' own ground, the discussion is perfectly in order, since nearly all the wrongs of which we complain grow out of the inequality, the injustice of the marriage laws, that rob the wife of the right to herself and her children—that make her the slave of the man she marries.

I hope, therefore, the resolutions will be allowed to go out to the public, that there may be a fair report of the ideas which have actually been presented here, that they may not be left to the mercy of the secular press. I trust the Convention will not vote to forbid the publication of those resolutions with the proceedings.[36]

The resolutions were retained in the record, but they were not accepted by the Convention.

Less than a year later, Stanton went before the New York legislature to advocate liberalized divorce laws. Although she was deeply disappointed by women's response to the 1860 debate and by the legislature's recalcitrance, she remained convinced that the marriage question affected women like nothing else. A decade later, stung by the suffrage defeats after the Civil War, Stanton took to the lecture circuit. In special sessions for women she discovered that "women responded to this divorce speech as they never did to suffrage."[37] Stanton shocked many even among the feminists by her refusal to deny freedom in the name of love:

> Freedom on this subject! Why that is nothing short of unlimited freedom of divorce, freedom to institute at the option of the parties new amatory relationships. . . . We are all free lovers at heart though we may not have thought so. . . . The men and women who are dabbling with the suffrage movement for women should be at once therefore emphatically warned that what they mean logically if not consciously in all they say is next social equality and next Freedom or in a word Free Love and, if they wish to get out of the boat, they should for safety get out now, for delays are dangerous.[38]

Stanton's increasingly strong stand on divorce helped split the woman's movement into the radical New York and the more conservative Boston factions. The scandal over Victoria Woodhull's public espousal of Free Love, the greater scandal in 1873 over Theodore Tilton's divorce trial, the growing concern with abortion, the impact of "Comstockery," and the general anxiety over America's supposed moral decline after the war, all meant that the national tide in the mid-1870s was turning against Stanton and those who sought further liberalization of marriage laws. The women who had responded to Stanton's divorce speech fell silent or turned their energies to the Social Purity Crusade. Their sense of women's sexual wrongs merged with a conviction of women's moral rectitude to fuel attacks not on marriage but on male immorality. When divorces increased from 9,937 in 1867 to 25,535 in 1886, many Americans (led by the new National Divorce Reform League) felt that something had to be done to stop the trend.[39] Permissive states such as Indiana and the Dakotas tightened their requirements; liberal Connecticut repealed its general misconduct clause. Laura Bullard, Stanton's successor at the *Revolution* could maintain bravely that "man has bound in wedlock many whom God has not joined together,"[40] but men like Greeley would prevent for at least a quarter century any significant loosening of the marriage bond.

IV

Marriage reform caused doubt and dissension among women; by the end of the period, suffrage had called forth their sustained, and indeed organized, opposition. In 1889 a group of prominent Englishwomen issued "An Appeal Against Female Suffrage," arguing that political equality would lead to a "total misconception of woman's true dignity and special mission." Mrs. Leslie Stephen, Mrs. Matthew Arnold, Mrs. Humphry Ward, Christina Rossetti, Eliza Lynn Linton, and others insisted that women lacked the experience, judgment, and physical strength necessary to undertake forceful action in the country's behalf. Moreover, they feared that women's participation in "the turmoil of active political life" would impair their "sympathy and disinterestedness"—the two moral qualities most essential for maintaining family stability and national integrity.[41] American opponents were even more organized. By 1890, the Boston Committee of Remonstrants had petitioned, distributed literature, hired male counsel to represent them at legislative hearings, and issued the first antisuffrage publication.[42] Such intense resistance indicates how radical a demand suffrage was. Women who sought the vote were asking to exercise power rather than influence. They were no longer Angels in the House, but persons pursuing equality in the body politic. Although they sometimes spoke of women's special qualities, the suffragists relied heavily on Enlightenment arguments for individual human rights. Most Victorians saw their campaign as a threat to the family and to larger political structures.[43]

As demonstrated in Volume I (Chapters 1 and 2), the right to vote had been claimed early in the period by feminists like William Thompson (1825), the Female Political Union at Newcastle (1839), Marion Reid (1843), Elizabeth Cady Stanton and other American women at the Seneca Falls Convention (1848), and Harriet Taylor (1851). Although some women's advocates regarded female enfranchisement as too controversial an issue to be publicly identified with, others spoke in detail about its moral, political, and social advantages. Women who believed that political activity was a selfless form of community service regarded the vote as a prerequisite for their real work of combatting the nation's wrongs; women who were oppressed saw the vote as a necessary defense against laws that were made and administered by men. In both countries, serious debate began during the 1860s when Congress and Parliament were considering proposals for enlarging the voting population through the Fourteenth Amendment and the Second Reform Bill.

In England, where the franchise was based on ownership or occupation of property, women had to start by trying to undo the effects of the First Reform Bill.[44] Passed in 1832, it had enfranchised about half the male middle class; agricultural laborers and most industrial workers were still excluded, but about one-sixth of the adult males—those who owned or rented property worth an annual rate of £10 or more—became eligible to vote. Unfortunately, the Bill's authors established the first statutory bar to female enfranchisement by using the words "male person." When Parliament took up discussion of the Second Reform Bill, political activists saw an opportunity for removing the barrier.

With the encouragement of John Stuart Mill, who was elected M.P. in 1865 despite his support of women's suffrage, Barbara Bodichon and Emily Davies prepared a petition of 1,499 signatures, including those of Harriet Martineau, Mary Somerville, and Frances Power Cobbe. The petition, which quickly gained the endorsement of the *Law Times*, stated:

> That it having been expressly laid down by high authorities that the possession of property in this country carries with it the right to vote in the election of Representatives in Parliament: it is an evident anomaly that some holders of property are allowed to use their right, while others, forming no less a constituent part of the nation, and equally qualified by law to hold property, are not able to exercise this privilege.

That the participation of women in the Government is consistent with the principles of the British Constitution, inasmuch as women in these islands have always been held capable of sovereignty and women are eligible to various public offices.

Your Petitioners therefore humbly pray your Honourable House to consider the expediency of providing for the representation of all householders, without distinction of sex, who possess such property or rental qualification as your Honourable House may determine.[45]

By maintaining the property qualification and avoiding such an extreme idea as universal suffrage, the women could argue that their proposal was consistent with the fundamental principles of English law.

Feminists like Bodichon, Lydia Becker, Cobbe, and Helen Taylor developed the argument in essays and speeches.[46] Mill stated the case in the House of Commons, presenting Bodichon's petition on June 7, 1866, and proposing an amendment to the Reform Bill on May 20, 1867. Although Mill believed that all women householders should be given the vote, he was reluctant to begin by attacking coverture; instead he asked only that suffrage be granted to single women who met the same property qualification as men.

There is nothing to distract our attention from the simple question, whether there is any adequate justification for continuing to exclude an entire half of the community, not only from admission, but from the capability of being ever admitted within the pale of the Constitution, though they may fulfil all the conditions legally and constitutionally sufficient in every case but theirs. . . . To lay a ground for refusing the suffrage to any one, it is necessary to allege either personal unfitness or public danger. Now, can either of these be alleged in the present case? Can it be pretended that women who manage an estate or conduct a business—who pay rates and taxes, often to a large amount, and frequently from their own earnings—many of whom are responsible heads of families, and some of whom, in the capacity of schoolmistresses, teach much more than a great number of the male electors have ever learnt—are not capable of a function of which every male householder is capable? Or is it feared that if they were admitted to the suffrage they would revolutionize the State—would deprive us of any of our valued institutions, or that we should have worse laws, or be in any way whatever worse governed through the effect of their suffrages? No one, Sir, believes anything of the kind.

And it is not only the general principles of justice that are
infringed, or at least set aside, by the exclusion of women, merely
as women, from any share in the representation; that exclusion is
also repugnant to the particular principles of the British Constitution. It violates one of the oldest of our constitutional maxims—a
doctrine dear to Reformers, and theoretically acknowledged by
most Conservatives—that taxation and representation should be
co-extensive. Do not women pay taxes? . . . If a stake in the
country means anything, the owner of freehold or leasehold property has the same stake, whether it is owned by a man or a
woman. . . .

The House, however, will doubtless expect that I should not
rest my case solely on the general principles either of justice or of
the Constitution, but should produce what are called practical
arguments. . . . I am prepared to state them, if I may be permitted first to ask, what are the practical objections? . . . Politics,
it is said, are not a woman's business. Well, Sir, I rather think
that politics are not a man's business either; unless he is one
of the few who are selected and paid to devote their time to
the public service, or is a Member of this or of the other House.
The vast majority of male electors have each his own business
which absorbs nearly the whole of his time; but I have not heard
that the few hours occupied, once in a few years, in attending at a
polling-booth, even if we throw in the time spent in reading
newspapers and political treatises, ever causes them to neglect
their shops or their counting-houses. . . . Is it not the very essence of constitutional liberty, that men come from their looms
and their forges to decide, and decide well, whether they are
properly governed, and whom they will be governed by? . . . The
ordinary occupations of most women are, and are likely to remain,
principally domestic; but the notion that these occupations are
incompatible with the keenest interest in national affairs, and in all
the great interests of humanity, is as utterly futile as the apprehen-
sion, once sincerely entertained, that artizans would desert their
workshops and their factories if they were taught to read. . . .

But perhaps it is thought that the ordinary occupations of
women are more antagonistic than those of men are to the com-
prehension of public affairs. It is thought, perhaps, that those who
are principally charged with the moral education of the future
generations of men, cannot be fit to form an opinion about the
moral and educational interests of a people; and that those whose
chief daily business is the judicious laying-out of money, so as to
produce the greatest results with the smallest means, cannot possibly give any lessons to right hon. Gentlemen on the other side of
the House or on this, who contrive to produce such singularly
small results with such vast means. . . . The notion of a hard and

fast line of separation between women's occupations and men's—of forbidding women to take interest in the things which interest men—belongs to a gone-by state of society which is receding further and further into the past. . . . The two sexes now pass their lives together; the women of a man's family are his habitual society; the wife is his chief associate, his most confidential friend, and often his most trusted adviser. . . . Sir, the time is now come when, unless women are raised to the level of men, men will be pulled down to theirs. . . .

We are told, Sir, that women do not wish for the suffrage. . . . But great numbers of women do desire the suffrage, and have asked for it by petitions to this House. How do we know how many more thousands there may be who have not asked for what they do not hope to get; or for fear of what may be thought of them by men, or by other women; or from the feeling, so sedulously cultivated in them by their education—aversion to make themselves conspicuous? . . . However this may be, those who do not care for the suffrage will not use it; either they will not register, or if they do, they will vote as their male relatives advise—by which, as the advantage will probably be about equally shared among all classes, no harm will be done. Those, be they few or many, who do value the privilege, will exercise it, and will receive that stimulus to their faculties, and that widening and liberalizing influence over their feelings and sympathies, which the suffrage seldom fails to produce on those who are admitted to it. Meanwhile an unworthy stigma would be removed from the whole sex. The law would cease to declare them incapable of serious things; would cease to proclaim that their opinions and wishes are unworthy of regard, on things which concern them equally with men, and on many things which concern them much more than men. They would no longer be classed with children, idiots, and lunatics, as incapable of taking care of either themselves or others, and needing that everything should be done for them, without asking their consent. If only one woman in 20,000 used the suffrage, to be declared capable of it would be a boon to all women. . . .

Then it is said, that women do not need direct power, having so much indirect, through their influence over their male relatives and connections. I should like to carry this argument a little further. Rich people have a great deal of indirect influence. Is this a reason for refusing them votes? . . . Sir, it is true that women have great power. It is part of my case that they have great power; but they have it under the worst possible conditions because it is indirect, and therefore irresponsible. I want to make this great power a responsible power. I want to make the woman feel her conscience interested in its honest exercise. . . . I want to awaken in her the political point of honour. . . .

But at least, it will be said, women do not suffer any practical inconvenience, as women, by not having a vote. The interests of all women are safe in the hands of their fathers, husbands, and brothers, who have the same interest with them, and not only know, far better than they do, what is good for them, but care much more for them than they care for themselves. Sir, this is exactly what is said of all unrepresented classes. The operatives, for instance; are they not virtually represented by the representation of their employers? Are not the interest of the employers and that of the employed, when properly understood, the same? To insinuate the contrary, is it not the horrible crime of setting class against class? Sir, we do not live in Arcadia, but, as we were lately reminded, *in faece Romuli*: and in that region workmen need other protection than that of their employers, and women other protection than that of their men. I should like to have a Return laid before this House of the number of women who are annually beaten to death, kicked to death, or trampled to death by their male protectors. . . .

I give these instances to prove that women are not the petted children of society which many people seem to think they are— that they have not the overabundance, the superfluity of power that is ascribed to them, and are not sufficiently represented by the representation of the men who have not had the heart to do for them this simple and obvious piece of justice. Sir, grievances of less magnitude than the law of the property of married women, when suffered by parties less inured to passive submission, have provoked revolutions. . . .

Amendment proposed, in page 2, line 16, to leave out the word "man," in order to insert the word "person,"—(*Mr. Mill*,)— instead thereof (see Illustration 1).

MR. KARSLAKE said, he had listened, as the rest of the House had done, with great attention to the argument of the hon. Member for Westminster, for there was this peculiarity in the subject—that there was not a man in England, whatever his rank in life, who was not interested in it:—for though the observations of the hon. Member pointed only to the admission of spinsters and widows to the suffrage, the hon. Member's argument, as well as the arguments in his published writings, which he (Mr. Karslake) had studied with great care, all pointed to the admission of married women. . . . If the hon. Member got in the thin end of the wedge by the admission of unmarried women to the electoral roll he would afterwards claim that married women should also be admitted to the franchise. . . . Now that was a question they ought to consider—first, with regard to the law of the land; and next, with regard to expediency. . . .

The law of the land at the present day had deliberately settled that the wife should be absolutely and entirely under the control of the husband, not only in respect of her property, but of her personal movements. For example, a married woman might not "gad about," and if she did her husband was entitled to lock her up; some held that he might beat her. He had his doubts about that, and if his advice were asked, as a lawyer, he would say do not do it:—but undoubtedly the husband had entire dominion over the person and property of his wife. He thought, then, it was clear that votes could not be given to married women consistently with the rules of law as regarded property and the husband's dominion over the wife's movements. Then how would it be in the matter of voting? In the course of his canvass, which was still vividly in his recollection, he often canvassed the wives of voters. And he generally found that the female persons were "blue" [conservative]. It was their usual reply—"Oh, I am blue; but my husband votes yellow" [liberal]. Sometimes, he admitted, it was the other way. How did the hon. Gentleman propose to deal with these differences of opinion between the head of the family and her whom the poet called "the lesser man?" . . .

As to the question of expediency, the hon. Gentleman in his works thought that advantage would arise from giving the suffrage to women, because among other things it would promote logical discussion between the man and his wife. In other words, hon. Members would have spent their Sunday evenings during the last six weeks in discussing with their wives the question of the compound-householder. He believed that the "unerring instinct" not only of the House of Commons, but of men themselves, would be utterly opposed to this innovation. . . .

Mʀ. LAING thanked the hon. Member for Westminster for the pleasant interlude he had interposed to the grave and somewhat sombre discussions on the subject of Reform, in which the Committee had hitherto been engaged. . . . But, to speak seriously on the subject, it would, he thought, be well in dealing with it to reflect for a moment how small a part mere logic played in political and social life. The instinct, he felt assured, of nine men out of ten—nay, of nine women out of ten—was opposed to the proposal which had been laid before the Committee by the hon. Member for Westminster with so much force and acumen, and although they might not be able to give a single argument for their opinion he would back their instinct against the logic of the hon. Member. . . .

Between the two sexes it was abundantly evident that Nature had drawn clear lines of distinction. . . . In all that required rough, rude, practical force, stability of character, and intellect,

man was superior: whereas in all those relations of life that demanded mildness, softness of character, and amiability, women far
excelled. . . . Who could fancy the Julias, Ophelias, and Desde-
monas, who were surrounded with so great a charm. . . , as
interesting themselves in and voting at municipal or Parliamentary
elections? Which was the most likely to figure in the character of a
ratepayer and elector—the gentle Cordelia or the hateful and
unattractive Goneril or Regan? . . . The contests of political life,
and the rude and rough work which men had so often to go
through, were not, however, he thought, suited to the nature of
woman, and, unless he was greatly mistaken, the majority of
women themselves were of that opinion. The question, he would
add, was not one of a purely speculative character. There was one
country in which women took a leading part in the concerns of
active life, in which they were regarded as constituting the safety
and ornament of the Throne, and monopolized the rewards of the
Court—even those which were the most seductive of all—the
rewards of military virtue and honour. That Court was the Court
of Dahomey. Now, he must confess he had no wish to see the
institutions of Dahomey imported into out own happy land; in
other words, he hoped the day was far distant when our women
should become masculine and our men effeminate.

  SIR GEORGE BOWYER: . . . Was there any reason for excluding women from the franchise? He thought that no such
reason existed, and that the claim of women to the suffrage could
not be answered logically. This country was governed by our
Sovereign Lady the Queen; and in other countries there were or
had been female Monarchs, among whom, indeed, on the page of
history, was to be found a larger proportion of great and distinguished Sovereigns than among male rulers. Women, moreover,
were qualified for churchwardens and for other parochical offices.
He was no advocate for strong-minded women; but he believed
they might exercise the suffrage without abrogating those qualities
which specially adorned their sex. He presumed, however, that the
hon. Member for Westminster would propose that they should use
voting papers, for it would be manifestly indecorous for them to
attend the hustings or the polling-booth; but voting papers, duly
guarded, would enable the sex to vote in a manner free from
objection. He approved the proposal in a constitutional point of
view, for it was a principle of our Constitution that taxation
should be as nearly as possible co-extensive with representation.
. . . Though, generally speaking, women do not occupy themselves with politics—nor was it desirable that they should do so—
he maintained that, being taxed, they ought to be represented.

  VISCOUNT GALWAY, believing that the Committee were anxious to proceed to more important business, would appeal to the

hon. Member for Westminster to withdraw his Motion, which, if pressed to a division, would place many Gentlemen who were great admirers of the fair sex in an embarrassing point. The hon. Member for Brighton (Mr. Fawcett) had said that the female sex had no representatives in the House. Now he thought they had a very able one in the hon. Gentleman himself, though his experience with regard to the sex was not very prolonged, as the hon. Gentleman, he believed, had not been married above a fortnight. . . .

Mr. J. STUART MILL: I will merely say, in answer to the noble Lord who requested me to withdraw the Motion, that I am a great deal too well pleased with the speeches that have been made against it—his own included—to think of withdrawing it. There is nothing that has pleased me more in those speeches than to find that every one who has attempted to argue at all, has argued against something which is not before the House: they have argued against the admission of married women, which is not in the Motion; or they have argued against the admission of women as Members of this House; or again, as the hon. Member for the Wick boroughs (Mr. Laing) has done, they have argued against allowing women to be generals and officers in the army; a question which I need scarcely say is not before the House. I certainly do think that when we come to universal suffrage, as some time or other we probably shall come—if we extend the vote to all men, we should extend it to all women also. So long, however, as you maintain a property qualification, I do not propose to extend the suffrage to any women but those who have the qualification. . . . I will only say that if we should in the progress of experience—especially after experience of the effect of granting the suffrage—come to the decision that married women ought to have the suffrage, or that women should be admitted to any employment or occupation which they are not now admitted to—if it should become the general opinion that they ought to have it, they will have it.[47]

Although the amendment was opposed by Disraeli and Gladstone and defeated 196 to 73, Mill said that "the honour of being the first to make the claim of women to the suffrage a parliamentary question" was "the most gratifying" and "the most important public service" he had been able to render.[48] Kate Amberley and Millicent Garrett Fawcett, later leaders in the suffrage movement, heard Mill's address in the Ladies' Gallery. "A masterpiece of close reasoning, tinged here and there by deep emotion," said Fawcett.[49] From America Stanton and Anthony requested a copy, which they reprinted for the American Equal Rights Association. New York activists who were preparing for an 1868 constitutional convention based their argument on Mill's theories and circulated his speech to delegates during the suffrage debates.[50]

However, in both countries, the terms of the controversy were quickly set. Many of the arguments against enfranchising women were also used against groups of men, such as immigrants, blacks, and argicultural laborers: they were said to be adequately represented already, to be ignorant and incompetent. The arguments that applied exclusively to women were built on contradictory assumptions. Speakers of both sexes declared that women were either too good for politics or too bad. Some politicians envisioned respectable widows assaulted at the polls, while their colleagues declared that only slatterns would dare appear at the hustings. Those who believed women to be religious denied them the vote because they might be under the influence of ministers and priests; those who believed women to be corrupt withheld it because they could be bribed. Many writers asserted that women did not really want the vote, but others protested that they wanted it too much, as a way to gain power and advance their own interests. When Mill argued that the vote should be granted to unmarried and widowed women, opponents denigrated his commitment to "society's failures." When married women were included in the proposals, speakers such as Karslake warned that wives who had the vote would quarrel constantly with their husbands about politics, and other legislators insisted that enfranchisement was unnecessary since women would always vote the way their husbands and fathers told them to. These arguments remained remarkably consistent throughout the century.[51]

When British and American feminists failed to alter the legislative processes, they turned to the courts. If they could not formulate new laws, they could perhaps wrest more favorable interpretations from existing statutes. In England legal controversy centered on the use of "man" in the 1867 Reform Bill. Lord Brougham's Act of 1859 had established that "in all Acts words importing the masculine gender shall be deemed and taken to include females unless the contrary . . . is expressly provided." Citing Lord Brougham's Act, some suffragists argued that women already had the vote. They were supported here by Chisholm Anstey, a barrister whose legal research implied that the right of appointing parliamentary representatives had been linked to property rather than sex in the Middle Ages; that some female landowners had exercised their voting rights in the past;

and that no statute had subsequently been enacted to deny them these rights. Relying on historical precedent, and on Lord Brougham's Act, 5,346 women householders from Manchester claimed the right to vote and went to court with Dr. Richard Pankhurst as their attorney. In their 1868 case, known as *Chorlton v. Lings*, the judge decided that if a precedent existed, it had been rendered nugatory by three hundred years of non-use, that women lacked the legal capacity to vote, and that the word "man" meant a "member of the male sex." (For many tax purposes, though, "man" remained generic.)[52]

American women encountered similar problems when they attempted to join the movement toward democracy. The 1865 freeing of the slaves had produced unwarranted optimism. Many feminists were abolitionists eager to see the woman's hour and the "Negro's hour" coincide; most assumed that legislators would grant the vote as readily to their wives as to their former slaves.[53] Unfortunately, the late 1860s brought setbacks at both the state and federal levels. In Kansas, the first referendum on women's suffrage was overwhelmingly defeated in 1867. In the nation's capital, discussions of the Fourteenth and Fifteenth Amendments had disconcerting implications. The second section of the Fourteenth Amendment, which was intended to make Confederate states enfranchise their ex-slaves, referred only to "male inhabitants"; it threatened to make women's inability to vote a matter of federal law. Alarmed by the prospect of having to challenge the United States Constitution in order to vote in federal elections, Stanton warned, "If that word 'male' be inserted, it will take us a century at least to get it out."[54] The Fifteenth Amendment explicitly prohibited disenfranchisement on grounds of race, but said nothing about sex: "The right of citizens of the United States to vote shall not be denied or abridged by the United States or by any State on account of race, color, or previous condition of servitude." To ratify it, charged Stanton, would give the vote to all men while leaving women utterly bereft of political privilege. Feeling betrayed by the abolitionists and increasingly hostile to black suffrage, Stanton sometimes gave way to racist rhetoric. She and Anthony fought bitterly to get "male" removed from the Fourteenth Amendment and "sex" added to the Fifteenth. But by 1870 both amendments were in force.

Like the Manchester householders, American women tried a practical tactic. Small groups attempted to vote—in New Jersey

(1865), Massachusetts (1869), the District of Columbia (1871), and other states. Feminists, such as Stanton and Victoria Woodhull, and a few legislators, such as S.C. Pomeroy and G.W. Julian, provided the theoretical justification: they argued that the first section of the Fourteenth Amendment—the "privileges and immunities" clause—had already enfranchised the female population.[55] Of these speakers trying to turn defeat into victory, Susan B. Anthony was the most eloquent. Arrested for voting in the 1872 presidential election, she took to the lecture circuit in Monroe County, New York. In this speech, Anthony invokes her inalienable natural rights; insists that the Fourteenth Amendment has given the vote to all persons, including women; and argues that the Fifteenth Amendment applies to married women because of their "condition of servitude."

Friends and Fellow-Citizens:—I stand before you under indictment for the alleged crime of having voted at the last presidential election, without having a lawful right to vote. It shall be my work this evening to prove to you that in thus doing, I not only committed no crime, but instead simply exercised my citizen's right, guaranteed to me and all United States citizens by the National Constitution beyond the power of any State to deny.

Our democratic-republican government is based on the idea of the natural right of every individual member thereof to a voice and a vote in making and executing the laws. We assert the province of government to be to secure the people in the enjoyment of their inalienable rights. We throw to the winds the old dogma that government can give rights. No one denies that before governments were organized each individual possessed the right to protect his own life, liberty and property. When 100 or 1,000,000 people enter into a free government, they do not barter away their natural rights; they simply pledge themselves to protect each other in the enjoyment of them through prescribed judicial and legislative tribunals. They agree to abandon the methods of brute force in the adjustment of their differences and adopt those of civilization. Nor can you find a word in any of the grand documents left us by the fathers which assumes for government the power to create or to confer rights. The Declaration of Independence, the United States Constitution, and the constitutions of the several States and the organic laws of the Territories, all alike propose to *protect* the people in the exercise of their God-given rights. Not one of them pretends to bestow rights. . . .

For any State to make sex a qualification, which must ever result in the disfranchisement of one entire half of the people, is to pass a bill of attainder, an ex post facto law, and is therefore a violation of the supreme law of the land. By it the blessings of liberty are forever withheld from women and their female posterity. For them, this government has no just powers derived from the consent of the governed. For them this government is not a democracy; it is not a republic. It is the most odious aristocracy ever established on the face of the globe. An oligarchy of wealth, where the rich govern the poor; an oligarchy of learning, where the educated govern the ignorant; or even an oligarchy of race, where the Saxon rules the African, might be endured; but this oligarchy of sex which makes father, brothers, husband, sons, the oligarchs over the mother and sisters, the wife and daughters of every household; which ordains all men sovereigns, all women subjects—carries discord and rebellion into every home of the nation. . . .

It is urged that the use of the masculine pronouns *he, his* and *him* in all the constitutions and laws, is proof that only men were meant to be included in their provisions. If you insist on this version of the letter of the law, we shall insist that you be consistent and accept the other horn of the dilemma, which would compel you to exempt women from taxation for the support of the government and from penalties for the violation of laws. There is no *she* or *her* or *hers* in the tax laws, and this is equally true of all the criminal laws.

Take for example the civil rights law which I am charged with having violated; not only are all the pronouns in it masculine, but everybody knows that it was intended expressly to hinder the rebel men from voting. It reads, "If any person shall knowingly vote without *his* having a lawful right." It was precisely so with all the papers served on me—the United States marshal's warrant, the bail-bond, the petition for habeas corpus, the bill of indictment —not one of them had a feminine pronoun; but to make them applicable to me, the clerk of the court prefixed an "s" to the "he" and made "her" out of "his" and "him;" and I insist if government officials may thus manipulate the pronouns to tax, fine, imprison and hang women, it is their duty to thus change them in order to protect us in our right to vote. . . .

Though the words persons, people, inhabitants, electors, citizens, are all used indiscriminately in the national and State constitutions, there was always a conflict of opinion, prior to the war, as to whether they were synonymous terms, but whatever room there was for doubt, under the old regime, the adoption of the Fourteenth Amendment settled that question forever in its first sentence:

> All persons born or naturalized in the United States, and subject to the jurisdiction thereof, are citizens of the United States, and of the State wherein they reside.

The second settles the equal status of all citizens:

No State shall make or enforce any law which shall abridge the privileges or immunities of citizens of the United States; nor shall any State deprive any person of life, liberty or property without due process of law, or deny to any person within its jurisdiction the equal protection of the laws.

The only question left to be settled now is: Are women persons? I scarcely believe any of our opponents will have the hardihood to say they are not. Being persons, then, women are citizens, and no State has a right to make any new law, or to enforce any old law, which shall abridge their privileges or immunities. Hence, every discrimination against women in the constitutions and laws of the several States is today null and void, precisely as is every one against negroes.

Is the right to vote one of the privileges or immunities of citizens? I think the disfranchised ex-rebels and ex-State prisoners all will agree that it is not only one of them, but the one without which all the others are nothing. . . .

If the Fourteenth Amendment does not secure to all citizens the right to vote, for what purpose was that grand old charter of the fathers lumbered with its unwieldly proportions? . . . For by the Thirteenth Amendment black men had become people, and hence were entitled to all the privileges and immunities of the government, precisely as were the women of the country and foreign men not naturalized. . . . Clearly, then, if the Fourteenth Amendment was not to secure to black men their right to vote it did nothing for them, since they possessed everything else before. But if it was intended to prohibit the States from denying or abridging their right to vote, then it did the same for all persons, white women included, born or naturalized in the United States; for the amendment does not say that all male persons of African descent, but that all persons are citizens.

The second section is simply a threat to punish the States by reducing their representation on the floor of Congress, should they disfranchise any of their male citizens, and can not be construed into a sanction to disfranchise female citizens, nor does it in any wise weaken or invalidate the universal guarantee of the first section.

However much the doctors of the law may disagree as to whether people and citizens, in the original Constitution, were one and the same, or whether the privileges and immunities in the Fourteenth Amendment include the right of suffrage, the question of the citizen's right to vote is forever settled by the Fifteenth Amendment. "The right of citizens of the United States to vote shall not be denied or abridged by the United States, or by any

State, on account of race, color or previous condition of servitude." How can the State deny or abridge the right of the citizen, if the citizen does not possess it? There is no escape from the conclusion that to vote is the citizen's right, and the specifications of race, color or previous condition of servitude can in no way impair the force of that emphatic assertion that the citizen's right to vote shall not be denied or abridged. . . .

If, however, you will insist that the Fifteenth Amendment's emphatic interdiction against robbing United States citizens of their suffrage "on account of race, color or previous condition of servitude," is a recognition of the right of either the United States or any State to deprive them of the ballot for any or all other reasons, I will prove to you that the class of citizens for whom I now plead are, by all the principles of our government and many of the laws of the States, included under the term "previous condition of servitude."

Consider first married women and their legal status. What is servitude? "The condition of a slave." What is a slave? "A person who is robbed of the proceeds of his labor; a person who is subject to the will of another." . . . I submit the question, if the deprivation by law of the ownership of one's own person, wages, property, children, the denial of the right as an individual to sue and be sued and testify in the courts, is not a condition of servitude most bitter and absolute, even though under the sacred name of marriage? Does any lawyer doubt my statement of the legal status of married women? I will remind him of the fact that the common law of England prevails in every State but two in this Union, except where the legislature has enacted special laws annulling it. I am ashamed that not one of the States yet has blotted from its statute books the old law of marriage, which, summed up in the fewest words possible, is in effect "husband and wife are one, and that one the husband."

Thus may all married women and widows, by the laws of the several States, be technically included in the Fifteenth Amendment's specification of "condition of servitude," present or previous. The facts also prove that, by all the great fundamental principles of our free government, not only married women but the entire womanhood of the nation are in a "condition of servitude" as surely as were our Revolutionary fathers when they rebelled against King George. Women are taxed without representation, governed without their consent, tried, convicted and punished without a jury of their peers. Is all this tyranny any less humiliating and degrading to women under our democratic-republican government today than it was to men under their aristocratic, monarchical government one hundred years ago?[56]

In an 1873 trial marked by procedural irregularities, Anthony was found guilty of having voted illegally. Although technicalities kept her case from going to the Supreme Court, a year later the Court did agree to hear a similar case. In *Minor v. Happersett*, the Supreme Court avoided the constitutional question of whether voting for national officials was covered by the provisions of the Fourteenth Amendment. Emphasizing legislative intent, the Court declared that women constituted a special category of citizens whose inability to vote did not infringe upon their rights as citizens or persons. Observing that states had withheld the franchise from other groups in the past—criminals, slaves, and those without property—*Minor v. Happersett* upheld the states' right to exclude women.

Forced to deal with the political rather than the judicial process, suffrage organizations proceeded according to different plans during the 1870s and 1880s. The American, led by Julia Ward Howe and Lucy Stone, tried to change laws on a state-by-state basis, while the National, under Stanton and Anthony, worked to amend the Constitution, particularly through the Anthony Amendment: "The right of citizens of the United States to vote shall not be denied or abridged by the United States or by any state on account of sex." Formulated in 1878 and reintroduced in every session of Congress, it gained committee approval in the 1880s only to be defeated 34 to 16 in 1887. American women did not win the vote until 1920.

In England, women flooded Parliament with suffrage bills during the 1870s. But when work began on the Third Reform Bill, they concentrated their efforts on amending it. The proposal to extend the franchise to unmarried women on the same terms as men seemed to have a promising future. Suffrage societies, journals, and petitions had proliferated, and women had gained some political power since Mill made his speech: they voted in municipal elections and held office on school boards. Moreover, many M.P.'s who supported women's suffrage had been returned to Parliament in the election of 1879. Although the opposition was firmly entrenched, several historians think that if Gladstone had supported the amendment, it would have carried.[57] Gladstone had favored women's suffrage earlier in his career, but he was not willing to jeopardize the Third Reform Bill. By removing the property restriction and by granting the franchise to agricultural laborers, the Reform Bill of 1884 left the male population almost fully enfranchised and the female population powerless. A farmhand could vote, but the woman who employed him could not.

Democracy had run its course, but women were denied political representation by virtue of their sex. After 1884, as the antisuffrage groups became increasingly well organized, many suffragists, including Millicent Garrett Fawcett, turned to volunteer campaign work as a way of building a power base and gaining expertise within existing parties. Others were entirely alienated. Looking back on the failure of the women's suffrage bills, one observer noted, "Not one woman took counsel with herself as to how and why the agricultural labourers had won their franchise. They had won it, as a matter of fact, by burning hay-ricks, rioting, and otherwise demonstrating their strength in the only way that English politicians can understand. The threat to march a hundred thousand men to the House of Commons unless the bill was passed played its part also in securing the agricultural labourer his political freedom. But no woman suffragist noticed that. "As for myself," said Emmeline Pankhurst, the leader of England's militant suffragettes during the early twentieth century, "I was too young politically to learn the lesson then."[58] In 1918, after a long and bloody battle, Englishwomen finally won the right to vote and to stand for Parliament.

2

SCIENCE

Most scientists and physicians throughout the Victorian period define woman's sphere narrowly. This puts science in an awkward position; the prestige of scientific arguments derives partly from their supposed "objectivity," and yet the scientific arguments about women are anything but unbiased. Recent historians have documented conclusively how Victorian science handpicked and egregiously bent facts to support foregone conclusions. The often desperate commitment to the domestic angel meant that the Woman Question was nowhere debated more emotionally than in its supposedly "scientific" aspects.

In science, as in all other phases of the debate, what changes are not the premises or the conclusions but the arguments. An innovative method or theory, a new body of data, a provocative or definitive book, draws particular attention in a particular decade to one of three basic areas of scientific controversy: woman's sexual capacity; her intellectual capability; her developmental potential.

Sexuality, which was increasingly considered unfeminine in the 1830s and 1840s, becomes the subject of two canonical books in the 1850s. *The Functions and Disorders of the Reproductive*

Organs (1857) by Dr. William Acton incorporates and authenticates sexual taboos millennia old; *The Elements of Social Science* (1854) by Dr. George Drysdale provides the first complete Victorian defense of woman's sexual equality. Although sexual equality continues to find advocates throughout the century, increasing worry about woman's moral and physical degeneration keeps Acton's attitudes dominant into the twentieth century. Woman's intellectual capability, debated since the late eighteenth century, becomes increasingly a matter of physiology for the Victorians. In 1873, Dr. Edward H. Clarke's *Sex in Education* uses the supposedly contrary demands of the cerebral and the reproductive systems to argue against equal education for women. Although the spectacular responses (pro and con) to Clarke help perpetuate the education controversy into the twentieth century, the "hard facts" of female achievement on competitive examinations and in professional life make education and medicine areas of substantial progress for woman. Her developmental potential is another matter. Where she stands on the evolutionary ladder, and specifically how she related to blacks, are debated in Britian and America before the Civil War and are tirelessly discussed by transatlantic anthropologists after 1865. Even when social scientists change from biological to psychological models around 1900, they continue to define woman as developmentally inferior, maternal.

Victorian "Scientific reasoning" was obviously circular. Assumptions about True Woman affected those physiological "analyses" which defined the female body, mind, and future in ways that justified traditional views of her. This circularity has prevented many nineteenth- and twentieth-century readers from seeing that more is at work here than simply women's victimization by men. Males were the creations as well as the creators of the True Womanhood cult; many of these males were motivated less by "chauvinism" than by deep needs and genuine concern; and the cult itself had benign as well as harmful effects. On the other hand, by proclaiming an objectivity which they could not live up to, Victorian scientists did betray an arrogance and dishonesty which no amount of anxiety can explain away. The patent speciousness of the brain-weight controversy [pp. 75–76] is a good example. Terrible suffering for both sexes was the inevitable outcome of society's willingness to let science serve ideology.

I

To understand Victorian attitudes toward sexuality,[1] readers today must understand such a figure as Dr. William Acton—both as a "repressive" writer on sexuality and as a "representative" voice of the age. For thirty years before Acton and for forty years after, most eminent and not so eminent physicians in America and Europe foster the fear of sexuality. Some doctors are undoubtedly misogynistic, but no single term like antifeminist can do justice to the intricate cultural phenomenon which produces Acton and his colleagues. Their desire is not primarily to thwart woman or to indulge man. They fear chaos, the chaos of sexual excess. Whether debilitation derives from masturbation or from conjugal incontinence, the result is the same—exhaustion of the individual and the race.

How to prevent such chaos? Although men were extolled tirelessly, most real attention falls upon women. Man is both too strong and too weak. So strong are his passions that society, despite encomia to the Knight of Continence, accept male sexuality as unregenerately animal. This attitude, in turn, often masks its opposite—the fear of male inadequacy. If a man spends his energy in masturbation or conjugal excess, he will fail in the daylight intercourse of business. Doctors join clerics in advancing two basic arguments for continence. The purpose of marriage, they maintain, is not recreation but reproduction, so that sexual energy should be "spent" on progeny, not pleasure. Doctors also defend this apparently effeminate ideal of moderation by citing the precedent of indubitably virile epochs. Dr. Theophilus Parvin quotes Solon, Zoroaster, and Mohammud who restrict intercourse to, respectively, once in ten days, once in nine, and once a week (on Friday).

Recognizing that these earnest arguments are no match for male animality, doctors lend their prestige to society's last, best hope—that woman does not want sex. Many American physicians second Acton and other British practitioners in maintaining that "It is a mistake to suppose that . . . the kiss and the loving embrace of a wife are, in general, the expression of sexual desire."[2] Behind this attitude lies assumptions, fears, and misinformation. Can sexual passion be acknowledged in woman if her reason is, as doctors assumed, far weaker than her emotions? Worse still, since the heart is closer than the head to the genital region, may not the heart-oriented woman be in fact more passionate than the head-oriented male? Victorians are thus hoist on their own paradox. That very idolization of Motherhood which was intended to control woman's sexuality gives primacy to her sexual organs, so a "true" woman can achieve the sexless ideal only by betraying it.

Acton's "repressive" writings on sexuality occur in this context of widespread cultural anxiety over woman's passion and thus raise the question of how "representative" a spokesman he is. Until recently, assumptions about Victorian repressiveness led scholars to assume that Acton was speaking for "the" Victorians. New research, establishing that daily Victorian practice did not conform to Acton's prescriptions, has refused to predicate to all Victorians what some "Victorian" writers said. Birth control, abortion, and female orgasm were unquestionably more frequent than Acton allows. The scholarly pendulum has now swung toward the opposite pole, and Acton has recently been called eccentric and extreme. At issue is the tension between prescription and practice. These two elements vary in each individual, and their proportions shifted repeatedly between 1837 and 1883, but once we acknowledge prescription and practice as variables we can go on to generalize about them.

"The" Victorians can be seen as a threefold group. Some share Acton's orthodox view of woman; some reject that view and act accordingly; some diverge from Acton in their practice but still approve of his sentiments. This third group's split between practice and prescription reveals an important tension between private needs and public concern. Publicly the upwardly mobile and the solidly middle-class Victorians want a rigorous standard maintained for the lower class, regardless of their own private conduct. What is safe innovation or utter necessity for the bourgeoisie can, they feel, lead others—and thus all society—quickly to chaos.

The tension between prescription and practice is endemic to the Victorian period. The substantial sale of Acton's books, and of the books of doctors, clerics, and laymen who agree with him, plus the testimony of memoirs and letters and scandals, can neither be dismissed as eccentric nor accepted as "the" Victorian position. Acton spoke for the practice of some and for the complexly-held ideas of many; the very earnestness of his pronouncements, however, indicates the amount of contradictory opinion and practice which he knew opposed him. Acton is caught between the need for old beliefs and the recognition of recent changes. And this anxiety-producing middle position is more representative and important than any single idea of his. Acton was an innovator, for example, in the prostitution debate. His *Prostitution* (1857) forced society to face realities which orthodoxy ignored—that the real causes of prostitution were the pauperizing power of Victorian economics and the predatory lusts of respectable males; that prostitutes were generally healthier than married women and passed frequently from the streets to holy wedlock; that only when we acknowledge our bodies and particularly our sexual-excretory systems are personal health and public sanity possible. Moreover, even Acton's "orthodox" attitude toward female sexuality can be interpreted fairly only in light of the many pages which precede his remarks on woman in *Functions and Disorders*.[3]

By beginning with childhood, Acton can establish a rule for both sexes. "In a state of health no sexual idea should enter a child's mind" (17). With adolescent males who *are* confronted with sexuality, Acton argues that "continence" can control masturbation completely. Acton's very doggedness here belies his insistence upon adolescent purity. Why argue for twenty pages against a nonexistent danger? With adult males, Acton continues to fear excess. "The whole being of the man cries out, at this period of his life for, not the indiscriminate indulgence, but the regulated use of his matured sexual powers" (101). What is regulated use? "Sexual congress ought not to take place more frequently than once in seven or ten days" (111). Among several examples of male excess, Acton cites the case of

> a medical man [who] called on me, saying he found he was suffering from spermatorrhoea. There was general debility, inaptitude for work, disinclination for sexual intercourse, in fact, he thought he was losing his senses. The sight of one eye also was affected. The only way in which he lost semen was, as he thought, by a slight occasional oozing from his penis. I asked him at once if he had ever committed excesses. As a boy, he acknowledged having abused himself, but he married seven years ago, being then a hearty, healthy man, and it was only lately that he had been complaining. In answer to my further inquiry, he stated that since his marriage he had had connection two or three times a week, and often more than once a night! This one fact, I was obliged to tell him, sufficiently accounted for all his troubles. (125)

Although he is generally fair to Acton, Steven Marcus is prompted by this case history "to wonder: if the consequences of sexual intercourse are indistinguishable from those of masturbation, then why marry?"[4] Acton's case shows not that marriage corrupts like masturbation, but that immoderation debilitates at any age. What *is* questionable, of course, is Acton's defining immoderation as three connections per week. Yet even here context is important. As Acton is more temperate about masturbation than "moralists" who advocated raising sores upon or tying bells to a child's penis, so his seven-to-ten-day interval for couples is less extreme than many Victorian prescriptions. Dr. John Cowan, Mrs. E.B. Duffey, and others allowed only one connection per month for most couples (the lower classes being conceded four); still more extreme were Dr. Augustus K. Gardner and those Purity Crusaders [Volume II, Chapter 3] who argued for complete continence.[5] Acton can insist that sexual intercourse is basic to health, but he cannot celebrate human passion. "When these [nocturnal emissions] are frequent, the sufferer may be intellectually in a worse plight than if he were married and occasionally indulged in sexual intercourse" (74). Acton agrees with St. Paul—better marry than burn.

It is in light of this view of sexuality and in the context of inevitable male excess that Acton introduces female sexuality in *Functions and Disorders*.

> . . . so many false ideas are current as to women's sexual condition, and are so productive of mischief, that I need offer no apology for giving here a plain statement that most medical men will corroborate.
>
> I have taken pains to obtain and compare abundant evidence on this subject, and the result of my inquiries I may briefly epitomize as follows:—I should say that the majority of women (happily for society) are not very much troubled with sexual feeling of any kind. What men are habitually, women are only exceptionally. It is too true, I admit, as the divorce courts show, that there are some few women who have sexual desires so strong that they surpass those of men, and shock public feeling by their consequences. I admit, of course, the existence of sexual excitement terminating even in nymphomania, a form of insanity that those accustomed to visit lunatic asylums must be fully conversant with; but, with these sad exceptions, there can be no doubt that sexual feeling in the female is in the majority of cases in abeyance, and that it requires positive and considerable excitement to be roused at all: and even if roused (which in many instances it never can be) it is very moderate compared with that of the male. Many persons, and particularly young men, form their ideas of women's sensuous feelings from what they notice early in life among loose

or, at least, low and vulgar women. . . . Any susceptible boy is easily led to believe, whether he is altogether overcome by the syren or not, that she, and therefore all women, must have at least as strong passions as himself. Such women, however, give a very false idea of the condition of female sexual feeling in general. . . . It is from these erroneous notions that so many unmarried men think that the marital duties they will have to undertake are beyond their exhausted strength, and from this reason dread and avoid marriage. . . .

Married men—medical men—or married women themselves, would, if appealed to, tell a very different tale, and vindicate female nature from the vile aspersions cast on it by the abandoned conduct and ungoverned lusts of a few of its worst examples.

I am ready to maintain that there are many females who never feel any sexual excitement whatever. Others, again, immediately after each period, do become to a limited degree, capable of experiencing it; but this capacity is often temporary, and may entirely cease until the next menstrual period. Many of the best mothers, wives, and managers of households, know little of or are careless about sexual indulgences. Love of home, of children, and of domestic duties are the only passions they feel.

As a general rule, a modest woman seldom desires any sexual gratification for herself. She submits to her husband's embraces, but principally to gratify him; and, were it not for the desire of maternity, would far rather be relieved from his attentions. No nervous or feeble young man need, therefore, be deterred from marriage by any exaggerated notion of the arduous duties required from him. Let him be well assured, on my authority backed by the opinion of many, that the married woman has no wish to be placed on the footing of a mistress. . . .

One instance may better illustrate the real state of the case than much description.

In —, 185-, a barrister, about thirty years of age, came to me on account of sexual debility. . . . His wife assured me that she felt no sexual passions whatever; that if she was capable of them they were dormant. Her passion for her husband was of a Platonic kind, and far from wishing to stimulate his frigid feelings, she doubted whether it would be right or not. She loved him as he was, and would not desire him to be otherwise except for the hope of having a family.

I believe this lady is a perfect ideal of an English wife and mother, kind, considerate, self-sacrificing, and sensible, so pure-hearted as to be utterly ignorant of and averse to any sensual indulgence, but so unselfishly attached to the man she loves, as to be willing to give up her own wishes and feelings for his sake.

In strong contrast to the unselfish sacrifices such married women make of their feelings in allowing cohabitation, stand out others, who, either from ignorance or utter want of sympathy, although they are model wives in every other respect, not only evince no sexual feeling, but, on the contrary, scruple not to declare their aversion to the least manifestation of it. Doubtless this may, and often does, depend upon disease, and if so, the sooner the suffering female is treated the better. Much more frequently, however, it depends upon apathy, selfish indifference to please, or unwillingness to overcome a natural repugnance for cohabitation. . . .

Perversion of Sexual Feeling.—Where, in addition to the indisposition to cohabitation which many modest women feel, we find a persistent aversion to it, so strong as to be invincible by entreaty or by any amount of kindness on the husband's part, a very painful suspicion may sometimes arise as to the origin of so unconquerable a frigidity.

The following is a case in which these suspicions seemed to be justified by the facts:—A gentleman came to ask my opinion on the cause of want of sexual feeling in his wife. He told me he had been married four years. His wife was about his own age (twenty-seven), and had had four children, but she evinced no sexual feeling, although a lively, healthy lady, living in the country. I suggested several causes, when he at last asked me if it was possible that a woman might lose sexual feeling from the same cause as men. "I have read your former edition, Mr. Acton," said he, "and though you only allude to the subject incidentally, yet from what I have learned since my marriage, I am led to think that my wife's want of sexual feeling may arise, if you can affirm to me that such a thing is possible, from self-abuse. She has confessed to me that at a boarding-school, in perfect ignorance of any injurious effects, she early acquired the habit. This practice still gives her gratification; not so connection, which she views with positive aversion, although it gives her no pain." I told him that medical men, who are consulted about female complaints, have not unfrequently observed cases like that of his wife. It appears that, at last, nothing but the morbid excitement produced by the baneful practice can give any sexual gratification, and that the natural stimulus fails to cause any pleasure whatever. . . . We offer, I hope, no apology for light conduct when we admit that there are some *few* women who, like men, in consequence of hereditary predisposition or ill-directed moral education, find it difficult to restrain their passions, while their more fortunate sisters have never been tempted, and have, therefore, never fallen. This, however, does not alter the fact which I would venture again to impress on the reader, that, in general, women do *not* feel any great sexual tendencies. The unfortunately large numbers whose lives would seem to prove the contrary are to be otherwise accounted for. Vanity, giddiness, greediness, love of dress, distress, or hunger, make women prostitutes, but do not induce female profligacy so largely as has been supposed. (133–37)

Among the few mid-century defenders of woman's sexuality is one who prompted Acton to pause in *Functions and Disorders* and say:

but if the benefits of continence be so great and the results of incontinence so deplorable . . . what reprobation can be too strong for those advisers, medical or not, who deliberately encourage the early indulgence of the passions, on the false and wicked ground that self-restraint is incompatible with health? . . . Unfortunately, it is not only among the dregs of either the medical or literary professions that these false teachers are to be found. The following opinions, enunciated by a writer of no mean standing or ability, may serve as an example of the kind of principles (if they can be so called) which I am deprecating. . . . "The ignorance of the necessity of sexual intercourse to the health and virtue of both man and woman, is the most fundamental error in medical and moral philosophy." (49)

This fiend in physician form is Dr. George Drysdale of Edinburgh, whose *The Elements of Social Science* appears three years before *Functions and Disorders*.[6] Drysdale advocates the opposite of continence: the regular exercise of all organs. "There is no *greater error* than this," Acton argues. "I may state that I have never seen a single instance of atrophy of the generative organs from this cause [continence]" (57). Despite Acton's sheep-goats stance, he shares much with his fellow practitioner. Both men are distinguished specialists of the reproductive system; they cite the same authorities and agree that masturbation is "unnatural," conjugal excess debilitating, and abortion unconscionable. Both men, moreover, go beyond clinical concerns and emphasize the social ramifications of sexuality. They share a humane attitude toward prostitutes, a critical view of brothel-goers, a cosmopolitan familiarity with continental authorities, and an informed concern about the eugenic effects of business competition. Both doctors write "scientific" books which are fiercely ideological and both prophesy debility for anyone ignoring them. Finally, both see women in light of men. As Acton requires female asexuality to control male excess, Drysdale finds in woman's sexual appetite another proof of her equality with man. This difference, plus their many fundamental similarities, makes George Drysdale a useful counterpoint to William Acton. *The Elements of Social Science* probably matched the sales of *Functions and Disorders*.[7] Like Acton, Drysdale faces many of the age's chief sexual concerns, but unlike Acton, Drysdale goes on to discuss such social issues as wages, competition, capitalism, and socialism. Drysdale thus resembles William Thompson in his ability to view woman's plight in terms of all social suffering and to develop a comprehensive remedy for that suffering. Like Thompson, Drysdale is largely unknown today and yet definitely influenced Victorian radicals. Although Drysdale expressly departs from socialism in his belief that population, not competition, is the chief cause of social ills, he shares Thompson's concern with cooperation, with the "distribution of pleasure," and with the relation of pleasure to wages. Both men recognize repression as an important cause of nineteenth-century unhappiness and recommend sexual expression as a cure. Finally, both men have the same goal—to create a social science (thus the title of Drysdale's book) which will improve the quality of all human life and will, in the process, allow women full sexual and political equality. Related less by direct influence (so little is known of Drysdale that his reading of Thompson cannot be established) than by a continuity of approach and of spirit, Drysdale and Thompson share that rare but premier capacity to embrace the whole of a problem and to propose a solution which challenges the very structure of society. To see Drysdale in light of both Thompson and Acton is to complicate considerably our understanding of the life of the mind in the nineteenth century.

As a physician, Drysdale begins his testament to female sexuality by relating woman's sexual needs to the diseases which occur when those needs go unsatisfied.

> Chlorosis and hysteria in the female are diseases quite analogous to spermatorrhoea in the male. Both are a general enfeeblement and prostration of the system, connected with genital enfeeblement. Now in man we have already seen, that the only real natural cure for spermatorrhoea, (without which in almost all cases the disease lasts indefinitely, causing its own insufferable miseries,) is a proper healthy exercise for the sexual organs, and a healthy outlet for the sexual emotions and passions. . . . In woman the

case is just the same; her nature languishes for the want of the natural stimulus to be imparted only through these organs: her mind and her feelings become morbid from the same cause, and the only true and permanent remedy is a proper amount of sexual exercise. . . . Sexual intercourse is particularly necessary, when chlorosis has been caused by masturbation; for here there is not only a natural habit to be established, but an unnatural one to be eradicated, and this in both sexes is sometimes a difficult matter. Indeed, there is no means, which can be relied upon in either sex for checking the habit of masturbation, except the supply of the normal gratification. . . .

There is a great deal of erroneous feeling attaching to the subject of the sexual desires in woman. To have strong sexual passions is held to be rather a disgrace for a woman, and they are looked down upon as animal, sensual, coarse, and deserving of reprobation. The moral emotions of love are indeed thought beautiful in her; but the physical ones are rather held unwomanly and debasing. This is a great error. In woman, exactly as in man, strong sexual appetites are a very great virtue; as they are the signs of a vigorous frame, healthy sexual organs, and a naturally-developed sexual disposition. The more intense the venereal appetites, and the keener the sense of the normal sexual gratifications, provided it do not hold a diseased proportion to the other parts of the constitution, the higher is the sexual virtue of the individual. . . .

For the *prevention* of this important disease every means must be taken to elevate the physical powers in woman, from her childhood upwards. Female education, and the cramping views as to female decorum, should be greatly altered. Their bodies should be strengthened, just as those of boys and young men, by active sports and exercises—such as all young people delight in. They should be taught that physical strength, courage, and blooming health are as excellent and desirable in woman as in man, and they should learn to take as much pride in the physical as in the mental virtues. It is not for themselves alone, that they elevate their bodily powers, but for their future offspring also; pale and sickly mothers beget pale and sickly children. Solid and real knowledge should be given them, as well as the graceful arts; and above all, that which is far the most urgently required in the education both of man and woman—a knowledge of the human body and the human mind, with their nature and their laws. . . . At present a morbid curiosity is excited by the general ignorance on these subjects; to gratify which, prurient and stupid books are written, which are read by immense numbers of all classes and sexes. . . . The mystery on sexual subjects keeps men and women constantly in a state of childhood. . . .

When the girl has been trained to the possession of a powerful and healthy frame, and a healthy mind, invigorated by sound knowledge for her guidance in life, puberty will be readily and easily established, menstruation will follow, and she will enter upon womanhood with the fairest prospect of happiness. But at this period it is absolutely requisite, in order to maintain and elevate the health, and prevent the occurrence of sexual disease, that she should have before long, a healthy exercise for the new organs, and the normal gratification of the new desires. If this be not attainable, all our former efforts will prove in vain, and we shall have elevated her powers only to their own destruction. . . . If the sexual organs are to remain, as at present, totally unexercised throughout a great part, and, in numberless cases, throughout the whole of life, and if chastity must continue to be regarded as the highest female virtue, it is impossible to give woman any real liberty . . . and it is out of human power to make the lot of woman other than an unhappy, a diseased, and a degraded one, as it is at present, when vast quantities of the sex pass their lives as involuntary nuns, or as prostitutes. (170–75)

Suffering and disease have social as well as physiological causes, so Drysdale must function not only as a medical scientist but also as a social scientist. The Elements of Social Science diagnoses, for example, the repressive effect of the Judeo-Christian tradition. "We have no longer voluntary nuns, but of involuntary ones there are myriads. . . . Chastity, or complete sexual abstinence, so far from being a virtue, is invariably a great natural sin. . . . [Nature] cares not for our moral code . . . she gives her seal of approbation to the sexually virtuous man or woman . . . while she punishes the erring by physical and moral sufferings" (162). Physical and moral suffering cannot be blamed upon religion alone, however. Drysdale directs his major attack against that ultimate social malady—the lack of physical and spiritual nourishment. "Poverty, taken in its widest sense, meant the want of love as well as of food" (335). In prescribing his remedy, Drysdale accepts Malthus' solution to the problem of food scarcity ("have fewer children"), but he protests emphatically against any birth control technique (such as the late marriages advocated by Malthus and J.S. Mill) which increases the scarcity of love.

POVERTY is the most appalling of all the evils which oppress mankind. Other great evils, such as war, or pestilence, are, when compared with poverty, but of little importance. They are evanescent. . . . They are, moreover, in general, nothing but *effects* of the poverty, in which, with its inseparable social misery, discontent, and angry passions, the majority of mankind are plunged; and which is the main root of the most important transitory evils that we are subject to at the present day. . . . If social discontent, and the angry and envious feelings that poverty engenders, were allayed by its removal, the standing armies (which are in the usual circumstances of modern States needed much more to keep in check the poorer classes, than to guard against foreign hostilities,) could be reduced; and international wars, together with civil wars, would become in all probability a thing of the past. . . .

Do not let us suppose either, that *we* escape from evils of an analogous nature to those, by which the poor are ground to death. The cares and anxieties of the business and professional men among us are proverbial. . . . The great principle of population moreover presses upon us in a different, but scarcely a less fearful manner, than upon the poor. It produces among us the want of *love,* just as it does the want of food among the poor; and the former is almost as blighting and withering an evil among the richer classes, especially the young ladies, as the want of food and leisure among the poor. It slowly undermines health and happiness, and has made our society, our parties, balls, promenades, a hollow and artificial masquerade, where the joyless gaiety ill-disguises the aching hearts beneath. . . .

The difficulty of comprehending the principle of population arises from the extraordinary *peculiarity* of the principle itself. It differs from all truths hitherto discovered in this awful feature: that two great natural laws of our constitution *cross each other,* and are in antagonism; or in the words of Mr. Malthus, that "human beings are brought into the world by one law of nature, who by another law of nature cannot be supported." . . . In all other matters it is by obedience to the laws of nature that our safety is secured, but in the case of the reproductive powers, to obey *their* natural laws is certain destruction; while on the other hand, to *disobey* them is no less certain destruction. . . .

Poverty and the present social difficulties are a *compromise* made by mankind in this and all preceeding ages, between the two fearful wants,—the want of food and of love. . . . Instead of less love, we need infinitely more love, to make this world other than a dreary desert, as it is at present to the sexual sufferers, whose name is legion.

Hence we see, that the remedy which Mr. Malthus proposed for the evils of over-population, was of itself such a frightful evil, that all men recoiled from it; and loaded with invectives the man, *the only man,* who had shewn them the true difficulties of their life. Rather than adopt his remedy, rather than renounce, as he advised, all sexual intercourse till a comparatively late age, they were content to remain sunk in the mire of poverty and hard work; and to palliate their miseries by the old routine of prostitution, masturbation, and other morbid sexual outlets. The great error in Mr. Malthus's reasoning was, that he, like most of the moralists of his and our own age, was unaware of the frightful evils, and fearful natural sin of sexual abstinence. *The ignorance of the necessity of sexual intercourse to the health and virtue of both man and woman, is the most fundamental error in medical and moral philosophy.* (331, 334, 335, 344, 345)

Drysdale's solution—preventive intercourse—raises immediate questions. "First—Is this preventive sexual intercourse possible, and in what way? second—Can it be done without causing physical and moral evil?" (347). After advocating a form of diaphragm and declaring limited childbirth "perfectly healthy," Drysdale faces the moral question. "Preventive sexual intercourse is unnatural, but the circumstances of our life leave us no alternative" (351). The alternative of sexual abstinence "is so unnatural, and therefore sinful, that it is totally incompatible with health and happiness"; the alternative of following "our sexual desires like the inferior animals . . . [would force us] to prey upon and check the growth of each other, just as they do" (351). And so "the only choice left to us is to take the course from which the smallest amount of physical and moral evil will result" (351). That this "course" does not lead necessarily to matrimony involves Drysdale in an argument as iconoclastic as his critique of Christianity. Premising that "the grand object of any social institution for uniting the sexes . . . is, that *each individual in the society, every man and woman, should have a fair share of the blessings of love and of offspring*" (353), Drysdale shows how monogamy can deny those blessings to individuals of either sex. Many people never marry; emotions (especially among the young) are so changeable that permanent bonds entrap those whose passion has expired; victims of diseased sexual organs cannot resort to wedlock for cure. Paradoxically, woman in particular is thwarted by the supposed goal of her life, monogamous wedlock.

Marriage is one of the chief instruments in the degradation of women. It perpetuates the old inveterate error, that it is the province of the female sex to depend upon man for support, and to attend merely to household cares, and the rearing of children—a belief which is utterly incompatible with the freedom or dignified developement of women on the one hand, and with the economical interests of society on the other. It is the emblem too of all those harsh and unjust views, which have given to woman so much fewer privileges in love than man, and have punished so much more severely a breach of the moral code in her case. For a man to indulge his sexual appetites illegitimately, either before or after the marriage vow, is thought venial; but for a woman to do so, is the most heinous crime. . . . Are not things like these a mockery? do they not make fools and puppets of us, and pour scorn upon our vaunted institutions? Marriage delivers woman bound into the hands of man . . . and tempts him to abuse his gift of superior strength; it is in short the instrument, in numberless cases, of making the man a tyrant and the wife a slave. . . . we see matches every day in which a young girl marries an old man, or where the fear of remaining an old maid, or the wish to obtain the social advantages and protection of marriage, is the real motive which influences the woman. Such marriages are in reality cases of *legalised prostitution*, and are utterly alien to the true spirit of love. It is not woman herself but her unfortunate social position, that is to be blamed for them.

When once the modes of preventive intercourse become universally known . . . it will be found to be totally impossible to confine woman by the present narrow sexual restrictions. In fact, preventive intercourse, if it be found to be really efficient and satisfactory, will put the two sexes almost on a par in sexual freedom. A woman will be able to indulge her sexual desires, with the same exemption from after consequences as a man; and it will rest entirely with herself, whether she shall have offspring or not. This cannot fail to make a signal alteration in the habits of woman; for there is no natural reason except the fear of getting children, which makes her less willing than man to gratify her sexual desires. . . .

Let those who will, marry; but those who do not wish to enter upon so indissoluble a contract, either on account of their early age, or from a disapproval of the whole ceremony, should deem it perfectly honourable and justifiable to form a temporary connection. If they refrain from undue procreation, rear their children carefully, and act in an open, sincere, and loving manner to their partner, they are fulfilling the *real* sexual duties; and although the world may for a time frown upon them, they will have the approval of their own consciences, the best and noblest of rewards, and will be laying the foundation of a truer sexual morality, than the world has yet known. (355-57, 375-77)

The tension between prescription and practice, the question of who was speaking for what percentage of the populace, becomes even more complex in the latter decades of the nineteenth century. Three generalizations can be made. Some writers carried on Drysdale's defense of woman's sexuality, but most perpetuated Acton's vision; considerably fewer children were born in America and England; and medical treatment of woman's sexual and psychological ills became more involved and severe.

Those who defend woman's sexuality are not only the scandalous Victoria Woodhull and Tennessee Claflin and the small band of "Free Lovers."[8] Such respectable conservatives as Dr. George H. Napheys have sales figures which indicate how many Victorians bought (in several senses) a message very different from Dr. Acton's.

> It is a false notion, and contrary to nature, that this passion in a woman is a derogation to her sex. The science of physiology indicates most clearly its propriety and dignity. There are wives who plume themselves on their repugnance or their distaste for their conjugal obligations. They speak of their coldness and of the calmness of their senses, as if these were not defects. . . . By following her [Nature's] counsel, women may escape from the hysterical and other disorders which often wait as well upon excess as upon too great denial of that passion, which claims satisfaction as a natural right.[9]

Phrenologists who champion female sexuality also reach large audiences. "That female passion exists is as obvious as that the sun shines," proclaimed Orson S. Fowler.[10] Despite the faddishness of his phrenology, Fowler gives to his argument a physiological grounding which few readers today would believe possible in a widely sold Victorian book.

> ITS [the vagina's] ERECTILE tissues are enclosed between layers of muscles; so that passion in woman creates her vaginal erection just as it does penile in man. . . . This mutual pressure [of the penis and cervix] is what gives mutual pleasure, and want of it dissatisfaction. . . .
> Love alone contracts her vagina which gives him pleasure, alone gives him that rigidity which presses against her organs and gives her pleasure. (732, 740)

Medical opinons are corroborated by some feminists. Isabella Beecher Hooker laments in 1874 that "men, full of their human passion and defending it as righteous and God-sent lose all confidence in womanhood when a woman here and there betrays her similar nature and gives herself soul and body to the man she adores"; Elizabeth Cady Stanton maintains in 1883 that "a healthy woman has as much passion as a man."[11]

Such voices are comparatively few, however, and sexual repressiveness increases generally in the 1860s and 1870s. Masturbation, for example, had already been viewed as a serious problem in the 1830s, but for the next quarter-century the chief offenders were assumed to be male, the chief dangers physical, the best remedy self-control. By the 1860s, attention turns increasingly to women. (Two best-selling authors, Dr. Gardner and Rev. John Todd, focus upon female audience-subjects in this decade.) The chief dangers of masturbation now seem to be psychological, and the remedies are, as we shall see, drastic.

First, however, this apparent increase in prescriptiveness must be viewed in light of Victorian practice—particularly that between 1800 and 1900 the birthrate fell dramatically in America and substantially in Britain. This fact is clear, but its meaning is not. Who, for instance, was deciding to limit family size? Were economic pressures forcing husbands to concentrate family resources on fewer members, or were wives gaining an increased role in family decision making? Or both? And how was pregnancy being limited? Contraceptives were almost certainly more pervasive than had been assumed by historians who stressed feminist opposition to contraception (George Eliot and Barbara Bodichon discussed their use of birth control devices in 1856[12]). Finally, how many pregnancies were aborted? Positive information is again fragmentary, but the proliferation of antiabortion literature and legislation (especially in America) argues for a much less "Victorian" situation than historians have traditionally assumed.[13]

Medical treatment of women's physical and psychological ills is better documented than marital sexuality, but again the situation resists easy generalizations. From 1830 to 1860 most doctors accepted the traditional association of womankind with emotional troubles and prescribed physical cures for psychological problems. "Heroic" medicine used acid and white-hot irons to cauterize "everything from cancer to cantankerousness."[14] These doctors bequeath to their successors the age-old belief that "the sex" was defined solely by her gender. Rousseau's 1764 pronouncement that "men are men only at times, but women always are female" was still being echoed in 1910 by the popular J.H. Kellogg: "A woman's system is affected, we may almost say dominated, by the influence of these two little glands."[15]

Heroic medicine is largely abandoned by 1870, but the tendency to treat psychological problems with physical cures continues and even increases. Doctors who persist in defining woman genitally are both alarmed by her apparent decline in health and encouraged by new treatments for "female complaints." When a patient behaved unconventionally—by masturbating, or becoming frigid or nymphomaniacal, or failing in other domestic duties, or advocating suffrage or birth control, or suffering from hysteria, or simply feeling sick in suspect ways—the health of the patient and of the race required drastic physical measures.

One of the new procedures is "rest cure." S. Weir Mitchell sought to bring the patient back to normalcy by force-feeding, bed rest, and complete submission to his will.[16] Male will, in fact, predominates in many gynecological encounters.

I [Dr. T.A. Emmet] was present . . . when a young lady had been lying in an apparently unconscious state, after an hysterical convulsion, and had taken no notice of my presence, although I felt satisfied that she was aware of it. The nurse had just introduced the rectal tube . . . and the patient began an attack . . . for my benefit. She suddenly threw herself into a position of opisthotonos, but . . . a loud escape of flatus took place. . . . I was in a position to see her as she opened her eyes, and the appearance of astonishment and mortification . . . as the flatus continued to escape was intense. I quietly asked if she had lost all of the delicacy of her sex. . . . She burst into tears and covered her face. She had, before coming under my care, been very willful, and had had these attacks of hysteria frequently. . . . But they were never repeated, as she was assured . . . that the instrument would again be introduced if she showed any symptoms of another seizure.[17]

Still more drastic are new surgical procedures. Cliterodectomy appears in England in the 1860s and persists in America until the 1890s. Medical logic here is brutally simple: the masturbator is disturbed psychologically; excise the clitoris and restore normalcy. Oomerotomy, or "normal ovariotomy," is still more pop-

ular, despite substantial evidence against its efficacy. Some surgeons claim credit for twenty thousand ovaries.

Even these enormities must be viewed in their cultural
context, however. Labeling medical treatments as "sadistic" and
seeing doctor-patient relations as "sexual conflicts" are dangerous, for several reasons. Some treatments, cauterization, for
example, were inflicted upon men as well as upon women;
others, like cliterodectomy, remain of questionable frequency;
and such innovations as Sims's procedure for vesico-vaginal
fistula saved women traditionally judged terminal. Moreover,
the doctor-patient relationship was itself complex. Doctors after
mid-century found themselves in the divided position of having
their prestige at an all-time high and their self-confidence eroded
considerably. The secularization of society which damaged the
prestige of the clergy had made physicians the new law-givers,
yet many doctors felt inadequate. Attacked by homeopaths and
health reformers since the 1830s and threatened by women
doctors in the 1860s, physicians knew that science had advanced
far enough to discredit venerable assumptions but had not yet
provided sufficient new theories and cures.[18] Women patients,
in turn, cannot be seen simply as passive victims. They often
sought out the gynecologist. The greater isolation of British and
American women after marriage may have made these wives
seek from doctors and health manuals the support traditionally
provided by a more extended family.[19] Illness, and particularly
forms of hysteria, provided culturally acceptable outlets. Some
women abused the invalid's privilege, of course; others sought
in the gynecologist the dominating authority which their husbands lacked. Frequently, however, hysteria was a mode of
communication. Women baffled by impossible duties and contradictory ideals expressed through illness what otherwise would
have remained repressed and destructive.

A comparably complex view must be taken of women who
handled sexual problems not by resorting to illness but by
espousing passionlessness. Woman was no more the simple
victim of this ideal than she was of the doctor. Denying her
sexuality meant that she was freed of her age-old role of use
object.[20] Safe from threat and safe to pursue the fuller life
beyond sexual service, woman could direct her attention to male
passion—not by striving to achieve the double standard for
herself, but by restricting him to the single standard of her
purity.

In the process of discarding simple theories of victimization and recognizing the advantages to woman of medicine and passionlessness, we must not, however, go too far. Woman by no means escaped entirely her role as sex object, and the double standard by no means vanished. Subjugation and repression were the high prices that many women had to pay. Science, if not the easy villain that scholars have recently portrayed it, did remain an often punitive force. Most doctors did not need to have aggressive feelings toward their patients. By accepting the century-long view of the sex as sexually suspect, physicians perpetuated the agony of both man and woman.

II

The conventional view of woman circumscribes her not only sexually, but also intellectually. Having defined her solely in terms of body, society throughout the Victorian period attributed woman's supposedly limited learning capacity to two physiological elements—her peculiar brain and her menstrual cycle.

Woman's brain is judged inferior both organically and functionally. To explain the organic inferiority, scientists offer the medical version of that tit-for-tat reasoning which sanctioned a double standard by equating women with purity and men with passion. Woman is praised for a superior nervous system, while man is credited with a brain organically superior in both quantity and quality. Quantity is important because the Victorians view intellection as a *function,* and conclude (erroneously) that the larger the engine, the more numerous and energetic its operations. Quantitative "evidence" confirming the male brain as heavier and the male cranium as larger than the female is advanced by many craniometrists (including Robert Boyd in 1839 and Veroidt in 1847).[21] The "obvious" conclusion about woman's intellectual inferiority is drawn endlessly.

There are hitches, however. Some geniuses had small brains, while the largest brain on record was a moron's. Moreover, the brain-weight "evidence" is itself questionable. As early as 1812 and as late as 1861, respected craniometrists who compared body and brain weights find that, proportionally, woman's brain actually outweighs man's. To this inconvenient finding, scientists react variously. Some ignore the comparative data and perpetuate into the twentieth century the argument from absolute brain weight. Most scientists who do recognize the comparative method seek more rewarding comparisons. By relating brain weight and body height, Alexander Sutherland confirms male superiority. So does the more novel comparison of brain and thighbone weights, and the comparative study of the brains' surface areas, and of the lobes (the parietal—supposedly the seat of the sensations—is larger in woman, whereas the frontal —supposedly the reasoning region—is larger in man). When the argument shifts from quantity to quality, the male brain again "proves" superior. Woman's greymatter is more watery, and its convolutions are both shallower and less intricate.

Among countering arguments, the general contention that science knew too little about the brain to draw definite conclusions comes not only from feminists but also from so dulcet a ladies' physician as J.V.C. Smith in 1875.[22] More specifically, apologists for woman argue that the evidence of comparative brain and body weights decides the case, if anything, in her favor, that the frontal lobes do not control rationality (a soldier with his forehead largely shot away had retained his rational powers), and that respected scientists find the brains of the sexes qualitatively indistinguishable in terms of greymatter and convolutions. Some feminists even argue, like Eliza W. Farnham, that physiology proves woman's *superiority*. "Life is exalted in proportion to its Organic and Functional Complexity; Woman's Organism is more Complex and her totality of Function larger than those of any other being inhabiting our earth; Therefore her position in the scale of Life is the most exalted—the Sovereign one."[23]

Contemporaneous with the organic argument is the controversy about woman's *functional* inferiority, a controversy that heats up as practical consequences—education and employment —become increasingly evident. Can woman's brain function successfully when faced with the supreme rigors of scientific and abstract problems? J. McGrigor Allan answers for the majority in 1869:

> In the highest realms of literature and science, man reigns supreme. The inventing, discovering, creating, cogitating mind is pre-eminently masculine; the history of humanity is conclusive as to the mental supremacy of the male sex. Men carry on the business

of the world in the two great departments—*thought* and *action*; the ideas on which depend all the marvellous acts of human intelligence, the discoveries in physical science, which have raised man from a savage to a civilised being; the jurisprudence, political, civil, military, and religious institutions which maintain the social structure, are all produced and elaborated by men. In the domain of pure intellect it is doubtful if women have contributed one profound original idea of the slightest permanent value to the world! Not only as thinkers, but as workers, are men pre-eminent. . . . So little demand is there for the direct assistance of women in the mental departments which are the special province of man, that could all the male intellect in the world be suddenly paralyzed or annihilated, there is not sufficient development of the abstract principles of justice, morality, truth, or of causality and inventive power in the female sex, to hold the mechanism of society together for one week.[24]

Those defending the functional potential of woman's brain point to her scholastic and professional achievement. On collegiate examinations, women score so well in the 1860s and 1870s that Lydia Ernestine Becker can boast in *Contemporary Review*, "wherever this test [of observation and experiment] has been impartially applied, by studies and examinations conducted without reference to the sex of the student, the honours have been fairly divided between men and women."[25] Woman's ability to put her scientific knowledge into practice professionally is also established by hard facts. In America in the 1850s and in Britain by the early 1870s, women begin earning medical degrees and some professional respect.[26] The terrible opposition facing these women appears in the rejection letters received by the first woman doctor, Elizabeth Blackwell, when she applies to medical schools in 1844.

Some of these refusals were based upon "the dependent position assigned to woman, as much by *nature* as by *society*, and upon the unheard-of presumption which had inspired the author of this request with the desire and hope of taking rank in a profession reserved and consecrated to the nobler sex." Others refused because "it would be unbecoming and immoral to see a woman instructed in the nature and laws of her organism."[27]

Instructing woman about her nature is one way to free her for moral fulfillment and action—according to Mary Gove Nichols who joins Emma Willard, Harriot Hunt, and Paulina Wright

Davis in teaching and lecturing (often to overflow crowds) on anatomy and physiology in the 1830s and 1840s.[28] The traditionalist objection that a medical career would be unladylike is turned around by several writers who argue that woman's "God-given . . . maternal nature" makes *her* the better physician.

Opposition to women becoming scientists is also severe, but here the stubborn facts of a long-standing tradition functioned as precedent. In mathematics there are Maria Gaetana Agnesi, Marquise Émelie du Chatelet, Sophia Germain; in astronomy, Caroline Herschel and Maria Mitchell; in natural science, Clemence Augustine Royer and Eleanor Ormerod.[29] Probably most important to the Victorians is the woman whose sister-in-law had urged her to give up this "foolish manner of life and studies, and make a respectable and useful wife" and whose husband had given lifelong encouragement to her research in astronomy, geography, and microbiology: Mary Somerville.[30]

In Somerville the Victorians see more than the era's foremost woman scientist; they see proof that potentially antagonistic roles—scientist and angel—can be harmonized. *Saturday Review* in 1874 speaks for the Anglo-American community when it describes Somerville's life as

> the unobstrusive record of what can be done by the steady culture of good natural powers, and the pursuit of a high standard of excellence, in order to win for a woman a distinguished place in the sphere habitually reserved to men, without parting with any of these characteristics of mind or character or demeanor which have ever been taken to form the grace and the glory of womanhood.[31]

One magazine does insist upon separating angel from scientist. *Godey's* praises Somerville for succeeding *not* by inspiration (like Lady Poets) but by "unremitting study and investigation" (like male scientists).[32] Most reviews and most Victorians, however, agree with Harriet Martineau that Somerville has a right to the telescope because she has one eye on the tea table.

The scientific community is of two minds. Although Somerville wins many prestigious awards and is offered membership in the American Philosophical Society in 1869 (along with two other women and Charles Darwin), the Royal Society of Great Britain and the French Academy refuse not only to abolish their rule against women members, but even to make an exception in this case. They deny membership to Mary Somerville as they did to Caroline Herschel before and to Madame Curie later.

What must be recognized, however, is that the traditional view of woman's intellectual limitations is something Mary Somerville herself cannot escape entirely. Her active support of political and educational equality prompted J.S. Mill to list her first on the Mill-Bodichon parliamentary petition for female suffrage in 1866 and prompted Oxford in 1879 to name one of its early women's colleges for her. Yet when this same Mary Somerville is asked by Alexander Buckland whether women should be admitted to his new British Association for the Advancement of Science, she answers, "no." Like most Victorians, including J.S. Mill, Somerville doubts the intellectual creativity of women. Compare her words—"we women are of the earth, earthy . . . that spark from heaven [original scientific] genius is not granted to the sex"—and the beliefs of two other women who rank with Somerville among the century's most brilliant minds, Mary Shelley before her and George Eliot after.

> My belief is—whether there be sex in souls or not—that the sex of our [woman's] material mechanism makes us quite different creatures [from men]—better though weaker, but wanting in the higher grades of intellect.—Shelley

> The woman of large capacity can seldom rise beyond the absorption of ideas; her physical conditions refuse to support the energy required for spontaneous activity; the voltaic-pile is not strong enough to produce crystalizations; phantasms of great ideas float through her mind, but she has not the spell which will arrest them, and give them fixity. This, more than unfavorable external circumstances, is, we think, the reason why woman has not yet contributed any new form to art, any discovery in science, any deep-searching inquiry in philosophy.—Eliot[33]

With her eighteenth-century birth and beauty, and with her utter commitment to home, Mary Somerville may seem anachronistic in the heyday of Sophia Jex-Blake and the public protest of aggressive women. But her very perpetuation of traditional values is what made Mary Somerville so important to an era which remained committed to woman's sphere. Somerville is thus a representative Victorian woman in several ways. She provided an example for both the young women who followed her into science and the orthodox who linked true intellectuality to True Womanhood. Somerville is also representative in her divided consciousness, her vision of woman as both entitled to political-educational equality and doomed to an earthy lack of genius. Seen in this intricate and self-dividing context, Mary Somerville's letter to Josephine Butler rings with the heroism of her life.

Naples, May 10, 1869.

DEAR MRS. BUTLER,

. . . the low estimation in which our intellect has hitherto been held has been a grief and mortification to me from my earliest years. While the improvement of man's education has occupied so much attention in the present age, it is wonderful that one-half of the human race should have been comparatively so much neglected. Great duties have been demanded from us, and our minds have not been prepared by solid instruction to fulfil them. Much prejudice still exists against high intellectual education for our sex, from the mistaken idea that it would render a woman unfit for the duties of a wife and mother. A woman that would neglect her family for her studies would equally neglect them for frivolous pursuits and dissipation. A solid course of instruction gives a high tone to any mind, whether male or female; it would render a wife capable of understanding and appreciating the pursuits of her husband; at any rate she would be an intelligent and agreeable companion.

Hitherto usefulness and duty to men have been thought the only objects worth caring for with regard to women; it would, at least, be generous to take the individual happiness of the sex into consideration in the scheme of education. Thousands of women never marry, and even those that do, have many solitary hours. I can only say from experience, that the higher branches of mathematical science as well as natural history have been inestimable blessings to me throughout the whole course of my life, and more especially in extreme old age, when other resources fail. As a source of happiness as well as of intellectual strength, mathematical science and classical learning ought to be essential branches of study in the higher and middle classes of women. Were these women highly cultivated, they would be followed, to a certain degree, by the lower ranks, but the general standard of all would be raised. Every assistance should be afforded, more especially to the numerous class who have to gain their livelihood by teaching or other employments, of which there are many peculiarly suited to the female sex, if, by instruction, they were fitted to fill them.

It has been assumed that the constitution of girls would be weakened by a classical and scientific education, in addition to the indispensable branches of study; but that is by no means the case, if they be taken progressively. Children at a very early age learn to speak several languages at the same time with perfect facility. . . . It is thus in the power of a highly educated mother or governess to make study agreeable, and gradually prepare the mind for its higher branches, when at a later age a girl is capable of understanding them.

Do not suppose that I undervalue accomplishments; on the contrary, I am a zealous advocate for refinement; but surely the graces of life are not incompatible with solid endowments. Even when every opportunity of improvement is given, education will necessarily be subservient to the natural disposition of the child. There is no need to fear that all will be too learned, though all may be improved; but the important point is, that a girl should be perfectly taught any branch of science or literature for which she shows an inclination, that she may be really learned. . . .

Yours, dear Mrs. Butler,
With much esteem,
MARY SOMERVILLE[34]

Somerville's mention of "the constitution of girls" pinpoints the second great area of scientific controversy. By mid-century Victorians are asking not only whether woman is too limited organically and functionally to learn science, but whether she is too limited "constitutionally" to learn much of anything. This debate over physiology centers upon a widely held misconception —that the cerebral and reproductive systems compete for the body's limited supply of blood. Debaters take up both the general question of woman's health and the specific issue of menstruation.

Health receives more of the attention in the 1840s and 1850s. Have woman's regimen, her bad diet and inadequate exercise and tight lacing and heavy skirts and low bodices, caused her to decline physically over the last two generations? Hawthorne's contrast of pale, flat-chested contemporaries and their robust, buxom grandmothers reflects the concern of Harriet Martineau, Catharine Beecher, Florence Nightingale, and other health reformers in Britain and America.[35] By 1873, the *Altantic Monthly* can say:

The falling off in the standard of the female constitution means national deterioration and degeneracy. It is a mistake to suppose it is peculiar to this country, though there is reason to fear that it has gone farther here than in other parts of the world. Miss

Nightingale speaks of "the fact so often seen of a great-grandmother, who was a tower of physical vigor, descending into a grandmother perhaps a little less vigorous, but still sound as a bell and healthy to the core, into a mother languid and confined to her carriage and house, and lastly into a daughter sickly and confined to her bed."[36]

Particularly in America, falling birthrates (with the corresponding spread of birth control and abortion), rising immigration figures (with the specter of dark, prolific foreigners), increasing female insanity (with its consequences for the infants who did get born)—all combine to make doctors and other patriots fear for the very future of the race.

Educators join the debate because the declining health of young women is repeatedly attributed to scholastic overwork. This theory fits nicely with the belief that True Women cannot sustain arduous lucubrations. The rise of coeducational colleges and women's schools in America and the struggle for similar facilities in Britain means that health and education are increasingly linked and debated throughout the 1850s and 1860s. Dr. Gardner's classic diatribe, "Physical Decline of American Women" (1860), is countered throughout the decade by medical testaments to female stamina.[37] In the 1870s, *Atlantic Monthly*, citing Mary Somerville's production of a major scientific work at the age of eighty-nine, espouses "the wholesome and preservative power of severe study, no less for a woman than a man." But Dr. Edward H. Clarke says no. His *Sex in Education, or, A Fair Chance for the Girls* (1873) goes beyond the general issue of health, introduces the specific question of menstruation, and sets off a controversy which *Harper's* says "has provoked more discussion, awakened more minds, incited to more investigation, than any book of its size which has been published in the past decade."[38]

Clarke, a humane and esteemed Harvard physician, shares William Acton's fear that the body-mind relation is a fragile balance of forces readily prone to and largely helpless before disaster. Whereas Acton stressed what bodily excesses do to the mind, Clarke stresses what mental excesses do the the body. In the process he summarizes orthodoxy's stands on the health, race, and education issues.

> The problem of woman's sphere, to use the modern phrase, is not to be solved by applying to it abstract principles of right and wrong. Its solution must be obtained from physiology, not from

ethics or metaphysics. The question must be submitted to Agassiz and Huxley, not to Kant or Calvin, to Church or Pope. Without denying the self-evident proposition, that whatever a woman can do, she has a right to do, the question at once arises, What can she do? And this includes the further question, What can she best do? (12)

. . . The first two of these systems [nutritive and nervous] are alike in each sex. . . . No microscope has revealed any structure, fibre, or cell, in the brain of man or woman, that is not common to both. . . . With regard to the reproductive system, the case is altogether different. Woman, in the interest of the race, is dowered with a set of organs peculiar to herself, whose complexity, delicacy, sympathies, and force are among the marvels of creation. . . . The growth of this peculiar and marvellous apparatus, in the perfect development of which humanity has so large an interest, occurs during the few years of a girl's educational life. No such extraordinary task, calling for such rapid expenditure of force, building up such a delicate and extensive mechanism within the organism . . . is imposed upon the male physique at the same epoch. . . .

The physiological principle of doing only one thing at a time, if you would do it well, holds as truly of the growth of the organization as it does of the performance of any of its special functions. . . . Nature has reserved the catamenial [menstrual] week for the process of ovulation, and for the development and perfectation of the reproductive system. Previously to the age of eighteen or twenty, opportunity must be periodically allowed for the accomplishment of this task. Both muscular and brain labor must be remitted enough to yield sufficient force for the work. If the reproductive machinery is not manufactured then, it will not be later. . . . The brain cannot take more than its share without injury to other organs. (32–43)

Periodicity characterizes the female organization, and developes feminine force. Persistence characterizes the male organization, and develops masculine force. Education will draw the best out of each by adjusting its methods to the periodicity of one and the persistence of the other. . . .

Let us look for a moment at what identical co-education is. The law has, or had, a maxim, that a man and his wife are one, and that the one is the man. Modern American education has a maxim, that boys' schools and girls' schools are one, and that the one is the boys' school. Schools have been arranged, accordingly, to meet the requirements of the masculine organization. . . .

It may be well to mention two or three details, which are so important that no system of *appropriate* female education, separate or mixed, can neglect them. . . .

One is, that during the period of rapid development, that is, from fourteen to eighteen, a girl should not study as many hours a day as a boy. . . .

Another detail is, that, during every fourth week, there should be a remission, and sometimes an intermission, of both study and exercise. . . . The organization of studies and instruction must be flexible enough to admit of the periodical and temporary absence of each pupil, without loss of rank, or necessity of making up work, from recitation, and exercise of all sorts. The periodical type of woman's way of work must be harmonized with the persistent type of man's way of work in any successful plan of co-education. (120–25, 154–58)

. . . "If the superior sections and specimens of humanity are to lose, relatively, their procreative power in virtue of, and in proportion to, that superiority, how is culture or progress to be propagated so as to benefit the species as a whole, and how are those gradually amended organizations from which we hope so much to be secured? . . . How should the race *not* deteriorate, when those who morally and physically are fitted to perpetuate it are (relatively), by a law of physiology, those least likely to do so?" The answer to Mr. Greg's inquiry is obvious. If the culture of the race moves on into the future in the same rut and by the same methods that limit and direct it now . . . —then the sterilizing influence of such a training, acting with tenfold more force upon the female than upon the male, will go on, and the race will be propagated from its inferior classes. The stream of life that is to flow into the future will be Celtic rather than American: it will come from the collieries, and not from the peerage. Fortunately, the reverse of this picture is equally possible. The race holds its destinies in its own hands. The highest wisdom will secure the survival and propagation of the fittest. . . . (138–40)

Besides a flurry of activity by the National Education Association and the Ladies Benevolent Association, responses for and against *Sex in Education* pour out from physicians and lay persons. Most doctors in America support Clarke, as does England's eminent Dr. Henry Maudsley who betrays the sexism latent in Clarke's premises. "Assuredly, if she [woman] has been a slave, she has been a slave content with her bondage." Scientific authority is by no means absent from woman's defense, however. T.H. Huxley says, "we have heard a great deal lately about the physical debilities of women. . . . nine-tenths of them [impediments] are artificial . . . the products of their mode of life."[39] Substantiating Huxley's contention by their very presence, women doctors join the attack. In 1874, Dr. Mary Putnam Jacobi replies to Clarke in America and Dr. Elizabeth Garrett Anderson answers Maudsley in England. Subsequent studies were undertaken by Dr. Antoinette Brown Blackwell (1875) and Dr. Sarah H. Stevenson (1880), and Mary Putnam Jacobi wins Harvard's Boyleston Prize for her *The Question of Rest for Women During Menstruation* (1876). Among lay responses, the reviews generally favor and the books generally oppose Clarke. The anti-Clarke anthologies of 1874—Julia Ward Howe's *Sex and Education* and Anna C. Brackett's *The Education of American Girls*—are followed in 1875 by Azel Adams' *Sex in Industry, a Plea for the Working Girl*, and in 1881 by Marion Harland's *Eve's Daughters*.[40]

The lay volume which exposes most fully the social consequences of "special education," *No Sex in Education, or An Equal Chance for Both Boys and Girls* (1874),[41] is written by the same Mrs. E.B. Duffey who advocated one connection per month for married couples. How does such a "conservative" attitude toward sexuality square with Duffey's "liberal" attitude toward education? Common to both is liberty. Duffey demands that women be granted the freedom to develop their minds, even as women must be free to control their bodies. Duffey begins *No Sex in Education* with woman's particular need for the freedom of self-definition.

> Instead of discovering that the physical ills of woman result from her following man's methods of life and study, I have become convinced that they first originate from, and are afterward aggravated by, a course of life which recognizes an element of imagined feminine weakness and invalidism to which it is necessary to yield, and which forbids the wholesome active physical life led by the normally healthful man. (7)

Committed to free-minded inquiry, Duffey goes on to question virtually every aspect of Clarke's book—his methodology, his science, his pedagogy, his eugenics, and his overall intent.

> "Without denying the self-evident proposition that whatever a woman can do she has a right to do, the question at once arises, 'What can she do?'"
> I thank Dr. Clarke for this statement, and I will add that the further question arises, "Who shall decide what she can do?" Dr.

Clarke says it must be the scientist—Agassiz or Huxley. But let us pause and consider. How do scientists arrive at their conclusions? By abstract reasonings based upon theories of their own invention? By no means. They delve deep for facts—for hard, incontrovertible facts—and reason from them. . . . Now, why not in all matters that pertain to her—especially in that question of what she can do—ask her directly, and pay some heed to her answer? If she does not know, who does? . . .

Dr. Clarke is himself unconsciously guilty of the very error of which he accuses the friends of co-education when he quotes a writer who says:

"Woman must be regarded as woman, not as a nondescript animal, with greater or less capacity for assimilation to man."

This is the very thing our author does. He does not comprehend her as a woman at all. His reasoning is something after this manner: "A *man* with such a drain upon him, and with only a man's capacity for endurance, would surely succumb unless counteracting measures were taken. His mental powers could be uninterruptedly educated only at the expense of his physical. Therefore a woman, who is like man in other particulars, stands in need of these counteracting measures." He does not comprehend—he seems never to have realized—the full sense of that which he tries to impress upon his readers, that a woman is *not* a man in any sense. Accompanying the demand upon her system which nature makes, nature has kindly and wisely—nay, more than that, justly—provided such supplies of strength, vigor and endurance as, if not wasted and frittered away by idle, pernicious habits, are equal to all feminine emergencies.

In his plea for periodicity he does not recognize the fact that there is no periodicity of brain action in a woman. . . .

Girls doubtless ruin their health by overstudy. Do not boys? Young women graduate from school and seminary semi-invalids. Do not young men also? . . .

President Fairchild of Oberlin, who is certainly as well qualified as any man in the country to testify on the point of the comparative health of male and female students, says:

"Nor is there any manifest inability on the part of young women to endure the required labor. A breaking down in health does not appear to be more frequent than with young men. . . . Of young ladies who have graduated since 1841, the deaths have been *one in twelve;* of the young men, a *little more than one in eleven.*" (10-12, 22-24, 55-57)

The doctor does not furnish us any working plans of his theories. We can hardly imagine how a school is to be properly conducted after his suggestions. If there were any uniformity in the sex in regard to the time of the monthly tides, there might be some possibility of special and practical arrangement. But each girl has her own time; and if each were excused from attendance and study during this time, there could be neither system nor regularity in the classes. . . . if, as sometimes happens, a male teacher is employed, how is a girl to account for her necessary absence at these regular periods and not do violence to her modesty and natural delicacy of feeling in the matter? (115–16)

Says Dr. Clarke: "Circumstances have repeatedly carried me to Europe, where I am always surprised by the red blood that fills and colors the faces of ladies and peasant-girls, reminding one of the canvas of Rubens and Murillo. . . ."

Not one word of the difference in climate; not even a hint of the active out-of-door life led by those ruddy European girls, who, in truth, think nothing of a five- or ten-mile walk for a constitutional. This is the real secret of their robust health and flushing beauty. When American women shall learn that out-of-door life means life indeed, and in-door existence a death in life, we may hope to see fuller and more rounded forms, stronger pulsating veins and more glowing cheeks. . . .

"Each succeeding generation, obedient to the law of hereditary transmission, has become feebler than its predecessor. . . ." It is something worthy of comment that in the history of mankind each new generation, viewing the evils which surround and characterize it, is inclined to look backward, and lamenting the degeneracy of the day, sigh for the good old times when such things were not.

But what is the truth in the matter? Mortuary tables and statistics of all sorts show that the average length of life has been steadily increasing for many generations back. The men and women of to-day are healthier and longer lived than any of their progenitors. . . .

Dr. Clarke is not the first one to find out that women are educated too much in a masculine manner. A writer of forty-five years ago . . . gives the following facts concerning the schools of our grandmothers and mothers, who Dr. Clarke assures us excelled us in physical and mental vigor:

"At the girls' schools kept by gentlemen (with the exception of the academy of Mr. F.) the studies are so multiplied, so abstruse, and I will add so *unfeminine*, that the minds of the pupils are worn out before they arrive at maturity, and frequently their bodies also."

Yet these girls actually survived and came in course of time to deserve the admiration of the doctor. In view of this fact, there is hope for their descendants yet. (27–28, 31–34)

Finally, Duffey recognizes that Dr. Clarke's argument has ramifications beyond schooling. For all of his sincere commitment to woman's health and education, Clarke leaves her little better off than more expressly hostile writers do. He demonstrates how changes in argument preserve the basically static ideal of True Womanhood. In fact, *Sex in Education* is attacked by William B. Greene for exactly what reviewers criticized in Eliza Lynn Linton—the failure to recognize that the ideal of Shrinking Delicacy is hopelessly antiquated in an industrial age where half of all women work and a third never bear children.[42] Clarke's ideal is attacked from another side by Duffey. She denies "sex" in the name of "liberty."

> But this book called "Sex in Education" is more than it seems to be. It is a covert blow against the desires and ambitions of woman in every direction except a strictly domestic one. The doctor has chosen to attack co-education as a representative of them all. His plan has been a crafty one and his line of attack masterly. He knows if he succeeds in carrying the points which he attempts, and convinces the world that woman is a "sexual" creature alone, subject to and ruled by "periodic tides," the battle is won for those who oppose the advancement of woman—the doors not only of education but of labor and any kind of physical and intellectual advancement are closed against her. He knows that labor is valued only as it is continuous and reliable, and that if women can be persuaded to become unreliable on principle, there is an end to the competition between the sexes in every department of employment. . . .
>
> I have called this book an attack, but it is rather the last, the most desperate struggle of the advocates of fogyism against the incoming new order of things. They have abandoned all their outposts, and are now defending their citadel, making the question of sex the stronghold upon which they place all their hopes of ultimate success. But their efforts are futile. The easily proven, or I should say the evident, fallacy of their position will awake multitudes to thought on the matter who without this book might have passed it by unnoticed. (117-19)

Throughout the rest of the century, women continue to make more progress in education than in any other area—partly because America needs school-marms for the developing west, partly because the sexist biases and deep needs which masquerade as "scientific facts" are most readily countered in both America and Britain by the real facts of woman's educational achievement. As early as 1874, a book entitled *The Building of a Brain* expresses concern for the health of young women in school, but does not advocate any form of "special education." The book's author is Dr. Edward H. Clarke.[43]

III

In the debate over woman's developmental potential, two assumptions important to the Woman Question predate Darwin by many years—that ethnic groups, like everything else in creation, exist on a hieratic scale of increasing perfection, with the white male supreme; and that woman is essentially a reproductive, domestic being. After 1859, traditional beliefs are buttressed by new methodologies, new theories, new "data," and by the increasing prestige of the new "sciences" of anthropology and sociology.[44] Despite Darwin's importance, the chief influence here is Spencerian. The Spencerian methodology is basically comparative: to achieve the ideal of synthesizing the physical and social sciences, principles of evolutionary biology are applied to the workings of the mind and society. Darwin himself sanctions this method insofar as he recognizes comparisons between man and the lower elements. But Darwin does not admire Herbert Spencer. Methodology was part of the problem. Not only does any comparative method invite false analogy, but also Spencerians are on particularly shaky ground because their "data" are often highly suspect and their analogical method encourages, rather than checks, biases.

Spencerians offer three basic theories to explain woman's inferiority. In the evolutionary struggle, woman survived not by her intellect, but by such attributes as fertility, docility, and attractiveness; man, on the other hand, survived precisely by using his brain to escape extinction and to win fertile mates. Since each sex transmitted its prime traits, women in successive generations move further and further from intellectual equality. In a second genetic argument, scientists—particularly William K. Brooks in 1879 and Patrick Geddes in 1889—hold that man transmits the innovative traits, woman the hereditary; thus males change, whereas females retain the earlier, more primitive aspects of the race.[45] A third argument assumes the priority of woman's reproductive role and maintains that she stopped at an earlier evolutionary stage than man because her procreative organs had to be assured maximum development. Woman's cranial sutures closed early so that no significant brain growth would draw blood away from the growing reproductive system.

All three theories, and much other speculation, lead to the conclusion that evolution proceeds toward increased specialization and that woman will therefore become ever more maternal as man becomes ever more intelligent. Unfortunately for Victorian women, "evidence" from five different areas seems to support this conclusion. Most harmful is probably the research of Gustave Le Bon and others which "proves" that the sexes in ancient Egypt were much closer to equal in brain size than Victorian men and women were. A similarly widening gap is found both by zoologists who contrast simple and sophisticated forms on the evolutionary ladder and by sociologists who contrast the brains of the lower and upper classes. Anthropologists, particularly McLennan, Lubbock, Morgan, and Spencer, see paternalistic monogamy as the triumphant species of social arrangement which had survived the evolutionary struggle with polyandry, polygyny, and of course matriarchy. Most anthropologists argue that civilization, like nature, moves from the supremacy of the female to the supremacy of the male, with the Victorian concern for equal rights being either a transitional moment or an evolutionary throwback. Although "optimistic" in its progressivist interpretation of evolution, Spencerian thinking is basically reactionary in its insistence upon geologic time. Amelioration is inevitable, but quick reform is impossible. (Even anthropologists who see an *increasing* role for woman as sensuality gives way to more feminine traits are so committed to geologic time that they can only advise women to wait quietly during the eons). Finally, Spencerians take very seriously the notion of "vital force." Addressing a public which had been regaled about the glories of "energy" since the 1830s, anthropologists assert that ideas are not innate but result from nutritive tendencies in the cerebral tissue.[46] The vigorous brain which can perform increasingly various and sophisticated operations can reach ever higher stages of civilization. Needless to say, the size and weight of man's brain means that his "vital actions" outnumber woman's and that his stage of civilization transcends hers.

Woman's supposed cerebral inferiority relates her to various groups which Victorian anthropologists find decidedly lower.

"The grown up Negro partakes, as regards his intellectual facilities, of the nature of the child, the female, and the senile White."[47] By "the female," Vogt means the angel of the house. Her relegation to the lower evolutionary level of children and blacks is "justified" by various wonders of the comparative method. Drawing upon authorities from Aristotle (women never transcend the childlike state) to Darwin (children of both sexes resemble women more than boys do men), scientists defined woman's traditional traits—intuition, fidelity, charity—as "infantile." Resembling children in cranial structures and dimensions, women are supposedly more susceptible to infant diseases. This susceptibility, and this cranium, also link women to blacks. Specific anatomical similarities—both are flat-footed, both stand less erect (more apelike) and have longer clavicles than the white male, and both turn readily to the left whereas he inclines to the right—reflect the more important *cerebral* limitations which white women share with black men. Sutures close early in both groups, so the terrific precocity often manifest in both ceases at puberty. Reproductive instincts win out, the sexual obsessiveness of the black male matching the maternal drives of the white female. Since both groups are more prognathous than the white male, the shallower angle of the jaw restricts the frontal lobes and hence rationality, whereas the enlarged parietal lobes make blacks as emotional as women. Like "savage" peoples past and present, both groups lack the powers of generalizing and abstracting; with their smaller hemispheres and shallower convolutions, both incline to showy dress and religious enthusiasm.

This equation of woman and black is one of the most important features of the Woman Question. While male-supremacists link women and blacks as inferiors, woman's apologists decry their mutual servitude. Woman as slave, like the counterimage of woman as angel, is widespread and long-lived—appearing in the eighteenth and continuing throughout the nineteenth century, in Britain no less than America, in the south as well as the north, in both literary and polemical works by writers ranging from extreme radicals to such male supremacists as Dr. Alexander Walker ("in all [countries], they [wives] are more or less slaves").[48] Britain shares America's concern because the absence of black slaves in Britain does not mean the absence of slavery there. Wilberforce's war against chattel slavery throughout the Empire and the subsequent concern over Jamaica and Haiti are part of a larger recognition that the prostitute, the proletariat, and the wife herself are all indentured to the white male's will. Victorians recognized not only that British and American males prey upon prostitutes and slave women, but that white women do too. The angel's purity costs her sister defilement. Again woman finds herself in an impossible position: her angel status is a form of slavery, but her only real alternative is a worse form of use. The white male too is impossibly caught. He needs to elevate and yet to degrade woman. The insurrections of women and workers which he foresees, he cannot forestall; the sexual drives which he regards as animal, he cannot forego.

Rather than present technical and largely outmoded scientific issues, the texts for this section will emphasize the aspect of the evolution controversy which has continued to affect woman most directly—her equation with blacks. The 1860s are, again, a crucial transition time. Before the end of the Civil War, the women's rights and abolitionist movements work closely together in Britain and America, as Margaret Fuller predicted. "It may well be an Anti-Slavery party that pleads for Woman. . . . As the friend of the negro assumes that one man cannot by right hold another in bondage, so should the friend of Woman assume that Man cannot by right lay even well-meant restrictions on Woman."[49] Expectably, apologists for slavery define woman's sphere narrowly. The most effective advocate of this position, and its most eloquent opponent, are both women. Louise Cheeves McCord and Sarah Grimké match up interestingly because they are in many ways so similar. Both are Southern intellectuals who begin with the Bible and agree on the linkage of woman and slave. They draw opposite conclusions, however. Grimké concludes that God's creation of man and woman as equals means that woman's slavery is morally heinous. McCord concludes that God's granting of supremacy to the white male means that women and blacks will be happiest if they accept their lower place in the divinely sanctioned hierarchy.

In her 1838 Letters on the Equality of the Sexes, [50] Sarah Grimké is among the first to recognize and support the common cause of white women and black slaves. Each letter ends, "Thine in the bonds of womanhood." Despite her belief that God himself sanctioned political equality, Grimké acknowledges how much religion and Christian women had contributed to the enslavement of humankind.

I am here reminded of what a slave once said to his master, a Methodist minister. The slave-holder inquired, 'How did you like my sermon to-day?' 'Very good, master, but it did not preach me free.' (41–42)

There is another class of women in this country, to whom I cannot refer, without feelings of the deepest shame and sorrow. I allude to our female slaves. Our southern cities are whelmed beneath a tide of pollution; the virtue of female slaves is wholly at the mercy of irresponsible tyrants, and women are bought and sold in our slave markets, to gratify the brutal lust of those who bear the name of Christians. . . .
Nor does the colored woman suffer alone: the moral purity of the white woman is deeply contaminated. In the daily habit of seeing the virtue of her enslaved sister sacrificed without hesitancy or remorse, she looks upon the crimes of seduction and illicit intercourse without horror, and although not personally involved in the guilt, she loses that value for innocence in her own, as well as the other sex, which is one of the strongest safeguards to virtue. She lives in habitual intercourse with men, whom she knows to be polluted by licentiousness. . . . Can any American woman look at these scenes of shocking licentiousness and cruelty, and fold her hands in apathy, and say, 'I have nothing to do with slavery'? *She cannot and be guiltless.* (51, 53–54)

Finally, however, Sarah Grimké places primary responsibility upon the legislators—civil and ecclesiastical—who assure that "woman has no political existence" and that "the very being of a woman, like that of a slave, is absorbed in her master" (74, 75).

This law that 'a wife can bring no action,' &c., is similar to the law respecting slaves. 'A slave cannot bring a suit against his master, or any other person, for an injury—his master, must bring it.' So if any damages are recovered for an injury committed on a wife, the husband pockets it; in the case of the slave, the master does the same. . . .

'The husband, by the old law, might give his wife moderate correction, as he is to answer for her misbehavior. The law thought it reasonable to entrust him with this power of restraining her by domestic chastisement. . . .'

Perhaps I may be told respecting this law, that it is a dead letter, as I am sometimes told about the slave laws; but this is not true in either case. The slaveholder does kill his slave by moderate correction, as the law allows; and many a husband, among the poor, exercises the right given him by the law, of degrading woman by personal chastisement. And among the higher ranks, if actual imprisonment is not resorted to, women are not unfrequently restrained of the liberty of going to places of worship by irreligious husbands, and of doing many other things about which, as moral and responsible beings, *they* should be the *sole* judges. Such laws remind me of the reply of some little girls at a children's meeting held recently at Ipswich. The lecturer told them that God had created four orders of beings with which he had made us acquainted through the Bible. The first was angels, the second was man, the third beasts; and now, children, what is the fourth? After a pause, several girls replied, 'WOMEN.' . . .

The laws above cited are not very unlike the slave laws of Louisiana.

'All that a slave possesses belongs to his masters; he possesses nothing of his own, except what his master chooses he should possess.'

'By the marriage, the husband is absolutely master of the profits of the wife's lands during the coverture. . . . 'With regard to the property of women, there is taxation without representation; for they pay taxes without having the liberty of voting for representatives.'

And this taxation, without representation, be it remembered, was the cause of our Revolutionary war. . . . That the laws which have generally been adopted in the United States, for the government of women, have been framed almost entirely for the exclusive benefit of men, and with a design to oppress women, by depriving them of all control over their property, is too manifest to be denied. . . . I have known a few instances where men have left their whole property to their wives, when they have died, leaving only minor children; but I have known more instances of 'the friend and helper of many years, being portioned off like a salaried domestic,' instead of having a comfortable independence secured to her, while the children were amply provided for. . . . Until such laws are annulled, woman never can occupy that exalted station for which she was intended by her Maker. . . . In ecclesiastical, as well as civil courts, woman is tried and condemned, not by a jury of her peers, but by beings, who regard themselves as her superiors in the scale of creation. Although looked upon as an inferior, when considered as an intellectual being, woman is punished with the same severity as man, when she is guilty of moral offences. Her condition resembles, in some measure, that of the slave, who, while he is denied the advantages of his more enlightened master, is treated with even greater rigor of the law. Hoping that in the various reformations of the day, women may be relieved from some of their legal disabilities, I remain,

Thine in the bonds of womanhood,

SARAH M. GRIMKE. (76–83)

Anomalous as she sounds today, Louise Cheeves McCord is by no means an idiosyncratic, or even a merely regional, figure. A year before Sarah Grimké's *Letters*, Catharine Beecher had addressed to Angelina Grimké *An Essay on Slavery and Abolitionism, with reference to the duty of American females*, which "present[ed] some reasons why it seems unwise and inexpedient for ladies of the non-slave-holding States to unite themselves in Abolition societies."[51] Besides denying to ladies any public role in abolition, Beecher attacked immediate emancipation with gradualist arguments which Angelina Grimké finds starkly racist ("Oh, my very soul is grieved to find a northern woman thus . . . fitting soft excuses for the slaveholder's conscience, whilst with the same pen she is *professing* to regard slavery as a sin. 'An open enemy is better than such a secret friend.'").[52] In her *de facto* advocacy of the subordination of both ladies and blacks, Beecher is subscribing to a social hierarchy which most Victorians—consciously or not—accepted. In "British Philanthropy and American Slavery" (1853) Louise Cheeves McCord accepts this hierarchy, and its cosmic and racial consequences.

"What American, North or South," triumphantly asks the reviewer, "would like to change places with the slave?" What scaly inhabitant of the deep, O most sapient brother, or the reviewing brotherhood, would like to change places with an oyster? and yet oysters *are*, and God made them; and, although the sportive denizen of the ocean, as he glances to and fro through its briny recesses, might not fancy being suddenly caught by the tail and glued down in some muddy shoal or gloomy submarine recess, yet have we a fair right to conclude that, as the oyster has, . . . his object and destiny in existence, so is he by nature suited to its functions and its contingencies; and yet we might imagine the poor devil of an oyster made exceedingly uneasy in his position, should some whispering demon of mischief set up a submarine school of communism, and lecture on the propriety of general abolition. "Liberty! liberty!" cries the oyster; "am I too not a brother of the deep?" . . . True liberty consists but in the freedom to exercise those faculties which God has given, and the oyster, upon his rock, is as free as his nature permits him to be.[53]

Responding to the 1852 *North British* appeal, "American Slavery and Uncle Tom's Cabin, The Affectionate and Christian Address of many thousands of the women of England to their sisters, the women of the United States of America," McCord goes beyond the obviously puerile contention that England enslaves too many of its own citizens to warrant any criticism of Dixie. McCord argues that abolitionist indignation derives from a moral double standard. If England regards the Irish as a lower race, then why criticize Southern slaveowners for espousing the same racial hierarchy? Still more important, if most English women, regardless of their feelings for the Irish, consider themselves "ladies," they are acknowledging the same hierarchy and accepting (along with blacks) the hegemony of the white male. McCord demands consistency. Women who accept the advantages of ladyhood must also accept the consequences of hierarchy.

There is evil in God's blessed world (why, God only knows), but there is also good,—deep, earnest good,—for those who will seek it deeply and earnestly. Below the nauseous froth-scum of sickly philanthropy and new-light Christianity, runs, quiet but clear, the pure stream of God-given reason and common-sense humanity. Ladies and reviewers, *God* is *God*, but *ye* are *not* his prophets. . . . We are accordingly a little amused, and not a little instructed by an article in the "North British," which happens . . . to have its place immediately following the one with which we have headed our remarks. . . . Here stands "American slavery and Uncle Tom's Cabin," treated of with all the gall and prejudice which the subject always seems to awake in those who ignorantly meddle with it; and immediately annexed is "The Modern Exodus, in its effects on the British Islands," wherein the sufferings leading to this Exodus (as the enormous emigration from the British islands is aptly termed) are treated of with a philosophic insight, a coolness of argument, and an apparent careful investigation of fact, which present a strange contrast to the sentimental slang, the careless assertion, and broad misstatements of the negrophilist article. . . . [According to "Exodus"] "Ireland is being depopulated at the rate of *a quarter of a million* per annum, a process which, if continued, will empty her entirely in the course of *twenty-four years.*" So much for the happiness of the subjects of Britain. . . .

The reviewer of the "Exodus" goes on to remark with regard to Ireland that not only is it necessary "to remove redundant numbers, but to replace them by a more energetic, more aspiring and more improvable race. The poor Celts must be pushed out, or starved out, to make place for more improvable Saxons: and why? Because their nature requires them to be "controlled, disciplined, and guided by others. Left to their own devices, a prey to their own indolent, slovenly, and improvident tendencies, all history shows how helpless and prone to degenerate they are". . . . The inferior people always have, always must it would appear, pass away before the wants of the superior, and the necessities of progress. "Begone, ye incompetent!" is surely the stern law of man's existence. . . . Wherever the Irish *congregate*, they carry Ireland about with them, for the simple reason that the peculiarities of one race can only be washed out by the commingled blood of others. The negro, under similar circumstances, brings to us, then, all the dark horrors of Negro-land. . . . Will our reviewer maintain that the same course is practicable,—conceivable even,—with regard to the negro? Can the ladies of Stafford-house coolly contemplate the feasibility of such an unraveling of this Gordian knot? Will their admiration for Mrs. Stowe not stop short of amalgamation? We answer for them boldly. We do them more justice than they have done to us. As Christian and civilized women, they shrink with horror from the idea. . . . Supposing then slavery to be even such as it has been described, what escape is there for the negro? Literally none. If there be upon him a curse (which we are not inclined to allow), the curse is of God's laying on—not of ours. But, we repeat, we believe it not a curse. Inferiority is not a curse. Every creature is suited for its position, and fulfilling that position can certainly not be called cursed. What God has made, dare we to call it cursed? No, ladies. As He has made you to be women and not men—mothers and sisters, and not (according to the modern improvement system), soldiers and legislators, so has He fitted the negro for his position and suited him to be happy and useful in it. (259–64)

Womanhood is McCord's basic concern. Womanhood is not characterized by the sentimentality which has unsexed such reformers as Wilberforce. "With a species of feminine pathetics and wailings . . . he set the example, and opened that sluice of sickly sentimentality which too often, taking the place of sound sense and argument, now inundates the world" (264). That British ladies have also unsexed themselves is implicit in McCord's claim that they lack "*pity*." Pity, the womanly counterpart to male "sound sense and argument," disappears and its opposite, sentimentality, surfaces when ladies become inconsistent, when they fail to recognize hierarchy throughout nature. By their pity for the blacks and by their otherwise ideal conduct—"*Ora et labora*—pray and strive" (279)—Southern women prove that they are True Women. Theirs is the true response to slavery, and, by implication, only a changed attitude toward slavery will restore British women to true ladyhood. However inhumane it sounds today, McCord is expressing with honest directness the attitude toward women and blacks which

Catharine Beecher and many Victorians—British and American, north and south, clerical and lay, male and female—cloak in rhetoric or in silence.

And now, "glory to God in the highest—on earth peace, and good-will toward men." Ladies of Stafford-house, thus you end your appeal; thus, too, dare we. Our tongue shrinks not the ordeal. We hold out to you the right hand of fellowship; we say to you, as women, slander not so your sex as to consent to believe, on the blind testimony of careless and misinformed, if not mischievous scribblers, the libels which you have so thoughtlessly accredited. Are we mothers without mothers' hearts? . . . Woman is woman still, and were this system what you represent it, long since would her heart have risen against it, and with pleading tears and earnest prayer, she would have taught the son of her bosom that truth is nobler than gain, and humanity better than power. . . . Strong as are the instincts of race—intensely as we are taught to feel that black men are not white men—and shudderingly as we turn from the impious and insane idea that would level in one sweeping equality of degradation what God has so distinctly severed, yet can we most acutely feel the human tie between us. We can weep with them, nurse them, and comfort them. . . .

By this exercise of charity, our whole being is the better attuned to love. The affections which pass from the child to the slave, descend still by gradation to the brute. The poor broken-down horse becomes dearer to us, and even the old ass, as we stroke his long ears, is from habit a friend. But, for heaven's pity! gentle ladies, be satisfied that we are kind to him, and do not insist that, because he cannot walk upright, we, for the sake of charity, equality and so forth, shall creep on all fours to keep him company. The white man may nurse and protect the negro—may pity the negro—may love the negro—but cannot consent to stoop to him. That position which is no degradation to the negro, because therein, as a really inferior man, he but conforms to nature, becomes to the white man a disgrace, and a reproach.

We have done. Brethren and sisters, in conformity with the *Christian* tone of your articles we conclude ours. . . . "Glory to God in the highest, on earth peace and good-will toward men." (277–80)

The war which ends black slavery in the United States did not end the subjugation of either blacks or white women—in either America or Britain. Traditional assumptions about physical inferiority are perpetuated by postwar "science." As physicians lament woman's apparent deterioration, numerous studies "prove" the declining health of the blacks. Supposedly both groups are increasingly prey to nervous breakdowns because reform has subjected them to competition beyond their developmental level. Politicians join physicians in warning that the overly emotional blacks and women are easy prey for demagogues and should be denied the franchise. Treating both groups differently from white men eliminates both as social and political threats.

> "A woman," said Miss Olive Logan, "has a right to vote, and to hold a seat in Congress, *because she is as good as a negro.*" We think, for our part, that a woman, especially if she is not a strong-minded one, is far better than a negro . . . or a white man either; and had, therefore, better keep within the high and holy sphere for which both nature and the God of nature intended her.[54]

Arguments like this one from an 1871 speech in Richmond, Virginia, are particularly serious because they are not limited to Southern "conservatives." On both sides of the Atlantic, reformers and feminists continue to deny full human status to blacks or women or both. "Emancipation—Black and White" (1864), for example, is written by an English reformer who defended Darwin and won increased educational opportunities for both sexes.[55] That Thomas Henry Huxley can advocate the full enfranchisement of black men and white women and can still continue to believe in the inferiority of both groups indicates how elemental sexual and racial prejudices are in the nineteenth century.

> QUASHIE'S plaintive inquiry, "Am I not a man and a brother?" seems at last to have received its final reply—the recent decision of the fierce trial by battle on the other side of the Atlantic fully concurring with that long since delivered here in a more peaceful way.
>
> The question is settled; but even those who are most thoroughly convinced that the doom is just, must see good grounds for repudiating half the arguments which have been employed by the winning side; and for doubting whether its ultimate results will embody the hopes of the victors, though they may more than realize the fears of the vanquished. It may be quite true that some negroes are better than some white men; but no rational man, cognizant of the facts, believes that the average negro is the equal, still less the superior, of the average white man. And, if this be true, it is simply incredible that, when all his disabilities are removed, and our prognathous relative has a fair field and no favour, as well as no

oppressor, he will be able to compete successfully with his bigger-brained and smaller-jawed rival, in a contest which is to be carried on by thoughts and not by bites. . . . But whatever the position of stable equilibrium into which the laws of social gravitation may bring the negro, all responsibility for the result will hence-forward lie between Nature and him. The white man may wash his hands of it, and the Caucasian conscience be void of reproach for evermore. And this, if we look to the bottom of the matter, is the real justification for the abolition policy . . .

The doctrine of equal natural rights may be an illogical delusion; emancipation may convert the slave from a well fed animal into a pauperized man; mankind may even have to do without cotton shirts; but all these evils must be faced, if the moral law, that no human being can arbitrarily dominate over another without grievous damage to his own nature be, as many think, as readily demonstrable by experiment as any physical truth. If this be true, no slavery can be abolished without a double emancipation, and the master will benefit by freedom more than the freed-man.

The like considerations apply to all the other questions of emancipation which are at present stirring the world—. . . . One of the most important, if not the most important, of all these, is that which daily threatens to become the "irrepressible" woman question. . . .

There are philogynists as fanatical as any "misogunists" who, reversing our antiquated notions, bid the man look upon the woman as the higher type of humanity. . . . On the other hand, there are persons not to be outdone in all loyalty and just respect for womankind, but by nature hard of head and haters of delusion, however charming, who not only repudiate the new woman-worship which so many sentimentalists and some philosophers are desirous of setting up, but, carrying their audacity further, deny even the natural equality of the sexes. They assert, on the contrary, that in every excellent character, whether mental or physical, the average woman is inferior to the average man, in the sense of having that character less in quantity, and lower in quality. . . .

Supposing, however, that all these arguments have a certain foundation; admitting for a moment, that they are comparable to those by which the inferiority of the negro to the white man may be demonstrated, are they of any value as against woman-emancipation? Do they afford us the smallest ground for refusing to educate women as well as men—to give women the same civil and political rights as men? No mistake is so commonly made by clever people as that of assuming a cause to be bad because the arguments of its supporters are, to a great extent, nonsensical. And we conceive that those who may laugh at the arguments of the extreme philogynists, may yet feel bound to work heart and soul towards the attainment of their practical ends.

As regards education, for example. Granting the alleged defects of women, is it not somewhat absurd to sanction and maintain a system of education which would seem to have been specially contrived to exaggerate all these defects?

Naturally not so firmly strung, nor so well balanced as boys, girls are in great measure debarred from the sports and physical exercises which are justly thought absolutely necessary for the full development of the vigour of the more favoured sex. . . . The possibility that the ideal of womanhood lies neither in the fair saint, nor in the fair sinner; that the female type of character is neither better nor worse than the male, but only weaker; that women are meant neither to be men's guides nor their playthings, but their comrades, their fellows and their equals, so far as Nature puts no bar to that equality, does not seem to have entered into the minds of those who have had the conduct of the education of girls.

If the present system of female education stands self-condemned, as inherently absurd; and if that which we have just indicated is the true position of woman, what is the first step towards a better state of things? We reply, emancipate girls. . . . "Golden hair" will not curl less gracefully outside the head by reason of there being brains within. Nay, if obvious practical difficulties can be overcome, let those women who feel inclined to do so descend into the gladiatorial arena of life, not merely in the guise of *retiariae*, as heretofore, but as bold *sicariae*, breasting the open fray. Let them, if they so please, become merchants, barristers, politicians. Let them have a fair field, but let them understand, as the necessary correlative, that they are to have no favour. Let Nature alone sit high above the lists, "rain influence and judge the prize."

And the result? For our parts, though loth to prophesy, we believe it will be that of other emancipations. Women will find their place, and it will neither be that in which they have been held, nor that to which some of them aspire. Nature's old salique law will not be repealed, and no change of dynasty will be effected. The big chests, the massive brains, the vigorous muscles and stout frames, of the best men will carry the day, whenever it is worth their while to contest the prizes of life with the best women. And the hardship of it is, that the very improvement of the women will lessen their chances. Better mothers will bring forth better sons, and the impetus gained by the one sex will be transmitted, in the next generation, to the other. . . . We see nothing for it but the old division of humanity into men potentially, or actually, fathers, and women potentially, if not actually, mothers. And we fear that so long as this potential motherhood is her lot, woman will be found to be fearfully weighted in the race of life.

The duty of man is to see that not a grain is piled upon that load beyond what Nature imposes; that injustice is not added to inequality.

Many feminists who fight sexual condescension like Huxley's share his racial biases. Immediately after the Civil War, white women led by Stanton and Anthony (who had fought so long and hard for emancipation) demanded the vote before negro men, if both groups cannot be enfranchised together. Stanton breaks with Frederick Douglass over this issue.

> Think of Patrick and Sambo and Hans and Ung Tung who do not know the difference between a Monarchy and a Republic, who never read the Declaration of Independence or Webster's spelling book, making laws for Lydia Maria Child, Lucretia Mott, or Fanny Kemble. . . . I do not believe in allowing ignorant negroes and foreigners to make laws for me to obey.[56]

The majority of Women's Rights advocates in the late 1860s reject the Stanton-Anthony position on black suffrage; and Stanton is later reconciled with Frederick Douglass. But the rift between women and blacks widens steadily over the next quarter century. In 1893, Ludwig Büchner writes in the *New Review:* "with what feelings must a highly educated American woman view a dirty, idiotic negro shoe-black or street sweeper going to the ballot-box while she herself remains excluded from it."[57] Several social and intellectual factors contribute to the rift. Evangelism, so important a force in prewar reform, saw many of its members unite with more traditionally-oriented groups whose influence became increasingly dominant. Also, much postwar abolitionist energy goes into the *white* slave crusade [Volume II, Chapter 3]. Intellectually, woman is stung by those opponents of her emancipation who pointed gleefully to the spectacle of emancipated blacks in Southern politics. To proliferating anthropological arguments which equate woman with the (supposedly) developmentally inferior black, she tends to reply that black debilities are genetic whereas woman's were environmental. *International Review* says in 1882:

> if the male Negro has the same brain-weight as the female European, —and being a man, a superior quality of brain—he ought

to be expected on the argument of brain-weight, not only to produce the same intellectual achievements, but on the argument of quality, to produce superior ones. The fact is, he produces not even equal achievements. The intimation is that, if intellectual achievements depend at all upon a superior quality of brain, that must be accredited to the female.[58]

Post-Darwinian arguments which defend woman and yet avoid racism appear as early as 1864 in Eliza W. Farnham's *Woman and Her Era* [Volume II, Chapter 4] and continue throughout the 1870s and 1880s. Thomas Wentworth Higginson, rests his lifelong defense of woman upon his belief that evolution is proceeding away from force and toward spirit, from the masculine to the feminine. "There are thousands to-day who are looking out of their loneliness, their poverty, or their crime, for the NEW AGE, when Women shall be truer to themselves than Men have ever been to Women; the new age of higher civilization, when moral power shall take the place of brute force, and peace succeed to war."[59] With coolly passionate urbanity Higginson writes in the late 1870s a series of *Woman's Journal* articles which defend women against Huxley and other "clerical gentlemen or physiological gentlemen."[60] The price of such urbanity is high, however. Higginson, who fought in the first black regiment in the Civil War, goes the way of Robert G. Ingersoll and many feminists who had known abolitionist fervor: he omits entirely that bond of woman and blacks which Sarah Grimké had recognized and which remains basic to both Victorian life and scientific debate.

The same silence echoes through the writings of the foremost female respondent to Huxley and Darwin and Spencer. Antoinette Brown Blackwell has by the 1870s largely abandoned that intensely Christian focus which characterized her stand in the Marriage Debate (see Chapter 1). Thoroughly versed in Victorian biology, Blackwell adopts three basic strategies in *The Sexes Throughout Nature* (1875). At times she meets specific arguments with specific refutations.

Herbert Spencer's theory, that, as the male exhales relatively more carbonic acid than the female, this fact must be taken as the measure of the oxygen consumed, and therefore of the amount of force evolved, takes no account of a differentiation of functions. The feminine system has other methods of eliminating waste matter along with the surplus nutritive elements, and perhaps even with the waste from the embryonic processes. Besides, at all ages of a woman's life, the skin and other tissues must be the more active in expelling refuse matter.[61]

Blackwell's second strategy is to move from the specific to the general. Arguing from the overall evolution of society and the continuing development of biology, she produces one of her most effective chapters, "The Trial by Science."

The editor of the *Popular Science Monthly*, comparing John Stuart Mill and Herbert Spencer as philosophers, refers to the unlike methods of these two eminent thinkers in their treatment of the Woman Question. Prof. Youmans claims that Mr. Mill might have written his treatise on *The Subjection of Woman* two thousand years ago, while Mr. Spencer has grounded his conclusions on principles of modern science which were beyond the reach of past generations.

This criticism seems to be entirely just. But it must be remembered that these two investigators belonged in reality to two different generations. By education and acquired habits of thought, Mr. Mill was as old as his own father [James Mill, Volume I, Chapter 2]. It is the more remarkable, therefore, that, using the older, speculative methods, he yet reached conclusions of a modern type; while Mr. Spencer, by modern scientific reasoning, has succeeded in grounding himself anew upon the moss-grown foundations of ancient dogma.

Yet it is to the most rigid scientific methods of investigation that we must undoubtedly look for a final and authoritative decision as to woman's legitimate nature and functions. Whether we approve or disapprove, we must be content, on this basis, to settle all questions of fact pertaining to the feminine economy. . . .

But science has not yet made the feminine constitution and its normal functions a prolonged and careful study. No investigator has attempted conclusively to determine the relative energy or endurance of the sexes from sufficient and carefully recorded data. . . .

Current physiology seems to be grounded on the assumption that woman is undersized man, with modified organs and special but temporary functions, which like all other more or less abnormal activities are a direct deduction from the normal human energy. When this being, so varied from the masculine type, has been studied as to these variations, then all that is over and above these is simply man—nothing more; but something less, as an exhausted potato is less by every sprout which has grown and been rubbed off from its dozens of germinal centres.

A *psychology* based on such a *physiology* can be no more scientific. It is not likely to rise even into the higher regions of psychological theorizing. It accepts the traditions which are allied to its authority. In the case of Mr. Spencer, even his ruling tendencies as an evolutionist have not been able to carry him a single step beyond. He accepts the popular, traditional estimate; but by masterly philosophical explanations, the philosopher dignifies the tradition; planting it firmly upon what he claims to be an unshaken scientific basis.

Mr. Darwin in his line of thought has done the same; he also has come by a fresh pathway to the old conclusion, and, building upon a mountain of evidence over which he has faithfully toiled in defence of another hypothesis, he announces authoritatively:"*Thus man has ultimately become superior to woman.*" He adds with delicious sympathy: "It is, indeed, fortunate that the law of the equal transmission of characters to both sexes has commonly prevailed throughout the whole class of mammals; otherwise it is probable that man would have become as superior in mental endowments to the woman, as the peacock is in ornamental plumage to the peahen."

When these two illustrious names, eminent in science, both thinkers who have more profoundly influenced the opinions of the civilized world than perhaps any other two living men—when these two, endorsed by other world-wide authorities, are joined in assigning the mete and boundary of womanly capacities; and when the physiologists assume to interpret physical limitations, announcing authoritatively to the world that the weaker sex is unfitted constitutionally for persistent work, physical or mental, it is time to recognize the fact that the "irrepressible woman question" has already taken a new scientific departure. Woman herself must speak hereafter, or forever holding her peace, consent meekly to crown herself with these edicts of her inferiority. She must consent to put in evidence the results of her own experience, and to develop the scientific basis of her differing conclusions. . . .

A belief in the more rapid and subtle action of the feminine mind, as a balance to the massiveness and weight of the sterner masculine type, is a spontaneous growth from modern culture. Few persons may be able to offer sufficient evidence of its truth; thousands may accord to it merely a courteous but unmeaning significance, yet the fact remains: that woman's intuitional, affectional, and moral traits are rapidly approaching par in current general estimation.

It was authoritatively decreed from time immemorial that man is the superior, physically, mentally, legally, and by Divine ordinance. This position remained unshaken in the early days of brute supremacy and dominant muscular strength. Now it is universally controverted. The higher the grade of culture in any community, the more nearly does woman gain recognition as the equal and peer of man. Mr. Herbert Spencer has very effectively used the argument of a presumptive evidence against any opinion which arose in an ignorant and barbarous era; but which is called in question in more enlightened times, and discredited by evidences accessible to us only after the race has made very considerable progress in science and philosophy. Nothing, therefore, but the most thoroughly sifted and undeniable scientific evidence, can now make us cling to the old dogma of feminine inferiority. The old theory of a righteous vassalage of one sex to the other, must be shown to us endorsed by the clear sign-manual of Nature herself; else we must continue to believe that equal halves make the perfect whole. . . .

Fortified by this significant change in recent opinion, I venture the more resolutely to suggest that all the learned authorities who have decided the intellectual inferiority of Woman from scientific data, will yet find that their conclusions require modification from the introduction of unforeseen elements into their premises.

There is no adequate Psychology of Womanhood. If Mr. Spencer had completed his entire *Sociology*, it is not probable that he either would or could have brought together sufficient data to enable us to determine whether, in all ages and nations, the aggregate amounts of masculine and feminine energy actually expended have or have not been equivalent factors. The woman of the past is little known in history. Her mental life has left almost no record of itself. The motives and influences under which she has acted can only be inferential. Even the present woman must be tested more by *physiology* than by *psychology*. We cannot directly compare mind with mind. Nor can we fairly estimate the intellectual work of men and women in comparison, unless we first determine that the work was done under equivalent conditions equally favorable to each. But such conditions do not exist; they have never existed hitherto. Therefore the earliest solution of the question must probably come through quantitative physical data. The mind works through the body. We must first establish estimates of the relative amounts of energy expended in thought, in feeling, in muscular action, and in reproductive functions, and must approach some standard of comparison as to the characteristic differences of male and female in all these respects; and we must reach some estimate as to their relative powers of appropriating and of using force, before there can be even an approximate basis for scientific comparison either of the physical or of the psychical characters of the sexes. . . .

Physiology must embrace the aggregate of physical characters in its estimate; Psychology must embrace the aggregate of psychical powers, and the real complexity of the question must be fairly apprehended. This will be done in this generation or in the next. (232–40)

To assure that this analysis-of-woman-by-woman is accomplished, Blackwell writes "Sex and Evolution," a long synthetic chapter which combines her general and specific strategies and makes an obvious claim to "scientific objectivity." Her basic argument is this: in evolution, nature devotes equal energy to the development of the special role of each sex; woman's role is direct nurture, man's is indirect; therefore woman is superior in those organic and psychological functions which contribute to Motherhood, and man is superior in those functions which make him a Provider. Blackwell compares the sexes this way:

MAN.

Males.			*Females.*
− Structure,			+ Structure,
+ Size,			− Size,
+ Strength,			− Strength,
+ Amount of Activity,			− Amount of Activity,
− Rate of Activity,			+ Rate of Activity,
+ Amount of Circulation,			− Amount of Circulation,
− Rate of Circulation,			+ Rate of Circulation,
− Endurance,			+ Endurance,
− Products,			+ Products,
− Direct Nurture,	=		+ Direct Nurture,
+ Indirect Nurture,			− Indirect Nurture,
+ Sexual Love,			− Sexual Love,
± Parental Love,			+ Parental Love,
+ Reasoning Powers,			− Reasoning Powers,
− Direct Insight of Facts,			+ Direct Insight of Facts,
− Direct Insight of Relations,			+ Direct Insight of Relations,
+ Thought,			± Thought,
± Feeling,			± Feeling,
± Moral Powers,			± Moral Powers.

Result in every Species.

The Females   =   The Males.

Comprehensive Result.

Sex   =   Sex.

Or,

Organic Equilibrium in Physiological and Psychological Equivalence of the Sexes. (58)

Blackwell can even say: "if Evolution, as applied to sex, teaches any one lesson plainer than another, it is the lesson that the monogamic marriage is the basis of all progress" (136). Spencer and most social scientists who limited woman's sphere severely would agree, of course, as they would agree with the traditionalist division of traits in Blackwell's chart. "Sex and Evolution" is thus both a triumph and a failure. It allows women to feel equal with the male provider and to see this equality as scientifically proven. On the other hand, Blackwell does what she criticizes in Spencer—she uses science to substantiate traditional beliefs. Her new arguments from evolutionary biology confirm the old doctrine of complementary spheres. Moreover, defining woman in terms of reproductive organs means that Blackwell, like the Spencerians, restricts womankind to motherhood and thus perpetuates that stereotyping which has shackled many women for so long. Moreover, Blackwell makes no mention of woman's shackle-mate, the black. She, like Higginson and many others, reflects the thinking of the woman's movement in the generation which follows, but does not follow, Sarah Grimké.

3

WORK

Victorians as different in their opinions as Harriet Martineau and Sarah Ellis agree that one event above all raised the Woman Question in the nineteenth century: the Industrial Revolution. That event, according to the prevailing Victorian view, had two important effects upon women. First, it drove needy women out of the home and into the factory and workshop. Second, it made women at home and in the family more vital to society than ever before, as the sole preservers of human values which found no place in the modern world of work. Removed from the competitive materialism of that world, woman's mission was, in Sarah Ellis' words, to "bring, as with one mind, their united powers to bear to stem the popular torrent now threatening to undermine the strong foundation of England's moral worth."[1] To most Victorians, these two effects of industrialization were radically in conflict. The modern world required apparently irreconcilable social roles for women: their work outside the home and their presence in it. Middle-class culture chose the second or domestic role for women, and thus effectively decided that women should not work. Exceptions were admitted for some spinsters and for working-class women, but one result of the preference for keeping women home was to reinforce the low wages and low status of work for all women. As Harriet Martineau observed in 1837, "Where it is a boast that women do not labour, the encouragement and rewards of labour are not provided. It is so in America."[2] It was so in Britain, too.

But the issue was far from settled. Throughout the century, fresh instances of women's disadvantaged position in the working world provoked proposals for improving that position. Yet each new proposal raised the same difficult question: do we *want* women to work, or do we want them to stay home? For many Victorians, this *was* the Woman Question. On perhaps no other issue were the arguments of both sides—of those who favored women's work, and those who opposed it—so impossibly and paradoxically intertwined. In the 1830s and 1840s, miserable conditions for working women in factories, mines, and workshops led to the first widespread demands for better work. Yet the supporters of these reforms were suspected, and not without cause, of being more interested in getting women out of the factories and back to their homes than in improving their working situations. Public attention shifted, in the more prosperous middle decades of the century, to demands for work from the middle class—ostensibly on behalf of a surplus of genteel but impoverished single women who had no homes to leave. These demands, however, expressed the social and psychological dissatisfactions experienced by a vocal minority of all middle-class women to whom "woman's mission" seemed unjust and inadequate as a social role. In the 1870s and 1880s, the middle class again rose to the defense of working-class women, this time employing broader arguments for work as a social right. The focus of concern was, unexpectedly, the prostitute. The arguments employed had very mixed implications for the old question of woman's proper place—in the home or in the work force.

The passionate debates over these three issues—the misery of women factory workers, the unemployment of single gentlewomen, and the exploitation of prostitutes—hardly resolved the underlying question. In each instance the proposed solutions to the immediate social problem tended to divide into the familiar alternatives: can we restore factory women, poor spinsters, and prostitutes to home and family—or can we make a better place for them in the world of work? Yet the debates are nonetheless illuminating. Middle-class Victorians, sometimes despite themselves, explored their strong desires to keep women home, their fears of the world of work, and the social conditions which made that world bear so oppressively on some groups, including most women.

Reading these debates, however, we must keep in mind that the middle-class perceptions that governed them were very often misperceptions. For example, when Victorians spoke of work for women, they meant work outside the home. Thus they often tended to speak as if work for women was a nineteenth-century phenomenon, a development which, because it was supposedly new, might also be unnatural.[3] This narrower definition of work also contributed to the perception of an absolute dichotomy between women's roles as worker and as wife, mother, and homemaker. Again, public discussions greatly exaggerated the place of wage-labor in the lives of actual working-class married women. In fact, as records clearly show, the great majority of women who worked outside the home were young and single; when they married, they tended to stay home (though often to combine home duties with part-time paid work in or near the home). In practice, the conflict between modern work and women's domestic roles was much less than the public mind imagined.[4] A third distortion in Victorian views of women's work was the disproportionate attention paid to the problems of single, unsupported middle-class women—a growing minority in the mid-nineteenth century but still a very small minority of the women who needed or wanted to work. In part this emphasis must have been a deliberate decision by feminists: to focus on work for single women was to avoid the threat to home and family perceived in the employment of married women.

Yet even a focus on single women could not really remove that threat. The facts of a particular social problem are sometimes less significant than the arguments it stimulates; the single-woman problem triggered a major discussion of woman's proper sphere. Of the several arguments put forward by those who felt that women must or should work, economic necessity was the most difficult to deny, at least for working-class and unsupported gentlewomen. But potentially broader arguments for social justice and psychological health were simultaneously voiced—directly challenging conceptions of social and moral health that required women to stay home. Harriet Martineau, describing working American women in 1837, begins by reminding her readers that most women are *not*, as Sarah Lewis assumed, safely removed from economic strife (see Volume I, Chapter 1). She goes on to relate miserable working conditions to sexual inequality in every sphere. Her leap from the plight of the working woman to that of all women is prophetic of the course of the woman's movement in the nineteenth century.

> During the present interval between the feudal age and the coming time, when life and its occupations will be freely thrown open to women as to men, the condition of the female working classes is such that if its sufferings were but made known, emotions of horror and shame would tremble through the whole of society . . . special methods of charity will not avail to cure the evil. It lies deep; it lies in the subordination of the sex: and upon this the exposures and remonstrances of philanthropists may ultimately succeed in fixing the attention of society; particularly of women. The progression or emancipation of any class usually, if not always, takes place through the efforts of individuals of that class: and so it must be here. All women should inform themselves of the condition of their sex, and of their own position. It must necessarily follow that the noblest of them will, sooner or later, put forth a moral power which shall prostrate cant, and burst asunder the bonds, (silken to some, but cold iron to others,) of feudal prejudices and usages. In the meantime, is it to be understood that the principles of the Declaration of Independence bear no relation to half of the human race? If so, what is the ground of the limitation? If not so, how is the restricted and dependent state of women to be reconciled with the proclamation that "all are endowed by their Creator with certain inalienable rights; that among these are life, liberty, and the pursuit of happiness?"[5]

The argument from economic need was also supplemented by a new demand for work as a psychological necessity. This demand was as moving as, and perhaps more threatening than, the appeal for social justice. "As society is at present constituted, women are educated not to do, but to suffer. . . . There is no greater question than that of woman's work," writes J.W. Kaye in the *North British Review* (1855).[6] Titling his article "The 'Non-Existence' of Women," Kaye suggests a link between work and existence which goes beyond mere physical survival. True, as society is constituted, work too often means suffering, especially for women. But the right to work is also a human right to self-definition. Work is an attempt to move from passive suffering to active doing, and from the restricted domestic sphere into the "real" (and male) world. The cultural bias against work for women, according to this argument, denies their human identity, declaring their psychological and social nonexistence. Such an argument implicitly applies to all women, regardless of class or commitments to home and family. It appealed especially to middle-class women who had internalized the work ethic that Thomas Carlyle had raised almost to the status of a new religion.[7] Even Sarah Lewis' description of domestic duties as woman's mission reflects something of this new religion. Woman's mission is a remedy not only for the evils of the working world, but also for women's discontent with their apparently frivolous lives. When productive labor is regarded as a moral duty, religious mission, and key to social progress, as well as both a cure for ennui, doubt, and despair and a route to the discovery and development of the self, it is not surprising that women too should want work. By the middle of the century, middle-class women were increasingly demanding their place in what Anna Jameson called "The Communion of Labour."[8] Male prophets of the gospel of work like John Ruskin encouraged women's desires to fulfill their human duties by expanding their spheres (see Volume I, Chapter 5).

The demand for work as personal fulfillment made both men and women uneasy, because it seemed to contradict the conception of woman's moral nature on which her role as preserver of essential human values was based. Woman, according to that conception, is above all selfless; her actions are motivated by self-denying love. If work is personally rewarding, encouraging economic and even emotional independence, then can the working woman be truly selfless? Suspicions about the psychological effects of work on women infected even the most generous efforts to help the needy. If work alters woman's nature, then it threatens not only the home and family but also the larger social and moral structures in which home and family have become essential if strictly segregated elements. Uneasiness about their own motivations bothered even those women who fought hard for the right to work. Some could reconcile their desires with the selfless ideal by the support they provided for their families; others accepted limits on the kind of work they might perform, choosing social services; still others expressed their hope that work for women was a passing phenomenon of a transitional age. Bessie Rayner Parkes, a leader in efforts to open new fields of employment, asks the familiar question:

> Do we wish to see the majority of women getting their own livelihood; or do we wish to see it provided for them by men? Are we

trying to assist the female population of this country over a time of difficulty; or are we trying to develop a new state and theory of social life? I feel bound to say that I regard the industrial question from a temporary point of view. . . . the fact remains clear to my mind, that we are passing through a stage of civilisation which is to be regretted, and that her house and not the factory is a woman's happy and healthful sphere.[9]

Perhaps not surprisingly, even the most ardent reformers pulled back from a wholly "new state and theory of social life." Public debates deal with immediate problems. For every Mill or Fuller who tried to stand outside controversy and raise the underlying questions, there were many Bessie Parkeses, writing and acting in the heat of the moment. But if Parkes and others were reluctant to justify their words and actions by rejecting the old theories of social life outright, they did explore the adequacies and inadequacies of those theories to meet the challenge of new social situations. The recurring problems of working women, from the factory worker to the single woman to the prostitute, posed just such a challenge in the Victorian period.

I

The first protests against the plight of the working woman in Britain occur in the "hungry forties," a period of economic depression and social unrest. They are part of a general alarm over bad conditions: an alarm heightened by growing protest from the working classes, especially as expressed in the Chartist movement. Reports from parliamentary commissions (the famous Blue Books), fiction by Frances Trollope, Charlotte Elizabeth Tonna, Elizabeth Gaskell, Benjamin Disraeli, Charles Kingsley, and Charles Dickens, and a report by the then-obscure Friedrich Engels describe how hard times in industrial and rural Britain reduce the working poor to misery.[10] The condition of women especially shocks these observers. Of all who describe women's work in this period, very few (Gaskell is an exception) portray it as a potential source of psychological and financial benefit or a natural part of women's lives. For most writers, working women are victims. The work which takes them from home and family is one of the evils inflicted on them by poverty.

Three figures represent the working woman to the early and mid-Victorian public: the needlewoman, the governess, and the factory girl. To the public mind they dramatize the problems of working women in the lower middle, educated, and working classes. As victims of the new economy, these three representative working women provide objects of pity and occasions for indignation for many who are uneasy with the consequences of industrialization, even if they have no particular commitment to the cause of woman. As with law, early discussions of women's work are concerned not to debate a right but to remedy a plight— to protect True Womanhood.

Much of what is written about working women describes deteriorating conditions in the traditional areas of sewing and teaching. The bitter poverty of the seamstress provokes the greatest attention in both Britain and America. Because she works at home or in small workshops, her woes are assumed to be a matter for private conscience, beyond the reach of legislation. She quickly becomes a familiar, perhaps too familiar, reminder to more fortunate Victorians of society's unsolved problems. In 1843, Thomas Hood published anonymously in *Punch* a poem that fixed the image of the needlewoman as helpless victim.

The Song of the Shirt

With fingers weary and worn,
With eyelids heavy and red,
A Woman sat, in unwomanly rags,
Plying her needle and thread—
Stitch! stitch! stitch!
In poverty, hunger, and dirt,
And still with a voice of dolorous pitch
She sang the "Song of the Shirt!"

"Work! work! work!
While the cock is crowing aloof!
And work—work—work,
Till the stars shine through the roof!
It's O! to be a slave
Along with the barbarous Turk,
Where woman has never a soul to save,
If this is Christian work!

"Work—work—work
Till the brain begins to swim;
Work—work—work
Till the eyes are heavy and dim!
Seam, and gusset, and band,
Band, and gusset, and seam,
Till over the buttons I fall asleep,
And sew them on in a dream!

"O! Men, with Sisters dear!
O! Men! with Mothers and Wives!
It is not linen you're wearing out,
But human creatures' lives!
Stitch—stitch—stitch,
In poverty, hunger, and dirt,
Sewing at once, with a double thread,
A Shroud as well as a Shirt.

"But why do I talk of Death?
That Phantom of grisly bone,
I hardly fear his terrible shape,
It seems so like my own—
It seems so like my own,
Because of the fasts I keep,
Oh! God! that bread should be so dear,
And flesh and blood so cheap!

"Work—work—work!
My labour never flags;
And what are its wages? A bed of straw,
A crust of bread—and rags.
That shatter'd roof—and this naked floor—
A table— a broken chair—
And a wall so blank, my shadow I thank
For sometimes falling there!

"Work—work—work!
From weary chime to chime,
Work—work—work—
As prisoners work for crime!
Band, and gusset, and seam,
Seam, and gusset, and band,
Till the heart is sick, and the brain benumb'd,
As well as the weary hand.

"Work—work—work,
In the dull December light,
And work—work—work,

When the weather is warm and bright—
While underneath the eaves
The brooding swallows cling
As if to show me their sunny backs
And twit me with the spring.

"Oh! but to breathe the breath
Of the cowslip and primrose sweet—
With the sky above my head,
And the grass beneath my feet,
For only one short hour
To feel as I used to feel,
Before I knew the woes of want
And the walk that costs a meal!

"Oh but for one short hour!
A respite however brief!
No blessed leisure for Love or Hope,
But only time for Grief!
A little weeping would ease my heart,
But in their briny bed
My tears must stop, for every drop
Hinders needle and thread!"

With fingers weary and worn,
With eyelids heavy and red,
A Woman sat in unwomanly rags,
Plying her needle and thread—
Stitch! stitch! stitch!
In poverty, hunger, and dirt,
And still with a voice of dolorous pitch,
Would that its tone could reach the Rich!
She sang this "Song of the Shirt!"[11]

Mathew Carey's one-man campaign for higher sewing wages in Philadelphia in the 1830s, Henry Mayhew's interviews with London seamstresses in 1849 and Horace Greeley's investigations of New York needlewomen in the *New York Daily Tribune* in 1845 and 1853 also help give them the peculiar dramatic reality they possess for Victorians. A few famous paintings and numerous *Punch* cartoons graphically repeat Hood's image of the lonely seamstress, or contrast her with her idle employer, the lady of fashion (see illustration 2).[12] The distressed needlewoman is an angel in trouble. The relief of her suffering does not imply a real change in women's roles.

2. The Sempstress
Richard Redgrave, 1846 (*Forbes Magazine* Collection)

3. The Daily Governess
London Society, 1862

Before she was reduced to sewing, the needy middle-class Victorian woman probably tried to teach. In America from the 1830s there are jobs to be had in schools, but in Britain until late in the century teaching usually means governessing. Of all Victorian working women, the most vivid and sympathetic figure for the middle-class imagination is the governess, for she is one of their own (see illustration 3). The cruelty of her position is felt to be psychological as well as physical: brought up as a lady, she is expected to behave like Sarah Ellis' self-sacrificing mother without any of the mother's rewards of love, influence, or honor. Nor is she to have adequate wages or even the separate downstairs social life of an acknowledged servant. The model held up for the governess may be the benevolent Sister of Mercy, but the realities of her situation, according to an 1848 *Punch*, render her one of the "Sisters of Misery."[13]

One feature of the governess' position sometimes complicates the sympathy expressed for her. Where the seamstress usually remains a silent victim, the governess can be a highly articulate advocate of her own cause. Charlotte Brontë writes her sister Emily in 1839:

> I have striven hard to be pleased with my new situation. The country, the house, and the grounds are, as I have said, divine. But alack-a-day! there is such a thing as seeing all beautiful around you—pleasant woods, winding white paths, green lawns, and blue sunshiny sky—and not having a free moment or a free thought left to enjoy them in. The children are constantly with me, and more riotous, perverse, unmanageable cubs never grew. As for correcting them, I soon quickly found that was entirely out of the question: they are to do as they like. A complaint to Mrs. Sidgwick brings only black looks upon oneself, and unjust, partial excuses to screen the children. I have tried that plan once. It succeeded so notably that I shall try it no more. I said in my last letter that Mrs. Sidgwick did not know me. I now begin to find that she does not intend to know me, that she cares nothing in the world about me except to contrive how the greatest possible quantity of labour may be squeezed out of me, and to that end she overwhelms me with oceans of needlework, yards of cambric to hem, muslin nightcaps to make, and, above all things, dolls to dress. I do not think she likes me at all, because I can't help being shy in such an entirely novel scene, surrounded as I have hitherto been by strange and constantly changing faces. I *used* to think I should like to be in the stir of grand folks' society but I have had enough of it—it is dreary work to look on and listen, I see now

more clearly than I have ever done before that a private governess has no existence, is not considered as a living and rational being except as connected with the wearisome duties she has to fulfil. While she is teaching the children, working for them, amusing them, it is all right. If she steals a moment for herself she is a nuisance. . . . I would not stay without some alterations. For instance, this burden of sewing would have to be removed. It is too bad for anything. I never in my whole life had my time so fully taken up.[14]

Brontë's sharp appraisal of her situation and her determination not to remain there are later dramatized in the governess heroine of her novel, *Jane Eyre* (1847). *Villette* (1853) explores the related problems of the school teacher. Prominent women who spoke out for higher wages and pensions for governesses were disturbed by resentment like Brontë's. Elizabeth Rigby (Lady Eastlake) pleads the cause of the governess but condemns the headstrong Jane Eyre (see Volume III, Chapter 3).[15] Elizabeth Sewell in her widely read *Principles of Education* (1865) advises the governess to accept her position and say with dignity:

"Yes. I am a governess; earning my own livelihood; dependent, in so far that I have certain duties to perform, for which I am paid. But my work is not the less God's work, because I receive payment from man. The Rector of a parish is not the less Christ's Minister, because he receives tithes. God appointed the circumstances of my lot. He ordained that I should have no means of living, except by labour; and in that very Providential arrangement of my life, He showed me what I have to do for Him. It is a great work, and I thank Him for it. My friends think I am lowered in social position, and they are correct. According to the world's estimate, I am lowered, and I am willing to be so. I should be admired if I worked gratuitously. I should be thought a saint and a heroine. But work for God can only be undertaken in the form in which He sees fit to give it. He will not value me the less because I perform two tasks instead of one; because, whilst working for His little ones, I also provide for my own maintenance, and perhaps help a mother, or a sister who cannot help herself. I accept, therefore, the world's commiseration, with the amount of gratitude which is due to it. It is meant kindly, but I do not need it. I take the materials of my life as God has given them, and do with them the best I can for His service. The prince upon his throne, the statesman in the senate, the philosopher in his closet, can do no more. I am content."[16]

The case of the factory worker is different. Although more than half of all working women were in fact domestic servants, public expressions of concern center on this newer, more distant, and much more anonymous figure (see illustration 4).[17] The factory epitomizes the working world that middle-class Victorians control and fear; the factory girl is both part of the alien world and the anonymous victim of it. The plight of needlewomen and governesses, dramatized and particularized in art and literature, spurs efforts to improve their position. Much of the debate over factory women, however, takes place in government reports, Parliament and state legislatures, and later in unions. The attitudes of the debaters toward the factory women are often profoundly ambivalent. The immediate issue is whether the state should interfere with private enterprise to legislate conditions for work. Short-hours laws, resisted as a dangerous extension of governmental control, are justified by their supporters as protection of the helpless: women and children. But the discussion touches a deeper issue, what role of woman such laws will protect. Should or can working-class women remain at home? The debate is of special interest because, unlike the more theoretical discussion of the middle-class woman's right to work which dominates the 1850s and 1860s, this controversy depends on middle-class perceptions of the effects of women's employment on marriage, family, and the home.

The factory woman becomes an object of public concern in Britain three decades earlier than in America. In the late 1820s and 1830s American mills, offering wages higher than teaching, attract many New England farmers' daughters seeking social and economic independence before marriage. The Lowell factory girl, banking her savings and contributing to a literary journal, is a famous though short-lived phenomenon. Disappointed by limited opportunities for advancement and crowded out by cheaper immigrant labor (mostly male), native American white women organize protests and push for legislation in the 1840s, without much success. By the 1850s, conditions in American factories decline to the level of those that alarm British Victorians in the 1830s and 1840s, although widespread protest does not develop until the 1870s. Except for the greater prominence of unions, however, protective legislation debates in the various American states resemble the national British debate of the 1840s.[18] In both countries women provide the occasion for laws which in fact affect all workers.

The debates are confusing because they conflate two issues: the role of the state, and the place of women in modern work. In the early part of the century those who argue in the name of woman are the proponents of protective legislation, defending short-hours laws as a means of protecting women (and ultimately all workers) *from* work by imposing state controls on private industry. Those who seem to oppose women's interests are in fact more concerned with opposing protective legislation. They invoke women's right to work, free from state regulation, but they also defend the rights of her employer to control her hours and pay without government interference, according to the "laws" of laissez-faire economics. By the 1870s and 1880s, however, the principle of state regulation of industry is established. The supporters of further protective legislation no longer speak as defenders of women, but as defenders of children from neglect by their working mothers. The opponents of protective legislation appear as the working woman's real friends.

The most publicized of the early debates are the moving speeches of Lord Ashley, seconded in print by Charlotte Elizabeth Tonna, and vigorously opposed by liberal manufacturers, economists, and members of Parliament. Anthony Ashley Cooper, stirred by Blue Book descriptions of long hours, low wages, and hard labor, mounted a campaign in the 1830s and 1840s to limit the working day of women and children in factories to ten hours. Lord Ashley (later the seventh Earl of Shaftesbury) was a lifelong proponent of philanthropic reforms. A Tory and an Evangelical, he appeals to a past of land and home against a present of factories and working women and children, urging the responsibilities of the rich toward the poor. On March 15, 1844, he delivered one of his most impassioned speeches before the House of Commons, graphically describing the hard life of overworked women but also appealing to the fear that working wives and mothers destroy families and homes. A domestic revolution among the working classes would have obvious implications for the rest of society. With the memory of the Chartist protests of 1839 and 1842 still fresh in their minds, Ashley's audience responded strongly to such fears. In the heat of the moment the bill was passed. (It was revoked a few nights later, but a Ten Hours Bill was passed in 1847.)

The tendency of the various improvements in machinery is to supersede the employment of adult males, and substitute in its place, the labour of children and females. What will be the effect on future generations, if their tender frames be subjected, without limitation or control, to such destructive agencies? Observe the appalling progress of female labour; and remember that the necessity for particular protection to females against overwork is attested by the most eminent surgeons and physicians. . . .

But there is a reason for this substitution [of women for men]; I will show, by an extract from a letter dated in March, 1842, the motives that actuate some minds:

"Mr. E., a manufacturer, (says the writer), informed me that he employs females exclusively at his power-looms; it is so universally; gives a decided preference to married females, especially those who have families at home dependent on them for support; they are attentive, docile, more so than unmarried females, and are compelled to use their utmost exertions to procure the necessaries of life."

Thus, Sir, are the virtues, the peculiar virtues, of the female character to be perverted to her injury—thus all that is most dutiful and tender in her nature is to be made the means of her bondage and suffering! . . .

"The small amount of wages," says inspector Saunders, "paid to women, acts as a strong inducement to the mill-occupiers to employ them instead of men, and in power-loom shops this has been the case to a great extent."

Now hear how these poor creatures are worked. . . .

"I found (says Mr. Horner, October 1843) many young women, just eighteen years of age, at work from half-past five in the morning until eight o'clock at night, with no cessation except a quarter of an hour for breakfast, and three quarters of an hour for dinner."

They may fairly be said to labour for fifteen hours and a-half out of twenty-four. . . .

Where, Sir, under this condition, are the possibilities of domestic life? how can its obligations be fulfilled? Regard the woman as wife or mother, how can she accomplish any portion of her calling? And if she cannot do that which Providence has assigned her, what must be the effect on the whole surface of society?

. . . But hear the history of their daily life from their own lips:—

"M.H., aged twenty years, leaves a young child in care of another, a little older, for hours together; leaves home soon after five, and returns at eight; during the day the milk runs from her breasts, until her clothes have been as wet as a sop." "M.S. (single) leaves home at five, returns at nine; her mother states she knows nothing but mill and bed; can neither read, write, knit, nor sew." "H.W. has three children; leaves home at five on Monday; does not return till Saturday at seven; has then so much to do for her children, that she cannot go to bed before three o'clock on Sunday morning. Oftentimes completely drenched by rain, and has to work all day in that condition. My breasts have given me the most shocking pain and I have been dripping wet with milk." . . .

So much, Sir, for their physical, and, if I may so speak, their financial condition; the picture of their moral state will not be more consolatory. . . . the females not only perform the labour, but occupy the places of men; they are forming various clubs and associations, and gradually acquiring all those privileges which are held to be the proper portion of the male sex. These female clubs are thus described:—Fifty or sixty females, married and single, form themselves into clubs, ostensibly for protection; but, in fact, they meet together, to drink, sing, and smoke; they use, it is stated, the lowest, most brutal, and most disgusting language imaginable. Here is a dialogue which occurred in one of these clubs, from an ear witness:—"A man came into one of the these club-rooms, with a child in his arms; 'Come lass,' said he, addressing one of the women, 'come home, for I cannot keep this bairn quiet, and the other I have left crying at home.' 'I won't go home, idle devil,' she replied, 'I have thee to keep, and the bairns too, and if I can't get a pint of ale quietly, it is tiresome. This is the only second pint that Bess and me have had between us; thou may sup if thou likes, and sit thee down, but I won't go home yet.'" Whence is it that this singular and unnatural change is taking place? Because that on women are imposed the duty and burthen of supporting their husbands and families, a perversion as it were of nature, which has the inevitable effect of introducing into families disorder, insubordination, and conflict. What is the ground on which the woman says she will pay no attention to her domestic duties, nor give the obedience which is owing to her husband? Because on her devolves the labour which ought to fall to his share, and she throws out the taunt, "If I have the labour, I will also have the amusement."
. . . Sir, under all the aspects in which it can be viewed, this system of things must be abrogated or restrained. . . . It disturbs the order of nature, and the rights of the labouring men, by ejecting the males from the workshop, and filling their places by females, who are thus withdrawn from all their domestic duties, and exposed to insufferable toil at half the wages that would be assigned to males, for the support of their families. It affects—nay, more, it absolutely annihilates, all the arrangements and provisions of domestic economy—thrift and management are altogether impos-

sible; had they twice the amount of their present wages, they would be but slightly benefited--everything runs to waste; the house and children are deserted; the wife can do nothing for her husband and family; she can neither cook, wash, repair clothes, or take charge of the infants; all must be paid for out of her scanty earnings, and, after all, most imperfectly done. Dirt, discomfort, ignorance, recklessness, are the portion of such households; the wife has no time for learning in her youth, and none for practice in her riper age; the females are most unequal to the duties of the men in the factories; and all things go to rack and ruin, because the men can discharge at home no one of the especial duties that Providence has assigned to the females. . . . But every consideration sinks to nothing compared with that which springs from the contemplation of the moral mischiefs this sytem engenders and sustains. You are poisoning the very sources of order and happiness and virtue; you are tearing up root and branch, all the relations of families to each other; you are annulling, as it were, the institution of domestic life, decreed by Providence himself, the wisest and kindest of earthly ordinances, the mainstay of social peace and virtue, and therein of national security.[19]

The most effective publicist of Ashley's views is Charlotte Elizabeth Tonna, author of religious stories and editor of the *Christian Ladies Magazine*. Tonna wrote a series of fictional accounts of working women, based on the Blue Books and Ashley's speeches, which she collected as *The Wrongs of Women* (1844). Unlike Ashley, Tonna does not write as if all working women are married and mothers, but she too invokes woman's sphere to attack the miseries of industrial labor. Tonna's viewpoint differs from Ashley's: he fears the effects of women's work on social structures; she demands women's rights—the right to stay home.

It is the monstrous abuse of forcing the female to forsake her proper sphere, that gives rise to such deplorable wretchedness. . . . We assert the unalienable right of woman to preside over her own home, and to promote the welfare of her own family; we cry out against the grievous wrong that drags her thence to minister to the coveting selfishness of men who will be rich, even in defiance of God's most plain, most stringent laws. . . . The dark system that selects *her* as the individual who must toil throughout the day at a wearisome and most unfeminine employment, because the yearnings of her heart towards those of her own flesh insure her toiling more steadily, and the comparative weakness of her frame compels her to toil more cheaply than man would do—such a system cannot be fairly designated by the word WRONG; it is the most grievous infliction with which powerful injustice can visit the body and the soul of the poor.[20]

Tonna's argument cuts both ways, however. If woman has the right to stay home, she also has the right to work. This right the parliamentary defenders of the factory system assert: "it is the opinion of this House that no interference with the power of adult labourers in Factories to make contracts respecting the hours for which they shall be employed be sanctioned by this House."[21] Harriet Martineau and J.S. Mill also argued against protective laws on the same grounds. But unlike Mill and Martineau, Ashley's opponents are not really interested in women's rights. "The power of adult labourers . . . to make contracts" is advanced as a principle of the new science of political economy. Bessie Parkes, who judged in 1865 that "no one now doubts that the bill was a right and good thing," explains the intensity of the objections to it.

> [I]t was impossible to defend it on the grounds of pure political economy; it is a restriction on the rights of capital, and makes it illegal for the work-woman to sell more than ten hours of her time. Accordingly, when it was proposed, the manufacturers and the political economists opposed it as a measure suggestive of the dark ages, flying right in the face of the new science. Women, regarded by them in the light of working animals, ought, said they, to be the best judges of how long they could work, and what wages they needed to earn.[22]

Ashley's opponents meet his emotional rhetoric on woman and the home with an appeal to economic fact and "the new science." Unlike Mill and Martineau, they do not challenge the True Womanhood ideal which they, like Ashley, believe to be unrealistic for the working class. John Arthur "Tear'em" Roebuck, known for his bold opinions and vehement speeches, was a disciple of Bentham and a friend of Mill. Although Roebuck writes his wife that he is appalled at what he sees at the factories,[23] in Parliament he is faithful to his economic principles, arguing that since factory work is better than other jobs available to women, their work there should not be restricted. Henry George Ward, an "advanced" liberal from Sheffield (a factory district), points out that to protect True Woman as Ashley wants, women must be excluded from factories altogether—an economic impossibility for both industrialist employers and working-class families.

Roebuck argues:

In the first place, I find that the factory labourer is as well paid as any other in the community. [*"Hear, hear."*] You say "Hear," but I say that at least the factory labourer is better paid than any other kind of operative in the community. Then, I find that the factory labourer is not subject to greater toil than the rest of the community. . . . I take one case now in this town,—and let not the House take it as a matter of merriment when I mention the class of labourers, for I do so in the belief that they are a more sorely taxed class of labourers than any other in the community,—I mean the women of all work in London. Compare them with the labouring girl in the factories, and you will find that the condition of the latter is a sort of Paradise. . . . It won't do to come down to this House with exaggerated descriptions of misery, of want, and of suffering. I deny them all.

. . . I now come to that which I know will be said to be the *ad captandum* argument on this occasion. "What," says the noble Lord, "have you such little regard for woman as to wish that she should be taken from those labours which are her peculiar sphere, which make her the solace of our lives, the instrument of our early education, and which, in fact, form her to be the framer of the mind of man? Are you to take her into the factory to destroy her vital powers, to make her a mere machine, to unfit her to raise her race in effect,—are you willing to degrade the human race by making their mothers miserable beings?" My answer is, first and foremost,—is the labouring woman in the factory worse off than she would be if she were not in the factory? Judging of her situation as an agricultural labourer, I should think that her situation is far better. I have this peculiar evidence in her favour—that all the medical men who investigated the subject in 1833 declared that the labouring woman is far better able to cope with the labour in factories than the man, and I can easily understand why. It is in-door work, warm and comfortable, and all that is required is continuous attention. It is their characteristic that they can give this continuous attention without hurting their health. A man feels all this when he is so tasked. Without one exception, medical men declare that women in factories bear the factory labour best—that it is suitable to their condition—to their habits—and to their physical and physiological development. I do not recollect any statement of theirs about hard labour, and so far from thinking that women are deteriorated thereby, the physicians were of opinion that they were a far better race for the propagation of the species than any other class of labourers.[24]

H.G. Ward observes:

The argument of the noble Lord, if legitimately carried out, goes against the system of manufacturers by human labour altogether. It is not merely a question between a twelve hours' Bill and a ten hours' Bill, but it is in principle an argument to get rid of the whole system of factory labour. The noble Lord said that the system would become aggravated unless restrained. Where is that restraint to stop? Would a ten hours' Bill do it? Would an eight hours' Bill do it? Would any such system cure those domestic evils of which the noble Lord so feelingly complains? Will it restore the mother to her children?

. . . What is the cause which obliges the people to labour to this excess? I believe that there is as much natural affection and as much desire to retain the woman in her own proper domestic circle among the working classes, as there exists among ourselves. No, it is not from a difference of nature that men and women and children toil during a long period of hours, but it is necessity that compels them to do so. . . . Dr. Hook wished that women should be released from the necessity of labouring at all, and this would be a most desirable condition of things if it could be accomplished. Would to God that such a blessed state of things could be created! . . .

We may suppose such a state of affairs in a most prosperous community, where a man at the end of his moderate day's labour shall be able to repair to his family circle and spend the evening in the company of his wife and in the education of his children; but I do not know in what part of the world such a condition of society exists, and I am quite sure that it has never existed in any part of the history of this country.[25]

In 1843, an article on the Blue Books in the *Athenaeum* criticized the positions of both Ashley and his opponents as argued the next year in Parliament. Anna Jameson, the author of "Woman's Mission and Woman's Position," had established a reputation as a skillful popular writer on travel, art, and literature. This, her only direct piece of social criticism before the mid-1850s, was first published anonymously. Like Ashley and Tonna, Jameson refuses to accept poor working conditions for needy women as a necessity of modern society. But like Roebuck and

Ward, she recognizes that keeping woman home is no solution; for how will such a woman live? Broadening the grounds of argument, Jameson protests vigorously on behalf of working women of all classes, caught between ideology and fact, whose anomalous position Victorian society will not recognize.

Such is the beautiful theory of the woman's existence, preached to her by moralists, sung to her by poets! Let man, the bread-winner, go abroad—let woman stay *at home;* let her not be seen in the haunts of rude labour any more than in those of vicious pleasure—for is she not *the mother?*—highest, holiest, dearest title to the respect and the tenderness of her "protector, man!" We really beg pardon of our readers for repeating these truisms—we merely quote them here, to show that, while they are admitted, promulgated, taught as indisputable, the real state of things is utterly at variance with them. Our social system abounds with strange contradictions in law, morals, government, religion. But the greatest, the most absurd, the most cruel of all is the anomalous condition of the women in this Christian land of ours. We call it *anomalous* because it inculcates one thing as the rule of right, and decrees another as the rule of necessity. "Woman's mission," of which people can talk so well and write so prettily, is irreconcileable with woman's position, of which no one dares to think, much less to speak. . . .

These future mothers of our labourers and operatives are described as wretched, diseased, debased, haggard, enfeebled creatures, whose offspring must, of necessity, be physically degenerate, who are not only incapable of performing the duties of a mother, but cannot be trusted with the lives of their own offspring. . . . Is she, therefore, a born monster? she *must* live: to live she *must* work, and make her children work as soon as they can use their little hands. We may shudder, and talk of the necessity of taking away the children to educate them, but by what right will you take the food out of the mother's mouth, procurable by no other means than through her own and her children's perpetual toil? what alternative do you leave her besides this course of unnatural cruelty and absolute starvation? These are questions to be asked and answered, or our merciful reforms are like to be only new forms of injustice and oppression. In extremity of want, "the pitiful mother hath sodden her own child." Go preach humanity to hunger! "Amid such abject wretchedness," says the Commissioner, "there is little hope of amending things;" and the only hope held out is a distant one—the better education of the women:—

". . . To the extreme ignorance of domestic management on the part of the wives of the mechanics, is much of their misery and want of comfort to be traced. . . ."

This is the *cause*, but where is the remedy? if to exist—to procure a pittance of food and hardly decent clothing, a young woman must toil incessantly at some handicraft from five years old and upwards, where and how is she to learn needlework, cookery, economy, cleanliness—and all the arts of *home*? These things are not taught in the "Sunday Schools," nor in the Dame Schools—and if they were, she has no time to learn them, nor opportunity to apply them, being learned: she must toil in womanhood as in childhood—always toil, toil;—unremitting, heart-sickening, soul and body-wearing toil! Where is the use of instituting a system of education if you continue a state of things in which that education is useless?—which renders it impossible for the woman to practise what the child has learned? in which incessant labour is the sole condition of existence? The women of these classes have *"no home;"*—can we wonder that they have *"no morals"*?

Let us go a step higher, to the class immediately above them. Attorneys and apothecaries, tradesmen and shopkeepers, bankers' clerks, &c.: in this class more than two-thirds of the women are now obliged to earn their own bread. This is an obligation which the advance of civilization, no less than the pressure of the times, has forced upon them—an obligation of which womankind, in the long run, will not have reason to complain; meanwhile it is not of her just share of hardship in hard times, that the woman complains at present; but she may well think it a peculiar hardship, a cruel mockery, that while such an obligation is laid upon her, and the necessity, and the severity of the labour increases every day, her capabilities are limited by laws, or custom strong as law, or prejudice stronger than either, to one or two departments, while, in every other, the door is shut against her. She is educated for one destiny, and another is inevitably before her. Her education instructs her to love and adorn her home ("the woman's proper sphere!!")—cultivates her affections, refines her sensibilities, gives her no higher aim but to please man, her protector—and allows her no other ambition than to become a good wife and mother. Thus prepared, or rather unprepared, her destiny sends her forth into the world, to toil and endure as though she had nerves of iron; she must learn to protect herself, or she is more likely to be the victim and prey of her *"protector, man,"* than his helpmate and companion. She cannot soothe his toils—for like him she must toil: to live she must work—but by working can she live? . . .

Is the picture exaggerated? Some may think so; but those who know the real state of things, know that it is so far from being overstated, that it rather falls short of the truth. This is what we mean when we speak of the *anomalous* condition of woman—a contradiction in itself, and disgraceful in the present advanced state of social opinion on every other subject. Every one admits the truth, every one acknowledges the hardship, but it remains unremedied, and "no man layeth it to heart."

. . .—and returning once more to the especial purpose of this article, we would ask one question of those best able to solve it: we would ask, what is the reason that in legislating in behalf of women (as in the recent case of the Custody of Infants' Bill), or in originating any measures, private or public, of which woman is the object, such strange, such insurmountable obstacles occur, as seem to daunt the most generous and zealous of their public advocates, and defeat all the aims of private benevolence, however well and wisely considered? It seems to argue something rotten at the very foundation of our social institutions, that such is so invariably the case.[26]

In the next decades legislation gave women factory workers some relief from physical hardship. But little help was provided for the working-class wife and mother who must manage home and family while competing in the labor market. Protective laws did not "restore the mother to her children," as Tonna and Ashley wished. Neither did they provide the legal, financial, and moral support for working women that Jameson had urged. To Ashley and Tonna it seems that the interests of women and of their families are the same: both will be benefited if women work less. Jameson points out that this is not always true; both women and their families need women's wages. Reformers like Ashley urge shorter hours to protect women under adverse circumstances. They do not wish to recognize wives and mothers as a permanent and equal part of the work force. Demands for better jobs and equal pay by the first women's unions are perceived by many supporters of protective legislation and many men's unions as threatening both to male workers and to the family.[27]

The latent antagonism toward the factory woman that Jameson detected in the speeches of the reformers, especially those who dwelt on tales of "monster mothers," becomes an open conflict between women's work and motherhood after 1858. Dr. John Simon, the respected health reformer, connects alarmingly high infant mortality rates with work by mothers.[28] The old fear of domestic revolution is partly displaced by another anxiety, that working women endanger the lives of the nation's children. The fear had some foundation. Recent research suggests that other "evils" attributed by middle-class observers to women's work in factories—poor housekeeping, wasteful spending, early and imprudent marriages, "cotton-mill morality"—were common throughout the working class, whether or not women worked outside the home. But a woman's absence from her family did substantially affect her infant's chances for survival. Until infant nutrition was better understood, until pasteurized milk was cheap and available to urban mothers and sterilizable bottles with rubber nipples in wide use, the health of babies who were not breast-fed was precarious. Though factory women were not the only mothers who did not nurse, their children were more seriously endangered by their absence because they could not afford to hire wet nurses as wealthier women could.[29] Another and more highly publicized danger was the widespread use of opium preparations like Godfrey's Cordial to pacify babies, hungry and colicky on their diet of indigestible "pap" (bread and water). Doctors summoned by panicky caretakers—usually young girls or old women—all too often found "half-a-dozen babies, some snoring, some squinting, all pallid and eye-sunken, lying about the room, all poisoned."[30] Such reports, appealing to deeply ingrained beliefs about woman's primary duty, could rouse even a noted economist like William Stanley Jevons, who supported the employment of women in factories as economically sound, to advocate restrictions on women's work. His proposal to bar new mothers from factories, in an 1882 article in *Contemporary Review*, would protect, not women, but children *from* their working mothers.

> Can such things be in a Christian country? is the exclamation which rises to the lips in contemplating the mass of misery, and, especially, the infinite, irreparable wrong to helpless children, which is involved in the mother's employment at the mills. . . . I do not think that it will be possible for the Legislature much longer to leave untouched the sad abuses which undoubtedly occur in the treatment of infants, especially in the manufacturing districts. . . .
>
> Such, then, is the progress of civilization produced by the advancing powers of science and machinery; two-thirds to three-fourths, or even as much as five-sixths, of the infants dying of neglect. On this point all the official reports concur so unanimously that they may well be described as "damnable iteration."
>
> . . . There are no duties which are more important in every respect than those which a mother is bound by with regard to her young children. The very beasts of the field tend and guard their whelps with instinctive affection. It is only human mothers which

shut their infants up alone, or systematically neglect to give them nourishment. . . . I go so far as to advocate the *ultimate complete exclusion of mothers of children under the age of three years from factories and workshops.*[31]

Though the solution proposed by Jevons and others in the 1870s was justified from the standpoint of infant health, it struck some Victorians as remarkably hostile toward the working mother. No provision for her welfare—on which that of her baby depended—is mentioned. This omission is noted by Richard Whately Cooke Taylor, a factory inspector who throughout the 1870s consistently opposes the passing of more protective legislation for working women. In two papers, one presented in 1874 to the National Association for the Promotion of Social Science (an important forum for the discussion of many women's issues, and one of the few at which women too could speak) and another published in the *Fortnightly* in 1875, Cooke Taylor argues that legislation that merely restricts the mother's freedom to work will destroy the family it is designed to preserve.

It might be argued, for instance, that the interference with liberty would be too great; that women have already a hard enough lot in life without increasing its hardship; that the cure would be likely to produce greater evils than the disease; the women, for instance, destroying their infants before birth rather than become mothers, and subject to such tyrannical legislation; perhaps even, that the world is not created exclusively for infants, and it is better that a few of them should die early than all adult women be oppressed.

. . . It appears always to be tacitly assumed that the workman's home must be naturally and inevitably the healthier, the happier, and the better for being in the continuous occupation of his wife and family, by being the arena in which all domestic operations are performed, and that some sort of indirect excuse for it is needful when a contrary policy is proposed; that this system is indeed needful to securing to him those home comforts to which he is so justly entitled. We are of quite a different opinion. Were it in our opinion required to point out with the most accurate particularity what are the *discomforts* of home, these and none others are precisely they. Nay, is it not notorious, is it not proverbial, that they are so? The robust operative who returns from work to find a languid wife nursing a peevish baby in a fearfully polluted atmosphere, will derive little satisfaction from the reflection that this atmosphere has been saturated beyond all expression with the fumes arising from the due discharge of her domestic and maternal duties during the day, and would not find himself less "at home" if they had been performed elsewhere.

. . . Let me speak plainly in this matter. We have hitherto prided ourselves in this country—and prided ourselves justly—on the liberty of the subject, on the sanctity of the domestic hearth, and on the decency and privacy of our family life. That unit, the Family, is the unit upon which a constitutional Government has been raised which is the admiration and envy of mankind. Hitherto, whatsoever else the laws have touched, they have not dared to invade this sacred precinct; and the husband and wife, however poor, returning home from whatsoever occupations or harassing engagements, have *there* found *their* dominion, *their* repose, *their* compensation for many a care. There has been a sanctity about this English home-life which even the vilest have acknowledged and the rashest have respected. But let such legislation as is now proposed be adopted, let the State step in between the mother and her child, and let us for ever abdicate this pretension—let us be prepared to remodel all that. Domestic confidence is destroyed, family privacy invaded, and maternal responsibility assailed. For the tender care of the mother is substituted the tender mercies of the State; for the security of natural affection, the securities of an unnatural law! Better by far that many another infant should perish in its innocence and unconsciousness than live to be the victim of such a state of things.

. . . Might it not rather seem that a simpler and more certain way of checking infant mortality would be to make some provision for infants not otherwise provided for, to offer some support to their mothers instead of depriving them of all and to encourage them to look on maternity as a high and proud privilege, instead of a disqualification and offence?[32]

Cooke Taylor's view did not prevail. Sixteen years later a law was passed in Britain excluding mothers from factories for four weeks after the birth of a child, with no provision for their economic support. Though not as drastic as Jevons' proposal, it indicates public sentiment in both Britain and America. Immigrant American as well as native English and American working - class women increasingly stayed home with their young children when they could afford it. And middle-class public opinion, while tolerating work for needy women, remained strongly opposed to work for wives and mothers.

II

When Victorians discussed work for the working-class woman, they were discussing a fact, however misperceived, but work for middle-class women was still the exception at mid-century. Particularly in Britain, jobs for middle-class women were scarce, and cultural opposition was strong. The majority of adult middle-class women were married and fully employed at home—either in the time-consuming labor of maintaining a household and raising children with minimal domestic help, or, for the wealthier few, in the equally time-consuming rituals of a social life whose major setting was the private home.[33] Of the 36 percent of British women over twenty listed as working or financially independent in the 1851 census, probably less than one quarter—about 7 percent of the total—were middle class, including about 4.5 percent who either had an independent income or worked as professionals (governesses, writers, artists) and another 3 percent who owned or managed businesses and farms. In America, too, professionals and business women were a tiny proportion of the 10.1 percent of women who worked in 1850, although teaching in the common-schools was opening up for middle-class women jobs not yet available in Britain.[34]

While public opinion objected primarily to working wives and mothers, the cult of True Womanhood affected work for all middle-class women. It was not uncommon for farmers' daughters in America to take jobs before marriage, and it was generally assumed in Britain that the working-class woman would be employed at some period in her life. But no such assumption was made for the lady. Brought up to marry, maintain a home, and fulfill the social obligations of gentility, she found it more difficult to work if she needed or wanted to than a woman with lower social status. Factory, farm, domestic service, or millinery employed many unskilled women from the rural or urban working classes. For only the last of these occupations was the lady at all prepared. She needed both professional training and more diverse job opportunities—especially in Britain, where women's colleges and teaching jobs were slower to develop—if she were to support herself. (For many Victorians the very fact of taking a paid job deprived a lady of her claims to gentility; nonetheless, it was highly unlikely that the impoverished middle-class woman would turn to domestic service or farm or factory work.) The debate over the middle-class woman's education could not finally be resolved until a prior question was decided: would society sanction work for such women?

Those who object to her working assume that every woman can, and of course should, marry, making work outside the home theoretically unnecessary as well as undesirable. Dora Greenwell echoes phrases long familiar to her readers in 1862: "To be Man's help-meet is woman's true vocation: for this, in the happy garden, she was given to the First Adam; and to be this, no longer Man's drudge or his plaything, the coming of the Second Adam has restored her."[35] A middle-class income makes this vision of a married woman's place at least economically possible. But what of the woman who marries late, or not at all? By the first part of the nineteenth century, the proportion of single women in Britain and New England has greatly increased, just when opposition to middle-class women's work outside the home hardens into social law. Observing America in the late 1830s, Harriet Martineau and Anna Jameson first point out the existence of a single-woman problem.[36] Emigration of men to frontier areas has created an artificial surplus of women in Britain and New England. At the same time, contemporary writers agree, a rapidly rising standard of living combined with the cultural prohibition against work for wives means that middle-class men cannot afford to marry young, and some never marry. By 1851, for every one hundred women in Britain there are only ninety-six men; of every one hundred women over twenty, only fifty-seven are married—thirteen are widowed, and thirty have not married. Nearly one half of the adult women in Britain—two and a half out of six million—have no spouse to support them. The figures are nearly comparable for New England. Many of these women will, of course, marry later, and most of them can in the meantime live at home. Nonetheless, the situation of the unmarried minority draws increasing attention in the mid-Victorian years. In 1858, Dinah Mulock Craik writes in her far from radical book *A Woman's Thoughts about Women:* "It is the single women, belonging to those supernumerary ranks which political economists tell us are yearly increasing, who most need thinking about." Craik concludes that "the chief canker at the root of women's lives, is the want of something to do."[37] It was increasingly probable that a Victorian woman would spend some portion of her adult life single and unsupported—yet middle-class women continued to be educated only to marry. The single-woman problem brought the question of work for ladies into new prominence.

Discussions of the single-woman problem appear in most of the major periodicals in the 1850s and early 1860s. Emigration is a popular though limited solution,[38] but Victorians are sharply divided over a more basic question: are single women a problem because they cannot marry or because society makes it difficult for them to support themselves? Is marriage or work the solution? W.R. Greg, a liberal manufacturer and frequent contributor to the periodicals, wrote a much-quoted response to this question in the *National Review*. "Why Are Women Redundant?" (1862) rejects any proposals which might make work and marriage equal alternatives. Like Roebuck, Mill, and Martineau, Greg has no objections to employing needy women for jobs they perform more cheaply or better than men. But the entry of women into the professions he opposes as unnatural, uneconomical, and unnecessary. (Note that Greg understates the size of the problem. The 1851 census, to which he refers, gives 1,767,194 spinsters and 795,194 widows, considerably more than Greg's "one million and a half adult unmarried women.")

Woman is the subject which for some time back our benevolence has been disposed to take in hand, fitfully and piecemeal. . . . The problem . . . appears to resolve itself into this: that there is an enormous and increasing number of single women in the nation, a number quite disproportionate and quite abnormal; a number which, positively and relatively, is indicative of an unwholesome social state, and is both productive and prognostic of much wretchedness and wrong. There are hundreds of thousands of women—not to speak more largely still—scattered through all ranks, but proportionally most numerous in the middle and upper classes, who have to earn their own living, instead of spending and husbanding the earnings of men; who, not having the natural duties and labors of wives and mothers, have to carve out artificial and painfully sought occupations for themselves; who, in place of completing, sweetening, and embellishing the existence of others, are compelled to lead an independent and incomplete existence of their own. . . .

It is because we think there is a tendency in the public mind at this conjuncture to solve it in the wrong way, to call the malady by a wrong name, and to seek in a wrong direction for the cure, that we take up our pen. In all our perplexities and disorders,—in social perplexities and disorders more perhaps than in any others,—there is one golden rule, if we will but apply it, which will suit great things as well as small, which is equally sound for all ages and all climes,—*consult Nature*; question her honestly and boldly, with no foregone determination as to what answer she shall give, with no sneaking intention to listen only to a fragment of her oracle, or to put a forced construction on her words. . . .

Now what does Nature say in reference to the case before us? By dividing and proportioning the sexes, by the instincts which lie deepest, strongest, and most unanimously in the heart of humanity at large in all times and amid all people, by the sentiments which belong to all healthy and unsophisticated organizations even in our own complicated civilization, marriage, the union of one man with one woman, is unmistakably indicated as the despotic law of life. This is *the* rule. . . . To a few, celibacy is a necessity; to a few, probably, a natural and easy state; to yet fewer, a high vocation. . . . [These] will not in their combined numbers exceed, if they even reach, that three or four per cent, for whom, as statistics show us, Nature has provided no exclusive partners. . . . The residue—the large excess over this proportion—who remain unmarried, *constitute the problem to be solved, the evil and anomaly to be cured.*

. . . all those efforts, on which chivalric or compassionate benevolence is now so intent, to render single life as easy, as attractive, and as lucrative to women as . . . to men, *are efforts in a wrong direction.* . . . To endeavor to make women independent of men; to multiply and facilitate their employments; to enable them to earn a separate and ample subsistence by competing with the hardier sex in those careers and occupations hitherto set apart for that sex alone; to induct them generally into avocations, not only as interesting and beneficent, and therefore *appropriate*, but specially and definitely as *lucrative*; to surround single life for them with so smooth an entrance, and such a pleasant, ornamented, comfortable path, that marriage shall almost come to be regarded, not as their most honorable function and especial calling, but merely as one of many ways open to them, competing on equal terms with other ways for their cold and philosophic choice:—this would appear to be the aim and theory of many female reformers. . . . Few more radical or more fatal errors, we are satisfied, philanthropy has ever made.

. . . *female servants do not constitute any part* (or at least only a very small part) *of the problem we are endeavoring to solve.* They are in no sense redundant; we have not to cudgel our brains to find a niche or an occupation for *them*; . . . they do not follow an obligatorily independent, and therefore for their sex an unnatural, career; on the contrary, they are attached to others, and are connected with other existences which they embellish, facilitate, and serve. In a word, they fulfil both essentials of woman's being; *they are supported by, and they minister to, men.* We could not possibly do without them.

. . . those wild schemers—principally to be found on the other side of the Atlantic, where a young community revels in every species of extravagant fantasies—who would throw open the professions to women, and teach them to become lawyers and physicians and professors, know little of life, and less of physiology. The brain and the frame of woman are formed with admirable suitability to their appropriate work, for which subtlety and sensitiveness, not strength and tenacity of fibre, are required. The cerebral organization of the female is far more delicate than that of man; the continuity and severity of application needed to acquire real *mastery* in any profession, or over any science, are denied to women, and can never with impunity be attempted by them; mind and health would almost invariably break down under the task. And wherever any exceptional women are to be found who seem to be abnormally endowed in this respect, and whose power and mental muscle are almost masculine, it may almost invariably, and we believe by a law of physiological necessity, be observed that they have purchased this questionable pre-eminence by a forfeiture of some of the distinctive and most invaluable charms and capabilities of their sex. . . .

We are not at all disposed to echo the cry of those who object to women and girls engaging in this or that industrial career. . . . It is clearly a waste of strength, a superfluous extravagance, an economic blunder, to employ a powerful and costly machine to do work which can be as well done by a feebler and a cheaper one. Women and girls are less costly operatives than men: what they can do with equal efficiency, it is therefore wasteful and foolish (*economically considered*) to set a man to do. . . .

Lastly, there are occupations for which single women are and always will be wanted,—occupations which none other can discharge as well, or can discharge at all. There are the thousand ramifications of charity,—nurses, matrons, *soeurs de charité*, "missing links";—functions of inestimable importance and of absolute necessity,—functions which if ill performed or unperformed, society would languish or fall into disorder. . . .

To sum up the whole matter. Nature makes no mistakes and creates no redundancies. Nature, honestly and courageously interrogated, gives no erroneous or ambiguous replies. In the case before us, Nature cries out against the malady, and plainly indicates the remedy. The first point to fix firmly in our minds is, that in the excess of single women in Great Britain we have a curable evil to be mended, not an irreparable evil to be borne. The mischief is to be eradicated, not to be counterbalanced, mitigated, or accepted.

To speak in round numbers, we have one million and a half adult unmarried women in Great Britain. Of these half a million are wanted in the colonies; half a million more are usefully, happily, and indispensably occupied in domestic service: the evil, thus viewed, assumes manageable dimensions, and only a residual half-million remain to be practically dealt with. As an immediate result of the removal of five hundred thousand women from the mother country, where they are redundant, to the colonies, where they are sorely needed, all who remain at home will rise in value, will be more sought, will be better rewarded. The number who compete for the few functions and the limited work at the disposal of women being so much reduced, the competition will be less cruelly severe, and the pay less ruinously beaten down. As the redundancy at home diminishes, and the value is thereby increased; men will not be able to obtain women's companionship and women's care so cheaply on illicit terms. As soon as the ideas of both sexes in the middle and upper ranks, on the question of the income and the articles which refinement and elegance require, are rectified,—as soon, that is, as these exigencies are reduced from what is purely factitious to what is indisputably real,—thousands who now condemn themselves and those they love to single life will find that they can marry without foregoing any luxury or comfort which is *essential* to ladylike and cultivated and enjoyable existence. Finally, as soon as, owing to stricter principles, purer tastes, or improved social condition,—or such combination of all these as the previous movements spoken of must gradually tend to produce,—the vast majority of men find themselves compelled either to live without all that woman can bestow, or to purchase it in the recognized mode,—as soon, to speak plainly, as their sole choice lies between marriage and a life of real and not nominal celibacy, the apparent redundance of women complained of now will vanish as by magic, if, indeed, it be not replaced by a deficiency. We are satisfied that IF the gulf could be practically bridged over, so that women went where they are clamored for; and IF we were contented with the *actualities* instead of the empty and unreal and unrewarding shadows of luxury and refinement; and IF men were necessitated either to marry or be chaste,—*all of which things it is a discreditable incapacity in us not to be able to accomplish*,—so far from there being too many women for the work that must be done, and that only women can do well, there would be too few. The work would be seeking for the women, instead of, as now, the women seeking for the work. We are disordered, we are suffering, we are astray, because we have *gone wrong*; and our philanthropists are laboring, not to make us go backward and go right, but to make it easier and smoother to persist in wrong.[39]

The reformers whom Greg attacks urge a changed attitude toward work for middle-class women as the only effective solution to the single-woman problem—and to the discontents of all women who have "nothing to do." One version of this argument, advanced in both Britain and America in the prosperous fifties, proposes that woman extend her sphere to social work but continue to think of herself as ministering to others' needs. A second version, exemplified by Florence Nightingale, urges women to enter professional careers as an antidote to the frustrations of inactivity. A third version, most radically formulated by Barbara Bodichon, claims woman's right to every kind of work as a human privilege and duty—whether she marries or not. Anna Jameson is typical of the first group of reformers. She asks in her 1856 lecture "The Communion of Labour" for the professionalization of women's service and philanthropy in hospitals, prisons, reformatory schools, refuges for prostitutes, and workhouses. Jameson's position is not egalitarian—"I return to the so called 'rights and wrongs of woman' only to dismiss them at once from our thoughts and our subject."[40] Like Greg, she believes in different kinds of work for men and women and in the primary importance of domestic duties for wives. Like Greg, too, she appeals to the needs of society and the nature of women, not to abstract justice, to decide what jobs they should fill. But Greg recognizes only the most traditional kinds of women's work, and then only where there is economic need. Jameson argues broadly that middle-class women have the right to work for society outside the domestic sphere, creating new jobs, for pay, when they are not needed at home. Greg, like Roebuck and Ward, justifies work by needy women as inevitable in a free economy; Jameson demands work for the middle-class woman by appealing to a shared ethic of work—the duty of women as well as men to contribute directly to the larger social good.

Jameson's opening definition of the problem indicates her different approach.

> Whether a more enlarged sphere of social work may not be allowed to woman in perfect accordance with the truest feminine instincts?
> . . .
> Work in some form or other is the appointed lot of all—divinely appointed; and, given as equal the religious responsibilities of the two sexes, might we not, in distributing the work to be done

in this world, combine and use in more equal proportion the working faculties of men and women, and so find a remedy for many of those mistakes which have vitiated some of our noblest educational and charitable institutions? Is it not possible that in the apportioning of the work we may have too far sundered what in God's creation never can be sundered without pain and mischief, the masculine and the feminine influences?—lost the true balance between the element of power and the element of love? and trusted too much to mere mechanical means for carrying out high religious and moral purposes?

. . . It appears to me that the domestic affections and the domestic duties—what I have called the "communion of love and the communion of labour"—must be taken as the basis of all the more complicated social relations, and that the family sympathies must be carried out and developed in all the forms and duties of social existence, before we can have a prosperous, healthy, happy, and truly Christian community. . . . to enlarge the working sphere of woman to the measure of her faculties, to give her a more practical and authorised share in all social arrangements which have for their object the amelioration of evil and suffering, is to elevate her in the social scale; and . . . whatever renders womanhood respected and respectable in the estimation of the people tends to humanise and refine the people. . . .

Here then I take my stand, not on any hypothesis of expediency, but on what I conceive to be an essential law of life; and I conclude that all our endowments for social good, whatever their especial purpose or denomination—educational, sanitary, charitable, penal —will prosper and fulfil their objects in so far as we carry out this principle of combining in due proportion the masculine and the feminine element.[41]

Jameson's "essential law of life" is part of the criticism of inhumane economic "laws" to which Lord Ashley, Tonna, and Carlyle had contributed. In the 1850s and 1860s, such men as F.D. Maurice and Ruskin make similar appeals to the "laws of life" against the prevailing practice of competitive economics, and like Jameson they include middle-class women in their redefinition of work as human duty (see Volume I, Chapter 5).[42] Believing with Tennyson (whose *The Princess* is often quoted) that "woman is not undevelop'd man, but diverse,"[43] they urge her to expand her horizon beyond the family and exercise her peculiar virtues—to minister and to serve—as philanthropist, reformer, teacher, and nurse. According to the American educator Horace Mann, the natural and divine "PRINCIPLE OF A

DIVISION OF LABOR" should be observed, but woman must nonetheless fill out her "hemisphere" in "the great circle of human duties."[44] The two hemispheres should fit together for social as well as domestic work, the womanly feeling complementing the masculine intellect "Like perfect music unto noble words" (Tennyson).[45] In practice, the principle is variously interpreted: Horace Mann thinks women can be doctors but not lawyers, while Jameson and Maurice see them as nurses but not doctors.

Jameson's middle-class woman social worker became a dramatic reality in the Crimean War and the American Civil War. Florence Nightingale, Clara Barton, Dorothea Dix, and "Mother" Bickerdyke visited wounded soldiers in army hospitals and on the battlefield, capturing the Victorian imagination as embodiments of the ministering angel, out of the house (see illustration 5). Before Nightingale, the popular image of the hospital nurse was that of Dicken's Sairey Gamp in *Martin Chuzzlewit* (1843): poor, uneducated, often rough, and always morally suspect. In 1857, Henry Wadsworth Longfellow helps fix the new image of the lady nurse-heroine with his "Santa Filomena," inspired by Nightingale and published in the first issue of the prestigious new Boston literary magazine, *Atlantic Monthly*. (Filomena is both Italian for Nightingale and the name of a medieval saint.)

> Whene'er a noble deed is wrought,
> Whene'er is spoken a noble thought,
>   Our hearts, in glad surprise,
>   To higher levels rise.
>
> The tidal wave of deeper souls
> Into our inmost being rolls,
>   And lifts us unawares
>   Out of all meaner cares.
>
> Honor to those whose words or deeds
> Thus help us in our daily needs,
>   And by their overflow
>   Raise us from what is low!
>
> Thus thought I, as by night I read
> Of the great army of the dead,
>   The trenches cold and damp,
>   The starved and frozen camp,—

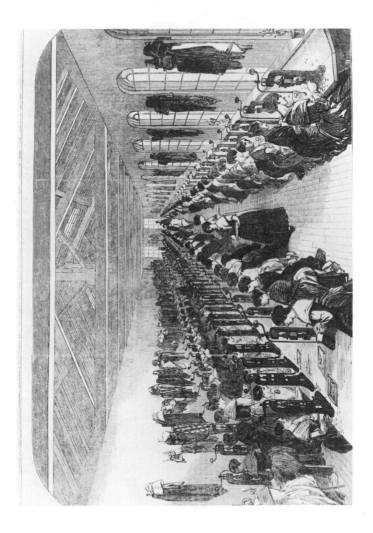

4. The Slitting Room for Pens
London Illustrated News, 1851

5. Miss Nightingale, in the Hospital at Scutari
London Illustrated News, 1855

The wounded from the battle-plain,
In dreary hospitals of pain,
   The cheerless corridors,
   The cold and stony floors.

Lo! in that house of misery
A lady with a lamp I see
   Pass through the glimmering gloom,
   And flit from room to room.

And slow, as in a dream of bliss,
The speechless sufferer turns to kiss
   Her shadow, as it falls
   Upon the darkening walls.

As if a door in heaven should be
Opened and then closed suddenly,
   The vision came and went,
   The light shone and was spent.

On England's annals, through the long
Hereafter of her speech and song,
   That light its rays shall cast
   From portals of the past.

A Lady with a Lamp shall stand
In the great history of the land,
   A noble type of good,
   Heroic womanhood.

Nor even shall be wanting here
The palm, the lily, and the spear,
   The symbols that of yore
   Saint Filomena bore.[46]

Nightingale herself was impatient with such sentimentaliza-
tions. To those government and army officials who saw her at
work, "the Nightingale power"—of which many disapproved—
referred to her administrative ability and reforming energy as
much as to the inspirational influence of "the lady with the
lamp." Queen Victoria was "very much struck" not only "by her
great gentleness and simplicity" but also by her "wonderful,
clear, and comprehensive head. I wish we had her at the War
Office."[47]

   Though Nightingale was not interested in serving as an
example for "Women's Missionaries" (as she wrote Harriet

Martineau in 1859),[48] the attitude with which she undertook her work, that of longing for a wider human duty than the domestic routine of a wealthy middle-class daughter, illustrates Jameson's argument. Nightingale was thirty-four when she went to the Crimea; for more than ten years she had struggled against family objections to train herself for regular, full-time work. Like Jameson and Carlyle before her, she claims the right to work as participation in a secularized religious duty. In 1843, reading Carlyle's "beautiful book" *Past and Present*, she singles out these sentences: "Blessed is he who has found his work: let him ask no other blessedness. He has a work, a life-purpose: he has found it and will follow it."[49] In a manuscript written in the early 1850s, Nightingale expresses all the bitter frustration of an educated woman, "chained to the bronze pedestal" upon which society had placed its angels, provided they marry and stay home. She called her work "Cassandra," and to that image of the mad, despised prophetess (who refused to become the consort of Apollo) she added another in her epigraph: "The voice of one crying in the crowd, 'Prepare ye the way of the Lord.'" John the Baptist's was a voice in the wilderness; Nightingale's would be a voice in the crowd of proper Victorian society. But though J.S. Mill in 1860 urged her to publish her manuscript (he drew on it for his own *The Subjection of Women*),[50] she followed the Oxford classicist Benjamin Jowett's more cautious advice and kept private this protest against the waste of woman's life.

Why have women passion, intellect, moral activity—these three—and a place in society where no one of the three can be exercised? . . . these three have never been satisfied in a woman. In this cold and oppressive conventional atmosphere, they cannot be satisfied. . . .

Look at the poor lives we lead. It is a wonder that we are so good as we are, not that we are so bad. . . . Women never have an half-hour in all their lives (excepting before or after anybody is up in the house) that they can call their own, without fear of offending or of hurting someone. . . .

If a man were to follow up his profession or occupation at odd times, how would he do it? Would he become skilful in that profession? It is acknowledged by women themselves that they are inferior in every occupation to men. Is it wonderful? *They* do *everything* at "odd times." . . .

Society triumphs over many. They wish to regenerate the world with their institutions, with their moral philosophy, with their love. Then they sink to living from breakfast till dinner, from dinner till tea, with a little worsted work, and to looking forward to nothing but bed.

When shall we see a life full of steady enthusiasm, walking straight to its aim, flying home, as that bird is now, against the wind—with the calmness and the confidence of one who knows the laws of God and can apply them? . . .

The family? It is too narrow a field for the development of an immortal spirit, be that spirit male or female. The chances are a thousand to one that, in that small sphere, the task for which that immortal spirit is destined by the qualities and the gifts which its Creator has placed within it, will not be found. . . .

How different would be the heart for the work, and how different would be the success, if we learnt our work as a serious study, and followed it out steadily as a profession! . . .

Women dream of a great sphere of steady, not sketchy benevolence, of moral activity, for which they would fain be trained and fitted, instead of working in the dark, neither knowing nor registering whither their steps lead, whether farther from or nearer to the aim. . . .

Dreaming always—never accomplishing; thus women live—too much ashamed of their dreams, which they think "romantic," to tell them where they will be laughed at, even if not considered wrong.

With greater strength of purpose they might accomplish something. But if they were strong, all of them, they would not need to have their story told, for all the world would read it in the mission they have fulfilled. It is for common-place, every-day characters that we tell our tale—because it is the sample of hundreds of lives (or rather deaths) of persons who cannot fight with society, or who, unsupported by the sympathies about them, give up their own destiny as not worth the fierce and continued struggle necessary to accomplish it. . . .

But if ever women come into contact with sickness, with poverty, and crime in masses, how the practical reality of life revives them! They are exhausted, like those who live on opium or on novels, all their lives—exhausted with feelings which lead to no action. If they see and enter into a continuous line of action, with a full and interesting life, with training constantly kept up to the occupation, occupation constantly testing the training—it is the *beau-ideal* of practical, not theoretical, education—they are re-tempered, their life is filled, they have found their work, and the means to do it. . . .

Women dream till they have no longer the strength to dream; those dreams against which they so struggle, so honestly, vigorously, and conscientiously, and so in vain, yet which are their life, without which they could not have lived; those dreams go at last. All their plans and visions seem vanished, and they know not where; gone, and they cannot recall them. They do not even remember them. And they are left without the food of reality or of hope. . . .

There is perhaps no century where the woman shows so meanly as in this. Because her education seems entirely to have parted company with her vocation; there is no longer unity between the woman as inwardly developed, and as outwardly manifested.

In the last century it was not so. In the succeeding one let us hope that it will no longer be so.

But now she is like the Archangel Michael as he stands upon Saint Angelo at Rome. She has an immense provision of wings, which seem as if they would bear her over earth and heaven; but when she tries to use them, she is petrified into stone, her feet are grown into the earth, chained to the bronze pedestal.[51]

Nightingale's Cassandra is a sister of George Eliot's Dorothea Brooke in *Middlemarch* (1872) and Gwendolyn Harleth in *Daniel Deronda* (1876); but Nightingale herself was not daunted by vague dreams or social restrictions. She objected, in 1873, when Eliot portrayed Dorothea as bound to give up a broader sphere of social action.[52] Elizabeth Barrett Browning's popular poem *Aurora Leigh* (1856) expresses better the aspirations of young women like Nightingale in the 1850s. Aurora begins her active pursuit of a literary career by refusing to marry her cousin, and before she finally joins him (he is a social reformer) for a future "communion of love and labour" she has established herself as a serious poet. Anna Jameson was much moved by the "beauty and power" of her friend's conception.[53] Barbara Leigh Smith Bodichon, one of the young women who turned Jameson's pleas into the beginnings of a feminist movement in the late 1850s, used as epigraph for her pamphlet *Women and Work* (1856) these lines from *Aurora Leigh*:

The honest earnest man must stand and work;
The woman also; otherwise she drops
At once below the dignity of man
Accepting serfdom.

Between 1858 and 1860, Barbara Bodichon, her close friend Bessie Parkes, and the women who joined them—Marie Rye, Isa Craig, Emily Faithfull, Jessie Boucherett, Emily Davies—established in offices at Langham Place the *Englishwoman's Journal*, the Society for the Promotion of Employment for Women, a reading room, and an employment bureau, and directed a middle-class emigration society, a law-copying office, the Victoria Press, and a school to train women for clerical work. The "ladies of Langham Place" approached work differently from Nightingale or Jameson. With the single-minded energy of a secular Sister, Nightingale had refused marriage in order to dedicate herself to nursing reform. The Langham Place women were high-spirited and practical, but no one thought of enshrining them as the celibate saints of True Womanhood. Bodichon's life was as unconventional as her views on women and work, though both are surprisingly little known today (her biographer does not mention that she was illegitimate, for example).[54] With her close friendship with George Eliot, her intellectual debt to Margaret Fuller, and her interest in European and American radicalism, Bodichon is perhaps the most important unstudied figure of mid-century English feminism.

The eldest child of what George Eliot called "the tabooed family,"[55] Barbara was liberally educated and given an independent income by her father, Benjamin Leigh Smith, a prominent radical and Unitarian. She experienced few of the restrictions that had troubled Nightingale. Unlike her close friend George Eliot, with whose tabooed position as Lewes' common-law wife she immediately sympathized, Bodichon did not lead a secluded life. She took advantage of her uncertain social position to move freely in and out of conventional society, working seriously as an artist while actively supporting women's rights in law, work, and education (see Chapter 1). In the early fifties she had an affair with John Chapman (with whom George Eliot had once been involved). She visited Eliot and Lewes at home, as proper women did not. And she arranged her marriage, at thirty, to an eccentric but romantic French Algerian doctor of radical views so that they spent six months of every year in Algeria for his work, and six in England for hers. Apparently she and Eliot discussed methods of birth control (both, by choice, had no children).[56] When Bodichon guessed that Eliot was the author of the successful *Adam Bede*, she rejoiced at the triumph of a friend, a social outcast, and a woman.[57]

Jameson thought of Bodichon and her friends as her "adopted nieces,"[58] but Bodichon's *Women and Work* makes a far more radical argument than Jameson's. Bodichon replaces Jameson's proposal for a middle-class woman social worker with an assertion of woman's right to every kind of work—with or without financial need, before and after marriage. In suggesting that marriage and work need not be incompatible, Bodichon goes further than Mill in his 1869 *Subjection*. She makes no appeal to woman's angelic nature, in or out of the house, in defending work for women.

Every human being should work; no one should owe bread to any but his or her parents. A child is dependent on its parents for bread as a child: idiots and imbeciles must be fed all their lives; but rational beings ask nothing from their parents save the means of gaining their own livelihood. Fathers have no right to cast the burden of the support of their daughters on other men. It lowers the dignity of women; and tends to prostitution, whether legal or in the streets. As long as fathers regard the sex of a child as a reason why it should not be taught to gain its own bread, so long must women be degraded. Adult women must not be supported by men if they are to stand as dignified rational beings before God. Esteem and friendship would not give nor accept such a position; and Love is destroyed by it. . . .

We do not mean to say work will take the place of love in life; that is impossible; does it with men? But we ardently desire that women should not make *love their profession*.

Love is not the end of life. It is nothing to be sought for; it should come. If we work, love may meet us in life; if not, we have something still, beyond all price. . . .

To many of you the question comes direct, whether you will accept a dependent, ornamental and useless position, or an independent and hard working one. Never hesitate for one moment; grasp the hand that points to work and freedom. Shake the hand with thanks of refusal, which offers you a home and "all the advantages of city society until you are married." Say that you prefer to pay your own way in the world, that you love an honorable independence better than to live on charity, though gilded with all the graces of hospitality and affection. Plan for yourselves a life of active single blessedness and usefulness. Be sure this is nobler and happier than many married lives, and not a hell at all, as some tell you; and is the way, too, to secure a happy marriage, if that is your destiny. . . .

"Certainly it would make unmarried women happier to have professions. But is it not discouraging to give a girl a training for a trade when we know that if she marries she will most surely give it up? She must, you know, if she has children, and nine out of ten women do marry and have children."

Taking your statement as true, which, by-the-bye, it is not, (for, of women at the age of twenty and upwards, 43 out of the 100 in England and Wales are unmarried,)* we can answer that it is worth while. 1st, A girl will make a better wife for having had such serious training. 2dly, Your daughter may not marry. It is your duty to provide for that possibility; and she will surely be ill, miserable, or go mad, if she has no occupation. 3dly, It may be years before your daughter finds a husband. It is your duty to give her worthy work, or to allow her to choose it; and certainly she is more likely to be attractive and to get a good husband if she is cheerful and happy in some work, than if she, being miserable and longing for a change, clutches at the first offer made her. 4thly, suppose the man she may love is poor, by her labor she can help to form their mutual home. Birds, both cock and hen, help one another to build their nest. 5thly, your daughter may be left to act as both father and mother to children dependent on her for daily bread.

But it is certain that a girl will give up her occupation when married? There are thousands of married women who are in want of a pursuit—a profession. It is a mistake to suppose marriage gives occupation enough to employ all the faculties of all women. To bring a family of 12 children into the world is not in itself a noble vocation, or always a certain benefit to humanity. To be a noble woman is better than being mother to a noble man: and also the best way of accomplishing that great work! . . .

Queen Victoria fulfils the very arduous duties of her calling, and manages also to be the active mother of many children. Each woman must so arrange her own life as best to fulfil all her duties. Women can be trusted to do the best for their young children; maternal love is too strong ever to be weakened by any love of a science, art, or profession. As the human being is larger and nobler, so will all the natural affections be. . . .

To sum up. Women want work both for the health of their minds and bodies. They want it often because they must eat and because they have children and others dependent on them—*for all the reasons that men want work*. They are placed at a great disadvantage in the market of work because they are not skilled laborers, and are therefore badly paid. They rarely have any training. It is the duty of fathers and mothers to give their daughters this training.

All experience proves that the effect of the independence of women upon married life is good.

*And a very large proportion in New England also, probably 30.

The time has arrived when women are wanted in the Commonwealth. John Milton said the Commonwealth "ought to be but one huge Christian personage, one mighty growth and stature of an honest man, as big and compact in virtue as in body." Our idea differs from this grand but incomplete conception. We rather think the Commonwealth should be—

"Inclusive of all gifts and faculties
On either sex bestowed, knit up in strengths
Of man and woman both; hers even as his,
And tempered with the finest tenderness
Of love betwixt these two."[59]

Few men or women were willing to go as far as Bodichon. Yet the middle-class woman's demand for work, as W.R. Greg certainly understood, was a more fundamental challenge to the doctrine of separate spheres than the limited case of the impoverished, genteel spinster might suggest.

III

"Practically, the command of society to the uneducated class is 'Marry, stitch, die, or do worse.'"[60] Boston feminist Caroline Dall reminded Americans in 1859 that prostitution was an ever-present alternative to starvation for Hood's poor seamstress. It paid better than stitching and might even offer a chance for social advancement to lower-class women: a prostitute might marry or save enough money to open a small business.[61] In the eyes of the Victorian public, however, prostitution was worse than death. Nonetheless, by mid-century Victorian discussions of prostitution shift from moral outrage to a new sympathy for the victimized woman. Her inability to earn a living except by marriage or prostitution brings women's underpaid work again to public attention. Then in the 1870s and 1880s the prostitute becomes the focus of a heated debate between doctors, legislators, and feminists. That debate, and the response it arouses in the many middle-class women who take up the defense of the prostitute and her working-class sisters, gives a new direction and a new tone to the Woman Question in the later decades of the century.

Rarely discussed in public before 1850, "the social evil" was at first largely a moral issue. The prostitute was an unknown, mythic figure from the "shadow side" of Victorian lives and minds. About 1850 information on the realities of contemporary prostitution prompts two new perspectives on "the oldest profession." Recognizing the ties of venereal disease that bind the prostitute to Victorian society, enlightened doctors shift discussion from mere sympathy or condemnation to social welfare, urging compulsory medical examinations for women suspected of prostitution. In the same period feminists begin to link prostitution with the depressed wages and inferior social status of all women. They object vigorously that health legislation not only ignores but effectively confirms women's deeper wrongs. Though women are idealized as the more spiritual sex, law and science, they argue, have once again deprived women of civil rights and defined them solely as sexual beings. For all practical purposes, the law recognizes two and only two occupations for women: marriage and prostitution.

By the 1870s and 1880s, liberal doctors and legislators clash head-on with an increasingly apocalyptic feminism. The prostitute becomes a symbol of the contradiction between woman's mission as the guardian of human values at home and woman's position as a sexually and economically exploited participant in the working world. That contradiction, as Jameson earlier claimed, puts women's work at the center of the Woman Question. Apocalyptic feminists, however, ultimately stress woman's power to reform society rather than her right to participate fully and equally in it. Their vision of a special social role for women fails once again to establish woman's place in the working world.

Those who view prostitution primarily as a moral state consider the prostitute either an evil to be punished and repressed or a victim to be pitied and redeemed. In either case, however, she is separated from respectable society by a moral abyss. *Meliora*, a British temperance journal, rises to impassioned denunciation of the sinning prostitute in 1859.

> . . . it is quite certain that, in this Christian land of England, many—very many—thousands of women are leading lives of open, notorious profligacy; many of the streets of our great cities are thronged at night with shameless creatures, who, not content

with parading their dishonour before the world, do not scruple to annoy and disgust even unwilling men with their solicitations; infamous houses are kept for the avowed purpose of prostitution; an acknowledged trade is carried on by panders and procuresses, in the bodies of women, both foreign and English. All this national disgrace and personal brutality has been carried on, and is spreading, in the very heart of us, to the disgust and scandal of the moral, the just horror of the pious, and the danger of all; yet, until within a short time, hardly an effort has been made to check this prodigious and abominable evil. . . . there is no clearer axiom in political morality than this—that it is the duty, the right, and the business of the state to punish such actions as are inconsistent with the virtue, the happiness, and the welfare of the people.[62]

But this view of woman as the carnal seducer is not dominant in the nineteenth century.[63] Henry Mayhew's interviews with London seamstresses who turned to prostitution, published in the *Morning Chronicle* in 1849, impressed many readers, contradicting the image of the deliberate temptress with portraits of social victims.

'I make moleskin trowsers. I get 7*d.* and 8*d.* per pair. I can do two pairs in a day, and twelve, when there is full employment, in a week. But some weeks I have no work at all. I work from six in the morning to ten at night; that is what I call my day's work. When I am fully employed I get from 7*s.* to 8*s.* a week. My expenses out of that for twist, thread, and candles are about 1*s.* 6*d.* a week, leaving me about 6*s.* a week clear. But there's coals to pay for out of this, and that's at the least 6*d.* more; so 5*s.* 6*d.* is the very outside of what I earn when I'm in full work. Taking one week with another, all the year round, I don't make above 3*s.* clear money each week. I don't work at any other kind of slop work. The trowsers work is held to be the best paid of all. I give 1*s.* a week rent. My father died when I was five years of age. My mother is a widow, upwards of 66 years of age, and seldom has a day's work. Generally once in the week she is employed pot-scouring—that is, cleaning publicans' pots. She is paid 4*d.* a dozen for that, and does about four dozen and a half, so that she gets about 1*s.* 6*d.* in the day by it. For the rest she is dependent upon me. I am twenty years of age the 25th of this month. We earn together, to keep the two of us, from 4*s.* 6*d.* to 5*s.* each week. Out of this we have to pay 1*s.* rent, and there remains 3*s.* 6*d.* to 4*s.* to find us both in food and clothing. It is of course impossible for us to live upon it, and the consequence is, I am obliged to go a bad way. I have been three years working at slop work. *I was virtuous when I first when to work, and I remained so till this last twelvemonth. I struggled very hard to keep myself chaste, but I found that I* *couldn't get food and clothing for myself and mother*; so I took to live with a young man. He is turned twenty. He is a tinman. He did promise to marry me, but his sister made mischief between me and him; so that parted us. I have not seen him now for about six months, and I can't say whether he will keep his promise or not. I am now pregnant by him, and expect to be confined in two months' time. He knows of my situation, and so does my mother. My mother believed me to be married to him. She knows otherwise now. I was very fond of him, and had known him for two years before he seduced me. He could make 14s. a week. He told me if I came to live with him he'd take care I shouldn't want, and both mother and me had been very bad off before. He said, too, he'd make me his lawful wife, *but I hardly cared so long as I could get food for myself and mother*. Many young girls at the shop advised me to go wrong. They told me how comfortable they was off; they said they could get plenty to eat and drink, and good clothes. There isn't one young girl as can get her living by slop work. I am satisfied there is not one young girl that works at slop work that is virtuous, and there are some thousands in the trade. They may do very well if they have got mothers and fathers to find them a home and food, and to let them have what they earn for clothes; then they may be virtuous, but not without. I've heard of numbers who have gone from slop work to the streets altogether for a living, and I shall be obligated to do the same thing myself, unless something better turns up for me. If I was never allowed to speak no more, it was the little money I got by my labour that caused me to go wrong. Could I have honestly earned enough to have subsisted upon, to find me in proper food and clothing, such as is necessary, I should not have gone astray; no, never! As it was, I fought against it as long as I could—that I did—to the last. I know know horrible all this is. It would have been much better for me to have subsisted upon a dry crust and water rather than be as I am now. But no one knows the temptations of us poor girls in want. Gentlefolks can never understand it. If I had been born a lady, it wouldn't have been very hard to have acted like one. To be poor and to be honest, especially with young girls, is the hardest struggle of all. There isn't one in a thousand that can get the better of it. I am ready to say again, that it was want, and nothing more, that made me transgress. If I had been better paid I should have done better. Young as I am, my life is a curse to me. If the Almighty would please to take me before my child is born, I should die happy.'[64]

Responding to Mayhew's interviews, W.R. Greg in 1850 broke conventions of public silence to plead for the prostitute as victim in an article for the *Westminster Review*. Like Dr. William

Acton, Greg sees the prostitute as essentially sexless, but unlike Acton, Greg ignores available information: Parent-Duchatelet's important observations of the prostitute's upward social mobility.[65] Greg shifts the moral responsibility from the woman to her seducers and accusers, but his vivid picture of her decline and death supports the popular image of the "fallen" woman.

> . . . we feel called upon to protest against the manner in which prostitutes are almost universally regarded, spoken of, and treated in this country, as dishonouring alike to our religion and our manhood. This iniquity pervades all classes, and both sexes. No language is too savage for these wretched women. They are outcasts, Pariahs, lepers. . . . It is discreditable to a woman even to be supposed to know of their existence. . . .
>
> If the *extremity* of human wretchedness—if a condition which combines within itself every element of suffering, mental and physical, circumstantial and intrinsic—is a passport to our compassion, every heart should bleed for the position of an English prostitute, as it never bled at any form of woe before. We wish it were in our power to give a picture, simple, faithful, uncoloured, but "too severely true," of the horrors which constitute the daily life of a woman of the town. The world—the unknowing world— is apt to fancy her revelling in the *enjoyment* of licentious pleasures; lost and dead to all sense of remorse and shame; wallowing in mire because she loves it. Alas! there is no truth in *this* conception, or only in the most exceptional cases. Passing over all the agonies of grief and terror she must have endured before she reached her present degradation; the vain struggles to retrieve the first false, fatal step; the feeling of her inevitable future pressing her down with all the hopeless weight of destiny; the dreams of a happy past that haunt her in the night-watches, and keep her ever trembling on the verge of madness;—passing over all this, what is her position when she has reached the last step of her downward progress, and has become a common prostitute? Every calamity that can afflict human nature seems to have gathered round her,—cold, hunger, disease, often absolute starvation. Insufficiently fed, insufficiently clad, she is driven out alike by necessity and by the dread of solitude, to wander through the streets by night, for the chance of earning a meal by the most loathsome labour that imagination can picture, or a penal justice could inflict. . . . The career of these women is a brief one; their downward path a marked and inevitable one; and they know this well. They are almost never rescued; escape themselves they cannot. . . .
>
> Then comes the last sad scene of all, when drink, disease, and starvation have laid her on her death-bed. On a wretched pallet in

a filthy garret, with no companions but the ruffians, drunkards, and harlots with whom she had cast in her lot; amid brutal curses, ribald language, and drunken laughter; with a past—which, even were there no future, would be dreadful to contemplate—laying its weight of despair upon her soul; with a prospective beyond the grave which the little she retains of her early religion lights up for her with the lurid light of hell,—this poor daughter of humanity terminates a life, of which, if the sin has been grievous and the weakness lamentable, the expiation has been fearfully tremendous.

. . . For that almost irresistable series of sequences, by which one lapse from chastity conducts ultimately to prostitution, we— the world—must bear the largest portion of the blame. What makes it *impossible* for them to retrace their steps?—almost impossible even to pause in the career of ruin? Clearly, that harsh, savage, unjust, unchristian public opinion which has resolved to regard a whole life of indulgence on the part of one sex as venial and natural, and a single false step on the part of the other as irretrievable and unpardonable. . . . She is driven into prostitution by the weight of all society pressing upon her.

. . . reason and religion are alike outraged when the sinner himself assumes a language of Rhadamanthine severity, which would sit ill upon the purest ermine, and pronounces the very same guilt which is held trivial and venial in him, to be unpardonable and irreparable in the more guileless accomplice whom he has led astray. . . . Till virtuous women and reflecting men can be persuaded to modify their verdict on the matter, much of the existing prostitution will lie at their door.[66]

The fallen woman as victim is an extraordinarily pervasive image in the art and literature of the late forties and early fifties. Thomas Hood again suggests the iconography that prevails. His poem "The Bridge of Sighs" (1844) focuses on the suicide of the starving and despairing woman, her drowned body found literally fallen under the arches of Waterloo Bridge. Artists including not only such Royal Academicians as G.F. Watts and Augustus Egg but also such rebellious Pre-Raphaelites as D.G. Rossetti and J.E. Millais paint variations on the victimized woman's death by drowning.[67] However, the focus on her physical prostration, which the painters and poets share with Greg, deflects attention from the social conditions at fault—conditions that Mayhew, who draws the clear connection between inadequate wages and prostitution, helped to expose.[68]

The nineteenth-century passion for statistics brings to light more new facts about the prostitute after the middle of the century. Acton and Caroline Dall draw on the pioneer research of Parent-Duchatelet in Paris and Dall on the further work of Dr. William Sanger in New York.[69] For Greg, even new facts are not enough to dispel the myth of the prostitute's fall, but for Acton and Dall they provide the basis for two new views of prostitution. In his important 1857 book Acton challenges social and medical attitudes based on misinformation. He insists that "prostitution is a transitory state, through which an untold number of British women are ever on their passage" not to a miserable death but to other jobs and perhaps even an improved social position. The harlot's fate is not death but marriage. Since she regularly rejoins the ranks of the respectable, and spreads disease both through her clients and through her children, the state of her body ought to concern society as much as the state of her soul. "If the race of the people is of no concern to the State, then has the State no interest in arresting its vitiation," he argues. "But if this concern and this interest be admitted, then arises the necessity for depriving prostitution not only of its moral, but of its physical venom also."[70] Acton in London, Sanger in New York, and others of liberal views convince doctors and administrators of the need for a more rational, "humane" attitude toward the prostitute. In the late 1860s and early 1870s, doctors campaign strongly in Britain and America for legislation requiring periodic examination and treatment for venereal disease of all women suspected of prostitution. Contagious Diseases Acts were first passed in Britain in 1864 and proposed in New York in 1867.[71]

Feminists, beginning with Dall in the early 1860s, draw very different conclusions from the same evidence. Using Sanger's investigations of New York prostitutes, Dall concludes that prostitution is not a doctor's but a woman's problem, the symbol of the low value placed on women's work. In "Death or Dishonor," the first of her Boston lectures on *Woman's Right to Labor* (1859–60), Dall urges middle-class women to see that the prostitute's economic and social position is intimately related to their own.

> I ask for woman, then, free, untrammelled access to all fields of labor; and I ask it, first, on the ground that she needs to be fed, and that the question which is at this moment before the great body of working women is "death or dishonor:" for lust is a better paymaster than the mill-owner or the tailor, and economy never yet shook hands with crime.

Do you object, that America is free from this alternative? I will prove you the contrary within a rod of your own doorstep.

Do you assert, that, if all avenues were thrown open, it would not increase the quantity of work; and that there would be more laborers in consequence, and lower wages for all?

Lower wages for *some*, I reply; but certainly higher wages for women; and they, too, would be raised to the rank of partners, and personal ill treatment would not follow those who had position and property before the law.

. . . I go farther, and state boldly, that women have, from the beginning, done the hardest and most unwholesome work of the world in all countries, whether civilized or uncivilized; and I am prepared to prove it. I do not mean that rocking the cradle and making bread is as hard work as any, but that women have always been doing man's work, and that all the outcry society makes against work for women is not to protect *women*, but a certain class called *ladies*. Now, I believe that work is good for ladies. . . .

O my sisters! why has God sheltered *us* in quiet homes? What have we done to deserve a happier fate? Why were we not left to writhe beneath the blows of the smith, or the outrage of a market-sale?

Because God has laid down a responsibility by the side of every privilege, and requires us to labor not merely to set such women free, but to establish a freedom and security *by law*,—the law of custom as well as the law of courts, which we only possess through usurpation or indulgence. . . .

It is pretty and lady-like, men think, to paint and chisel: philanthropic young ladies must work for nothing, like the angels. *Let* them, when they rise to angelic spheres; but, here and now, every woman who works for nothing helps to keep her sister's wages down,—helps to keep the question of death or dishonor perpetually before the women of the slop-shop.

Why? Because she helps to depress the estimate of woman's ability. What is persistently given for nothing is everywhere thought to be worth nothing. . . .

Plenty of employments are open to them; but all are under-paid. They will never be better paid till women of rank begin to work for money, and so create a respect for woman's labor; and women of rank will never do this till American men feel what all American men profess,—a proper respect for Labor, as God's own demand upon every human soul,—and so teach American women to feel it.[72]

In 1870 feminism and science collide. The controversy is heated and prolonged in both Britain and America. There is no conservative position. For women who agree with Dall that their own wrongs are reflected in the position of the prostitute, the Contagious Diseases Acts are intolerable because they amount to official recognition of prostitution as a permanent social fact. To recognize the prostitute, they argue, is to accept woman's low economic status, and to deny the influence of her supposed moral superiority. Because the Acts allow women to be detained on the suspicion of prostitution, the Acts also deprive women of basic civil rights. In America the opposition to Contagious Diseases Acts, in which Susan B. Anthony is active, is known as "New Abolitionism." Its appeal to feminists who have already linked liberty for blacks with liberty for women, and seen their expectations disappointed after the war, is doubly powerful. But supporters of the Acts also speak in the name of progressive ideas—a rational, humane science and the state's responsibility for public health. In response to a public manifesto against the Acts signed by many prominent British women, John Morley, then a rising man of letters and liberal ideas, protests that opponents of the Acts are sentimental, blind, and finally inhumane. Morley's "A Short Letter to Some Ladies" is published in 1870 in the review he edited, the *Fortnightly*.

You assert that these Acts *"indirectly admit prostitution to be a necessity."* It is truer to say that they recognise it as a fact. There is no more ground for charging the framers and advocates of these Acts with a belief in the necessity of prostitution, than there is for bringing the same charge against the surgeon who treats the diseases incident to it. Whether necessary or not, prostitution does actually confront us, and like any other evil of our social condition, has to be dealt with in one way or another. Do the various Acts for promoting the health of towns, indirectly admit the necessity of uncovered cesspools, over-crowded lodging-houses, and so forth? Prostitution is at present so widespread and deep-rooted that it is practically for our generation just as if it were a necessity.

"This admission," you say finally, "we resist with all the strength of our belief in the sanctity of pure and faithful love, and in the progress of the human race." Surely these sound the very windiest words I have heard for many a day. We others believe in the progress of the human race, too, but only on condition of enlightened and strenuous effort on the part of persons of superior character and opportunity; and though this effort to prevent the redemption of a portion of an unborn generation from a deadly disease may be strenuous, its enlightenment strikes us as questionable. To sacrifice the health and vigour of unborn creatures to the "rights" of harlotry to spread disease without interference, is a doubtful contribution towards the progress of the race. As to the sanctity of pure and faithful love, a time may come when such words will describe the relations of all men and women as truly as they describe those of a very great many among them now. But can you seriously think that the Satyr is on the very point of parting company with man?

. . . Reluctance to admit that so many human creatures are irreclaimably brutalised in their natures by influences at work from the first moment of susceptibility is natural, but it is a strange reason why we should refuse not only to mitigate the sufferings which the poor wretches, with characters for which they are partially responsible, bring on themselves, but also to stretch out a hand to stay the plague from innocent offspring.

. . . You speak of the "practical contempt for womanhood" displayed by the legislature in these Acts. This practical contempt for womanhood may be seen every hour of every day in its supreme form in the leaden inconsiderateness of nine ladies out of ten for their dressmakers, domestic servants, nurses, and dependents generally.

It is for women, for courageous women like those of whom your Association is composed, to spread and realise such an idea of the family and of all forms of service and of the moral obligation against indifference which they instantly erect, that on this most dangerous of all sides the approach to the pit may be fenced off. This, however, and all other action dictated by the contrition of which you speak, so far as it cuts off the roots and sources of the evil, must be prospective. It cannot redeem those who are already fully committed to courses and, what is still more, to a habit of mind, which nothing short of a directly miraculous interposition of divine grace could change. For those who are not thus irretrievably committed, restoration to health is a first condition of any rise from degradation, and the influence of the Acts against which you protest is to promote this sanatory condition of the case.[73]

Other reactions to respectable women's discussion of prostitution are far more extreme. The *Saturday Review* calls them "shrieking sisters," "frenzied, unsexed, and utterly without shame." Sir James Elphinstone tells the House of Commons in 1872, "I look upon these women who have taken up this matter as worse than prostitutes."[74] Even Charles Kingsley, a supporter of social work for middle-class women, writes privately to Mill that unmarried women will damage the cause of woman by speaking out on an issue about which they are supposed to be innocent.[75]

From "New Abolitionism," the campaign to abolish prostitution by reforming male morals, many American women move directly to the broader goals of the Social Purity Reform Movement. Taking everything from temperance to municipal reform as their province, these women become a powerful social force, although they largely relinquish efforts to win the vote or access to more and better jobs. The American movement draws not only on Stanton and Anthony's arguments for women's rights, but more importantly on apocalyptic feminism—the belief that the moral superiority of woman gives her a leading role in the imminent establishment of a more perfect world (see Chapter 4, and Volume I, Chapter 3). This apocalyptic strain is rare among English feminists (though Lady Morgan's 1840 *Woman and Her Master* may have influenced the American Eliza Farnham). The Contagious Diseases campaign in Britain is an exception, and one which any account of the Woman Question must consider. Its leader, Josephine Butler, appeals both to the justice of equal rights and to the hope of redemption through woman. British as well as American Victorians were enormously responsive to *both* appeals.

Why did women like Butler choose to face the insults and stones hurled at them when they claimed the prostitute's cause as woman's? Butler's father had been an antislavery speaker, and she herself felt from her youth a particular sympathy with sexually exploited women. As a young wife in Oxford, she was shocked to hear how enlightened men judged fallen women like Elizabeth Gaskell's Ruth. When Butler's small daughter died, she deliberately redirected her grief toward those who had earlier aroused her imagination. At the Liverpool workhouse she befriended vagrant women, later nursing some of them in her home. She found justification for her activities not only in her feeling for women but also in a radical reading of the gospels: "Among the great typical acts of Christ which were evidently and intentionally for the announcement of a principle for the guidance of society, none were more markedly so than His acts toward women; and I appeal to the open Book and to the intelligence of every candid student of Gospel history for the justification of my assertion, that, in all important instances of His dealings with women, His dismissal of each case was accompanied by a distinct act of Liberation," she wrote in 1869.[76] Later the same year, Butler began her thirteen-year crusade to repeal the Contagious Diseases Acts.

The first of Butler's two arguments invokes the justice of equal rights, including the right to work. "The Constitution Violated"—an 1871 speech reprinted for use in several American campaigns—claims the English political right to individual liberty guaranteed by due process, in the name of the working-class women most threatened by the Acts.

We who have combined to oppose this legislation maintain that this Act is unconstitutional, because it submits a case, in which the result is to the party concerned of the most enormous consequence, to trial without jury. . . .

In answer to our objections to these Acts, it is utter vanity and folly in anyone to plead that they apply only to women who are prostitutes. Can it be supposed that there is any man in England so foolish as to think that the safeguards of English law exist for the sake of the guilty only? They exist for the sake of the innocent, who may be falsely accused, as well to protect them when accused, as to lessen the chances of unjust accusation. And can it be supposed that we are so blind as ever to be able to fancy that it is impossible that under this law an innocent woman may be accused? On the contrary, it is obvious that the question of a woman's honour is one in which mistaken accusations are peculiarly likely to occur.

For the rich and great there may be little danger in dispensing with jury trial in this particular instance. As there are classes in society whose position and wealth place them above any chance of being erroneously accused of theft, so there are classes whose position, wealth and surroundings place the women belonging to them equally above any chance of being erroneously accused of being prostitutes. . . . Ladies who ride in their carriages through the streets at night are in little danger of being molested. But what of working women? What of the daughters, sisters, wives of working men, out, it may be on an errand of mercy, at night? And what most of all of that girl whose father, mother, friends are dead, or far away, who is struggling hard in a hard world to live uprightly and justly by the work of her own hands—is she in no danger from this law? Lonely and friendless and poor, is she in no danger of a false accusation from malice or from error, especially since one clause of the Act particularly marks out *homeless* girls as just subjects for its operation? And what has she, if accused, to rely on, under God, except that of which this law has deprived her, the appeal to be tried "by God and my country, by which she is understood to claim to be tried by a jury, and to have all the judicial means of defence to which the law entitles her."

We have been reproached for making this question a class question. We accept the reproach, if reproach it be, because we say that it is a question for the poor rather than for the rich. It was not we who initiated this distinction, but the majority of the upper classes soon taught us that they considered it no question of theirs. They told us plainly that the subject was too unpleasant to be treated as one of public interest. But while with this plea they endeavoured to silence us, we found that they generally lent the weight of their influence, and not always apathetically or ignorantly, to the promotion of this legislation. To them this legislation involved no present and immediate diminution of freedom for themselves, and they seem to have been blindly ignorant, or selfishly forgetful, that their children and children's children would be, as well as the children of the poor, inheritors of the fatal consequences of violated liberties, and that the chains which they now weave for others will in time entangle themselves. But when we turned to the humbler classes we found that they knew that it *is* a question for them, and that they, more intelligent in this than the upper classes, knew that it was also a question for this whole country of England, whose political liberty depends on the preservation of the rights of all. . . .

If any of my readers then came to the consideration of this matter with the idea that there might be something to be said for this law medically, and that though there might be something undefinedly wrong in it, yet it embodied at least a benevolent intention, let him then remember that he has, at the next election, to answer for himself and his country: Shall we have liberty in lust, or shall we have political freedom? We cannot retain both.[77]

Butler's second argument, probably more powerful for Victorians, appeals to the belief that women can redeem their moral inferiors, the men who sexually exploit them. Speaking in the fervent tones of a crusader, Butler calls on women to lead the moral reform of a male-dominated society. Responses to Butler's speeches fulfill her promise that woman's influence can become woman's power—a power exercised politically in speaking, lobbying, and organizing to influence laws and votes. She and those she inspires defeat at least one political candidate, change the minds of a parliamentary committee, and are instrumental in persuading Parliament to repeal the Contagious Diseases Acts. Speeches in 1871 and 1874 give some idea of the emotional energy released by her invocation of woman as society's savior.

. . . Valuable as individual efforts are, they can never accomplish the work, to which we are surely called at this time, of a wide, a national purification; nay, they will not even prevent the increase of the evil on every hand. . . . Women have been told that they must be silent on this subject. Can the soul of my sister be defiled, and my own soul not be the worse for it? It cannot; unless indeed I rise up in wrath for her redemption, and through the long toils and pains and anguish of my life I render back to God my soul for hers. Is it possible that pure and Christian women can bear any longer to look on in silence at this costly and impious sacrifice of souls, this wholesale destruction of women born with like capacities with themselves for a life of honour and an eternity of peace? I do not believe they can; and when they rise by thousands to the rescue, it will not be as now, for the reclamation of their own sex only, but in order to penetrate to the causes of the evil and to elevate the moral standard of men. . . .

It is as if we were passengers in a water-logged ship, when all hands are called to the pumps. We are all called to labour for the salvation of our country. It is absolutely necessary to get rid of all unjust, partial, oppressive, and impure laws; for the laws may have little power to make men good, but they have very great power to increase wickedness. Certain laws for the protection of children, and to remove injustice to which women are subject, are rightly and loudly called for, and we mean to have them. But the great thing that has to be done is to create a pure moral tone among men. It will be our duty to require sternly of men that they be pure; to demand it of them as they have hitherto demanded it of us.

. . . It is manifest that on all sides it begins to be felt that the principle is to be decided whether male profligacy, at the expense of women, is to be condoned, excused, and darkly perpetrated, or to be sternly condemned and pertinaciously resisted. This question has got to be answered—to be answered first by England, before Europe and the whole world. The answer to this question involves the sweeping away of that whole corrupt fabric of injustice and inequality in matters moral, and in the relations of men and women, upon which, alone, was it possible for men to erect this last abomination of legalized vice and slavery. . . . In the contest against slavery in America, men and women gave up fortune, home, friends, and life itself. The system against which we contend is one which has as deeply corrupted the life of nations as Negro Slavery has done; the evil we oppose is rooted in a *yet more cruel negation of human brotherhood, and a more immoral violation of the principle of liberty.*

. . . Our battle belongs to a great and extensive field of spiritual war; we are standing at a key position, and are called to promote a revival of faith on the earth, with higher views of righteousness and purity. No matter, if we, the pioneers, lay our bones in the dust, others will pass over them to victory. Let us remember the cry of the Crusaders (and ours is a better crusade), 'God wills it, God wills it!'[78]

In 1883 the Contagious Diseases Acts are suspended in England, and attempts to pass them in America are defeated. Spurred on by these successes, the Social Purity Reform Movement sweeps America. Elizabeth Cady Stanton and Susan B. Anthony join women like Frances Willard, founder of the Woman's Christian Temperance Union, to demand that woman's special nature reform a male world. This, too, is to be women's work, and as with women's hard-won new professional and clerical jobs, women's reform leadership earns respect. But many issues are left unresolved. The economic position of woman and her political rights are not affected by her access to power as a social reformer. There is no support for working wives and mothers. Except among American blacks and, to a lesser extent, the British working class, work for women continues to mean work for *single* women. Equal pay is seldom even an issue. The separation of jobs into men's and women's work, fostered by arguments like Jameson's and the apocalytic feminists', is almost complete by the end of the century, and "women's work" continues to mean low prestige and low pay. In almost every instance, middle-class Victorians still see woman's work as directly threatening her essential social role at home. Anthony ironically entitled one of her speeches "Bread—not the Ballot." Victorian women in 1883 still have need of both bread and the ballot.

4

RELIGION

The Bible in the Victorian period draws fire from many sides, from science, anthropology, the Higher Criticism, and from feminists.[1] Does Scripture establish woman's equality or condone her subjection? The answer depends upon who is interpreting the text. For example, the Hebrew word describing Eve's relation to Adam is "'ēzer." Orthodoxy throughout the nineteenth century accepts the traditional interpretation of "ēzer"—that Eve as Adam's "helpmate" is his servant, his inferior. Some Victorians, however, insist upon what has become generally recognized today—that "ēzer" has in Hebrew no connotations of subservience and that Eve the "helper" is Adam's peer in Eden. Exegesis is particularly important for the Victorians because male-oriented translations and interpretations are not woman's only difficulty. The Bible itself proves ambiguous and contradictory. Various Old Testament passages seem irreconcilable, and St. Paul, a paramount figure for Protestants, seems repeatedly to deny in one place what he affirms in another. For a sense of how problematic scripture can prove for believers (and for those wavering), here are a few of the many Old and New Testament passages relating to women.

Most blessed of women be Jael she struck Sisera a blow, she
crushed his head, she shattered and pierced his temple (Judg.
5:24, 26)

A certain woman threw an upper millstone upon
Abimelech's head and crushed his skull. Then he
called hastily to the young man his armor-bearer,
and said to him, "Draw your sword and kill me,
lest they say of me, 'A woman killed him.'" (Judg. 9:53–54)

The daughter of any priest, if she profanes
herself by playing the harlot, profanes her
father; she shall be burned with fire. (Lev. 21:9)

I will not punish your daughters
   when they play the harlot,
nor your brides when they commit adultery;
for the men themselves go aside with harlots,
   and sacrifice with cult prostitutes. (Hos. 4:14)

And your sons and your daughters
shall prophesy. (Joel 2:28)
But I suffer not a woman to teach,
nor to usurp authority over the man,
but to be in silence. (1 Tim. 2:12)

There is neither Jew nor Greek, there is neither
bond nor free, there is neither male nor female,
for ye are all one in Christ Jesus. (Gal. 3:28)
And if they will learn anything, let them ask
their husbands at home. (1 Cor. 14:35)

Interpreting these and other scriptural passages has sparked
debate since patristic times. For the Victorians three issues are
particularly controversial: Woman and Genesis, Woman and the
Church, and Woman and Christianity. The first involves
woman's role in the creation and the fall; the second, the issue
of female ministry; the third, the larger question of Christianity's
effect upon women.

That these questions were front-page Victorian news is
difficult to imagine today, not only because interest in religion
has declined, but because most recent books have limited their
focuses distortingly.[2] The spiritual crises of figures like John
Henry Newman, the political and denominational battles of
Lyman Beecher, the notorious quarrels over *Essays and Reviews*
(1860) or Colenso's critical examination of the Pentateuch (1862),

are obviously major moments in Victorian religion, but they cannot be allowed to obscure entirely the daily controversies involving innumerable parishioners on both sides of the Atlantic. Catherine Booth, for example, responds to Rev. Arthur Augustus in 1859; Gail Hamilton to Rev. John Todd in 1867; Emily Faithful to Rev. Charles Dunbar in 1882; Lillie Devereux Blake to Rev. William Morgan in 1883. In these and other controversies, fierce at the time and unknown today, the age was speaking forth. Although most clerics joined with physicians in defending True Womanhood, the clergy knew that women had become the mainstays of religion. Increasing female influence in Anglo-American religious life was one of the clearest instances of woman's widening sphere.

I

Genesis, a perennial battleground, proves particularly controversial as Victorian women strive to see for themselves what scripture said. With the precedent of Mary Wollstonecraft's having reinterpreted key biblical passages, Sarah Grimké becomes the first important female exegete in 1837. In 1853, Julia Evelina Smith takes the additional step and becomes the first woman to translate the Old and New Testaments—though she did not publish her audacious venture until 1876. Seven years later, Mary Baker Eddy supplements her *Science and Health* with a scriptural commentary which supported her religion of Christ Scientist. Finally, in 1898, Elizabeth Cady Stanton and her committee of female scholars completes the *Woman's Bible*, which offered text and commentary for all passages relevant to women.[3]

The Genesis controversy centers upon two stories: the creation and the fall. By creating Adam first, did God intend to establish male hegemony? Most Victorians side with St. Paul:

For the man is not of the woman; but the woman of the man. Neither was the man created for the woman; but the woman for the man. (1 Cor. 11:8–9)

I suffer not a woman to teach, nor to usurp authority over the man, but to be in silence. For Adam was first formed, then Eve. (1 Tim. 2:12–13)

In 1859, William Landels, Minister of Regents' Park Chapel, London, writes an advice book for young women which goes through eight editions in ten years. Drawing indirectly upon St. Paul and directly upon the immensely influential French divine Adolphe Monod, Landels' *Woman's Sphere and Work Considered in the Light of Scriptures* sums up the majority position on woman's creation.

"The place which God assigns to woman has reference to this vocation of love. It is no inferior position; the woman is not merely a help *for* man, but a help *like* man; therefore should she walk his equal, and it is only on this condition that she brings to him the help which he requires. But it is, nevertheless, a position secondary and dependent; for the woman was created *after* the man, made *for* the man, and, in fact, derived *from* the man. This last remark speaks for itself. . . . She owes to him both the air she breathes and the name she bears. By what right, then—I ought to say, with what heart—could she deny to him the first rank? Her *position* by birth is a position of humility."
. . . If the Bible did not say that she was created for man, and that the wife ought to be in subjection to her husband, her nature would testify no less plainly that she yearned to be dependent on, and, by consequence, subject to, the other sex.[4]

Disagreement with such traditional interpretations of the creation story is abetted by St. Paul himself. Unequivocal though 1 Cor. 11:8–9 and 1 Tim. 2:12–13 seem, other Pauline passages apparently affirm equality in creation. Two verses after 1 Cor. 11:8–9, Paul says, "Nevertheless neither is the man without the woman, neither the woman without the man, in the Lord. For as the woman is of the man, even so is the man also by the woman; but all things of God." Gal. 3:28 seems expressly egalitarian: "There is neither Jew nor Greek, there is neither bond nor free, there is neither male nor female, for ye are all one in Christ Jesus." Besides quoting these passages, critics of the traditional interpretation of creation use other arguments against Paul's antifeminist passages. Sarah Josepha Hale, caricatured today as the arch-eulogist of True Womanhood, indicates the subversive potential of orthodoxy. Sanctioned by the Protestant tradition of individual interpretation, and supported by pre-Darwinian theories of evolution, *Woman's Record* (1853) challenges male-oriented exegeses by arguing that the creation story shows Eve's moral superiority. The logic of Hale's argument suggests a potentially subversive conclusion—that wo-man's moral superiority makes *her* the dominant sex. Not until the 1860s and 1870s, however, do writers more daring than Hale follow her logic to its subversive conclusion. Hale, like most Victorians, accepts the logical contradiction inherent in orthodoxy's attitude toward woman—that her moral superiority is compatible with her biblically-ordained subordination to man.

> Go not to Milton, or the Fathers, but to the Word of God. . . .
> Men, ay, good men, hold the doctrine of woman's inferiority, because St. Paul says she was created "for man." Truly she was made "for man," but not in the sense this text has heretofore been interpreted. She was not made to gratify his sensual desires, but to refine his human affections, and elevate his moral feelings. En-dowed with superior beauty of person, and a corresponding delicacy of mind, her soul was to "help" him where he was deficient,—namely, in his spiritual nature.
> . . . He was formed of the earth, and had in the greater development those powers of mind which are directed towards objects of sense; she, formed from his flesh and bones, had in greater development those powers of mind which seek the affec-tions. . . . She was the *last work* of creation. Every step, from matter to man, had been in the ascending scale. Woman was the crown of all,—the *last*, and must therefore have been the *best* in those qualities which raise human nature above animal life; the link which pressed nearest towards the angelic, and drew its chief beauty and strength from the invisible world. . . .
> . . . I am not aiming to controvert the authority of the husband, or the right of men to make laws for the world they are to subdue and govern. I have no sympathy with those who are wrangling for "woman's rights;" nor with those who are foolishly urging women to strive for equality and competition with men. What I seek to establish is the Bible doctrine, as I understand it, that woman was intended as the teacher and the inspirer for man, morally speaking, of "whatsoever things are lovely, and pure, and of good report." The Bible does not uphold the equality of the sexes.[5]

The story of the fall is a second traditional source of argu-ments for female subservience. Woman must atone for bringing sin into the world. The Genesis story is buttressed by the prestigious pronouncements of St. Paul and the Fathers. In 1 Tim. 2:14–15, Paul maintains that "Adam was not deceived, but the woman being deceived was in the transgression." Among the Fathers, Tertullian is particularly antifeminist.

You are the Devil's gateway. *You* are the unsealer of that forbidden tree. *You* are the first deserter of the divine Law. *You* are she who persuaded him whom the Devil was not valiant enough to attack. *You* destroyed so easily God's image man. On account of *your* desert, that is death, even the Son of God had to die.

This tradition is perpetuated in the Renaissance by John Calvin's declaration that "it was not only for the sake of complying with the wishes of his wife, that he [Adam] transgressed the law laid down for him; but being drawn by her into infatuation, he became partaker of the same defection with her."[6] The English Renaissance authority most influential for Victorians is John Milton. His differentiation in *Paradise Lost* between Adam and Eve—"Hee for God only, shee for God in him" (IV.299)—is quoted endlessly. *Paradise Lost* establishes Eve expressly as "first/ To offend" (X.110–11), and Milton's Adam gives males the all-time lesson in blame shifting.

> This Woman whom thou mad'st to be my help,
> And gav'st me as thy perfect gift, so good,
> So fit, so acceptable, so Divine,
> That from her hand I could suspect no ill,
> And what she did, whatever in itself,
> Her doing seem'd to justify the deed;
> She gave me of the Tree, and I did eat. (X.137–43)

Milton's God censures Adam not for being prideful or ambitious, but for being seduced. "Because thou hast heark'n'd to the voice of thy Wife . . ./In the sweat of thy Face shalt thou eat Bread" (X.198, 205).

In the Victorian period, women still regard childbirth pains as God's curse and still hear the fall described as woman's work. Christians who do not equate her directly with sin do so indirectly by continuing to associate women with the emotions. According to William H. Holcombe in *The Sexes Here and Hereafter* (1869), "whenever conscience chides us for a lapse, we shall find that it comes of some misdirection of the affections. As the historical Fall had its origin in the surrender of the woman, so does its reiteration in her descendants come of a corresponding surrender of the feminine elements of themselves."[7]

Even many progressive Christians perpetuated the traditional link of woman and sin. Charles Kingsley, for example, publicly supports Elizabeth Blackwell's campaign for women physicians and privately espouses other aspects of the woman's movement; yet the sexual and racial condescension of "The Tree of Knowledge" (1874) undercuts Kingsley's defense of woman's desire for knowledge and perpetuates the patronizing tone so frequent in even "progressive" Victorian discussions of woman.

> The sacred story is only too true to fact, when it represents the woman as falling, not merely at the same time as the man, but before the man. . . . A missionary, preaching on this story to Negroes; telling them plainly that the "Serpent" meant the first Obeah man; and then comparing the experiences of that hapless pair in Eden, with their own after certain orgies not yet extinct in Africa and elsewhere, would be only too well understood: so well, indeed, that he might run some risk of eating himself, not of the tree of life, but of that of death. The sorcerer or sorceress tempting the woman; and then the woman tempting the man; this seems to be, certainly among savage peoples, and, alas! too often among civilised peoples also, the usual course of the world-wide tragedy.
>
> But—paradoxical as it may seem—the woman's yielding before the man is not altogether to her dishonour, as those old monks used to allege who hated, and too often tortured, the sex whom they could not enjoy. It is not to the woman's dishonour, if she felt, before her husband, higher aspirations than those after mere animal pleasure. To be as gods, knowing good and evil, is a vain and foolish, but not a base and brutal, wish. She proved herself thereby—though at an awful cost—a woman, and not an animal. And indeed the woman's more delicate organisation, her more vivid emotions, her more voluble fancy, as well as her mere physical weakness and weariness, have been to her, in all ages, a special source of temptation; which it is to her honour that she has resisted so much better than the physically stronger, and therefore more culpable, man.[8]

Victorians who balk at such interpretations of the fall find some support in tradition. Paul's epistle to the Romans establishes unequivocally that Adam was responsible for sin.

> Wherefore, as by one man sin entered into the world, and death by sin; and so death passed upon all men, for that all have sinned:. . . .
>
> Therefore as by the offence of one *judgment came* upon all men to condemnation; even so by the righteousness of one *the free gift came* upon all men unto justification of life.

For as by one man's disobedience many were made sinners, so
by the obedience of one shall many be made righteous. (5:12, 18–19)

Besides citing this passage against Adam's heirs, Victorians also
defend Eve's conduct before and after the fall. Sarah Grimké
makes two points. Like St. Ambrose she argues that the greater
severity of Eve's temptation made her less culpable than Adam;
like many biblical scholars Grimké claims that in Hebrew the
pronouncement of woman's subjection was not a curse but a
prophecy.

> Here the woman was exposed to temptation from a being with
> whom she was unacquainted. She had been accustomed to associate
> with her beloved partner, and to hold communion with God and
> with angels; but of satanic intelligence, she was in all probability
> entirely ignorant. Through the subtlety of the serpent, she was
> beguiled. . . .
> We next find Adam involved in the same sin, not through the
> instrumentality of a supernatural agent, but through that of his
> equal, a being whom he must have known was liable to transgress
> the divine command, because he must have felt that he was him-
> self a free agent, and that he was restrained from disobedience
> only by the exercise of faith and love towards his Creator. Had
> Adam tenderly reproved his wife, and endeavored to lead her to
> repentance instead of sharing in her guilt, I should be much more
> ready to accord to man that superiority which he claims; but as the
> facts stand disclosed by the sacred historian, it appears to me that
> to say the least, there was as much weakness exhibited by Adam as
> by Eve. They both fell from innocence, and consequently from
> happiness, *but not from equality.*
> Let us next examine the conduct of this fallen pair, when
> Jehovah interrogated them respecting their fault. They both
> frankly confessed their guilt. . . . And the Lord God said unto the
> woman, 'Thou wilt be subject unto thy husband, and he will rule
> over thee.' That this did not allude to the subjection of woman to
> man is manifest, because the same mode of expression is used in
> speaking to Cain of Abel. The truth is that the curse, as it is termed,
> which was pronounced by Jehovah upon woman, is a simple
> prophecy. The Hebrew, like the French language, uses the same
> word to express shall and will. Our translators having been
> accustomed to exercise lordship over their wives, and seeing only
> through the medium of a perverted judgment, very naturally,
> though I think not very learnedly or very kindly, translated it *shall*
> instead of *will*, and thus converted a prediction to Eve into a

command to Adam; for observe, it is addressed to the woman and not to the man. The consequence of the fall was an immediate struggle for dominion, and Jehovah foretold which would gain the ascendency; but as he created them in his image, as that image manifestly was not lost by the fall, because it is urged in Gen. 9:6, as an argument why the life of man should not be taken by his fellow man, there is no reason to suppose that sin produced any distinction between them as moral, intellectual and responsible beings.[9]

Two more defenses of Eve and womanhood are offered by Sarah Josepha Hale in *Woman's Record*: that the divine curses upon Adam and Eve establish her superiority, and that Eve's motive is superior to Adam's.

That Adam intended, in thus accusing his wife, covertly to throw the blame on God for creating her, seems probable from the severity with which his sentence is worded. He is judged as though he was the *selfish* criminal, disobeying God from sensuous inclinations—"of the earth, earthy;"—his sin is so great, that the ground is "cursed for his sake;"—like a felon he is condemned to hard labour for life; and his death, connected with his origin from *dust*, is set before him in the most humiliating light. The only ray of hope to which he could turn was the promise made to his wife; thus showing him that she was still considered worthy of trust, and must therefore have been the least culpable. A corroboration of this is found in the sentence pronounced against the serpent or spirit of Evil which had deceived her; the clause reads thus:—"And I will put enmity between thee and the woman, and between thy seed and her seed; it shall bruise thy head, and thou shalt bruise his heel." Gen. III.5. . . . The conflict with sin was to be first waged by her and with her. How could this be, unless she was then endowed with the germ of divine grace, which, unfolded by the breath of the Holy Spirit, would, in the fulness of time, be honoured by her glorious "Seed," the Saviour, who would "put all His enemies under His feet?"
. . . Commentators have imputed weakness of mind to the woman, because the tempter assailed her. But does it not rather show she was the spiritual leader, the most difficult to be won, and the serpent knew if he could gain her the result was sure? Remember that her husband was *"with her"*—the serpent addressed them both—*"Ye shall be as gods,"* &c. Now, is it not reasonable to suppose that the nature (the human pair was then one,) best qualified to judge of these high subjects, would respond? The decision was, apparently, left to her. The woman led; the man

followed. Which showed the greatest spiritual power, the controlling energy of mind? In the act of disobedience the conduct of the woman displayed her superior nature. (xxxviii, 39)

Hale once again verges on the subversive. "In the act of disobedience the conduct of the woman displayed her superior nature." From here Eliza W. Farnham goes on a decade later to do for Eve what Shelley did for Milton's Satan. Eve becomes a heroic rebel. In *Woman and Her ERA* (1864), Farnham faces directly a question which most Christians sidestepped: what kind of God can create a creature in His image and yet prevent that creature from becoming "like unto God." Farnham makes Eve a female Prometheus, a heroine of the rights of humanity.

First, God is the very embodiment of Wisdom and Love, *i.e.*, knowledge of Good, and choice of it; second, man was made in His image and likeness, yet was without the one, and necessarily, therefore, destitute of the other; third, *a moral obedience, notwithstanding this original incapacity, was required of him*—he was expected to remain in his bondage and darkness. . . .

In these difficult circumstances, it seems clear that the first service which humanity could possibly do itself, would be to vindicate its alleged noble creation, by developing its likeness to God in the very act with which Eve stands charged—the act which clothed it in the divine power to know good and evil. . . .

But the case of Woman is specially illustrated in the alleged fact that she took the initiative, in this great service to humanity, of developing, or we might perhaps as properly say, creating, its moral likeness to God; and that she was moved thereto by an appeal which could only *address itself to a spiritual nature*, the assurance that she should thereby become as a god! And, whether the serpent represents Wisdom or Wickedness in this transaction, the compliment to the feminine nature is equally distinct, because of the purity and Godlikeness of the motive presented to it. Woman rose out of bondage, *in the love of freedom—that she might become wiser and diviner. Man followed her.* So early dates the spiritual ministration of the feminine. . . . To "become as a god," who would not joyfully face certain death?[10]

II

Farnham's phrase "the spiritual ministration of the feminine" echoes Victorian concern for woman's place in the Church. Reexamination of virtually every aspect of religious life sparks sharp disagreement over female preachers. These preachers threaten more than an ancient clerical tradition; they threaten male supremacy itself. Woman in the pulpit is literally elevated— not on the insubstantial pedestal of chivalric respect, but in the very place of traditional authority. A woman handing down the law from on high, like Moses, is especially threatening because female silence in church is traditionally associated with wifely subordination in marriage.

> Let your women keep silence in the churches; for it is not permitted unto them to speak. . . . And if they will learn any thing, let them ask their husbands at home: for it is a shame for women to speak in the church. (I Cor. 14:34–35)

St. Paul is again at the center of the controversy because he once again speaks on both sides of the question. I Cor. 14:34–35 is supported by 1 Tim. 2:12 ("I suffer not a woman to teach, not to usurp authority over the man, but to be in silence"). But the very Corinthian epistle which apparently forbids female preaching also seems to recognize it.

> Every man praying or prophesying, leaving his head covered, dis-honoureth his head. But every woman that prayeth or prophe-sieth with her head uncovered dishonoureth her head. (I Cor. 11:4–5)

Controversialists on both sides can point to Hebrew, patristic, and Reformation precedents. British Protestantism itself teaches contradictory lessons. The Society of Friends recognizes female preachers since the seventeenth century; yet Quaker women in England do not achieve full equality with men until 1896. John Wesley, responding to his mother's urging and example, allows women to preach in the 1770s; by 1800, however, English Methodism has already begun—as Dinah Morris learns in *Adam Bede*—that exclusion of women preachers which is complete by 1850.

Victorian opposition to woman's ministry varies directly with how "high" the particular church is. Most of the cele-brated female preachers are Quaker or evangelical: Sarah Grimké, Lucretia Mott, Phoebe Palmer, Maggie van Cott, Amanda Smith, Catherine Booth, Frances E. Willard. These denominations tend to stress the common sinfulness of *all* mankind and to celebrate what every believer can partake of—the *experience,* as opposed to the *theology,* of Christianity. In America, the strength of evangelism, the absence of an established church, and the particular influence of Charles G. Finney and Dwight L. Moody make the new world the leader in advocating woman's ministry.[11] In 1851, the theology department of the first co-educational college, Oberlin, graduates its first woman, Antoinette Brown; also in 1851, Lydia Sexton of the Church of the United Brethren becomes the first ordained female minister. Brown herself is ordained in 1853, and as the ordinations of more women follow, the debate over woman's ministry heats up. Before turning to the actual arguments, we must recognize a fact about Victorian Christianity: women are offered a middle way between rigorous exclusion and ministerial status.

Church work independent of actual ordination is opened to women by the end of the eighteenth century.[12] Sunday schools, benevolent societies, domestic and foreign missions grow to impressive size by the 1860s. With various Societies—"Dorcas" and "Mite," Pastoral Aid, Waifs and Strays, Woman's Help— plus the Deaconess Movement, various Anglican sisterhoods, and ultimately the opportunity for mission work itself, Protestantism attempts to harness the increasingly restless energy of its female majority. Although these movements can be seen as a step toward full ministerial status, they can also be seen as an alternative to equality.

In 1883, Annie C.F. Cunningham declares that "the way is opened as it never has been before for Christian women in their own sphere to 'serve their generation by the will of God,' as well as for men in a sphere more extended."[13] The unequal spheres of man and woman have not slipped into the argument inadvertently: they are consciously introduced by a Christian who expressly disclaims equality in religion. Denomination and nationality are not at issue here. Believers so different as the Swedenborgian Elizabeth Strutt and the Baptist William Landels agree with Presbyterian Cunningham, though they reach agreement by opposite paths. Strutt in *Feminine Soul* (1857) argues that women should be restricted to catechism because they cannot accomplish more. "From the very inmost nature of Woman's soul, she is not capable of severely impartial and logical reasoning; or, in other words, of convincing, or being convinced, by truth alone."[14] Landels in *Woman's Sphere and Work* suggests that women should teach catechism because they are so ideally suited to it.

It were strange if, while on his reception of the gospel, man's less susceptible nature is moved to effort for its diffusion, woman could be content to enjoy its blessings without communicating them to others. It would be a violation of every womanly instinct . . . her greater sensitiveness, her deeper and quicker sympathies . . . and if what we have previously said of woman's peculiarities shews that her sphere in the diffusion of the truth is not that prominent and public one which properly pertains to men, it also shews that hers is no trifling or unimportant part. (217–18, 221)

Anglicanism agrees heartily. In 1872 illustrious Anglicans received a questionnaire about women: "What are the best means of associating the organized or individual efforts of women with the missionary and educational work of the church?" The very question precludes certain answers. Woman is restricted to her traditional sphere, education, and to her traditional associates, children and blacks. The inferiority proclaimed in the brain-weight controversy (Volume II, Chapter 2) is thus reaffirmed by religion's insistence that woman can teach catechism but not theology. Most Protestants would agree with the way Miss Langley, daughter of the late Archbishop of Canterbury, answers the questionnaire's first query, *"How far may women be employed as evangelists?"*: "As teachers in day-schools; mistresses of boarding schools for high-caste girls, and as teachers in Zenanas. In all cases under the direction and control of the president missionary."[15] The good which sacrificing Christian women do in the Victorian period is enormous. Not only do these women help millions of human beings throughout the world; they also help themselves by finding in church work a way to expand their sphere and yet remain True Women. Today we must also recognize, however, that all the offshoots and counterparts of the Deaconess Movement do not make women deaconesses, do not give women major ecclesiastical positions, let alone full equality in the churches. Woman's ministry must finally be fought out on the dark, bloody ground of scripture itself.

The controversy over women mounting the pulpit flares openly in America as Victoria mounts the throne. An 1837 Pastoral Letter from "The General Association of Massachusetts (Orthodox) to the Churches under Their Care" attacks as "unnatural" those women who went beyond "unostentatious" efforts and usurped man's role as public reformer. Among various counterattacks, John Greenleaf Whittier's is probably most indignant ("Now, shame upon ye, parish Popes!"), but another poet proves more devastating. Relying not upon indignation but upon point of view, Maria Weston Chapman lays the Pastoral position open to ridicule by letting the clergy speak (supposedly) for themselves.

"THE TIMES THAT TRY MEN'S SOULS."

Confusion has seized us, and all things go wrong,
    The women have leaped from "their spheres,"
And, instead of fixed stars, shoot as comets along,
    And are setting the world by the ears!
In courses erratic they're wheeling through space,
In brainless confusion and meaningless chase.

. . . .

They insist on their right to petition and pray,
    That St. Paul, in Corinthians, has given them rules
For appearing in public; despite what those say
    Whom we've trained to instruct them in schools;
But vain such instructions, if women may scan
And quote texts of Scripture to favor their plan.

Our grandmothers' learning consisted of yore
    In spreading their generous boards;
In twisting the distaff, or mopping the floor,
    And *obeying the will of their lords*.
Now, misses may reason, and think, and debate,
Till unquestioned submission is quite out of date.

. . . .

Could we but array all our force in the field,
    We'd teach these usurpers of power
That their bodily safety demands they should yield,
    And in the presence of manhood should cower;
But, alas! for our tethered and impotent state,
Chained by notions of knighthood—we can but debate.

Oh! shade of the prophet Mahomet, arise!
    Place woman again in "her sphere,"
And teach that her soul was not born for the skies,
    But to flutter a brief moment here.
This doctrine of Jesus, as preached up by Paul,
If embraced in its spirit, will ruin us all.

                           —*Lords of Creation*.[16]

The most serious and extended reply to the Pastoral Letter comes from one of the women whom the Association was expressly attacking, Sarah Grimké.

'We appreciate,' say the Association, 'the *unostentatious* prayers and efforts of woman in advancing the cause of religion at home and abroad, in leading religious inquirers TO THE PASTOR for instruction.' Several points here demand attention. If public prayers and public efforts are necessarily ostentatious, then 'Anna the prophetess, (or preacher,) who departed not from the temple, but served God with fastings and prayers night and day,' 'and spake of Christ to all them that looked for redemption in Israel,' [Luke 2] was ostentatious in her efforts. Then, the apostle Paul encourages women to be ostentatious in their efforts to spread the gospel, when he gives them directions how they should appear, when engaged in praying, or preaching in the public assemblies. Then, the whole association of Congregational ministers are ostentatious, in the efforts they are making in preaching and praying to convert souls.

But woman may be permitted to lead religious inquirers to the PASTORS for instruction. Now this is assuming that all pastors are better qualified to give instruction than woman. This I utterly deny. I have suffered too keenly from the teaching of man, to lead any one to him for instruction. The Lord Jesus says,—'Come unto me and learn of me.' He points his followers to no man; and when woman is made the favored instrument of rousing a sinner to his lost and helpless condition, she has no right to substitute any teacher for Christ. . . .

The General Association say, that 'when woman assumes the place and tone of man as a public reformer, our care and protection of her seem unnecessary; we put ourselves in self-defense against her, and her character becomes unnatural.' Here again the unscriptural notion is held up, that there is a distinction between the duties of men and women as moral beings; that what is virtue in man, is vice in woman; and women who dare to obey the command of Jehovah, "Cry aloud, spare not, lift up thy voice like a trumpet, and show my people their transgression," [Isa. 58] are threatened with having the protection of the brethren withdrawn. If this is all they do, we shall not even know the time when our chastisement is inflicted; our trust is in the Lord Jehovah, and in him is everlasting strength. The motto of woman, when she is engaged in the great work of public reformation should be,—"The Lord is my light and my salvation; whom shall I fear? The Lord is the strength of my life; of whom shall I be afraid?" [Ps. 27:1] She must feel, if

Religion   179

she feels rightly, that she is fulfilling one of the important duties laid upon her as an accountable being, and that her character, instead of being "unnatural," is in exact accordance with the will of Him to whom, and to no other, she is responsible for the talents and the gifts confided to her.[17]

The next important stage of the controversy occurs at Seneca Falls. The Declaration of Sympathies and the unanimously adopted Resolutions raised the issue of woman's ministry four times; on the last day, Lucretia Mott specifically proposed "the overthrow of the monopoly of the pulpit."[18] Part of that overthrow occurs in 1853, when Rev. Luther Lee's sermon at the ordination of Antoinette Brown raises the issue of the early church figure, Phoebe. Lee argues that the King James translation of Paul's expression διακογοζ—"servant of the church"—reveals the bias inherent in traditional opposition to female ministry.

> Out of the thirty instances of the use of the word [diakonos] in the Greek testament, twenty two of them are in the language of Paul. Note, Paul uses the word twenty two times, and in eighteen cases out of the twenty two, the translators have rendered it *minister*; in three they have rendered it *deacon*, and in the one remaining case they have rendered it *servant*, and that is where it is applied to Phebe. Poor Phebe is made a single exception out of the twenty two instances of the use of the word. . . . We see then if we conform the translation to the almost undeviating course of the translators, we shall make it read, "I commend unto you Phebe our sister, which is a *minister* of the Church which is at Cenchrea," and so reading as it ought to read, the question of a woman's right to preach the gospel is settled.[19]

A Phoebe also features in the next flare-up of the controversy which now spreads to England. Phoebe Palmer, the American evangel who tours successfully through the British Isles in 1859, draws intense crowds and criticism for daring to preach publicly to "promiscuous" (mixed) audiences. Palmer's reply, *Promise of the Father*, provides a defense of women's ministry which countless later defenses draw upon.[20] Another reply, by the then-unknown Catherine Booth, constitutes the first major argument for female preachers in Victorian England and helps change the course of Christianity.[21] Booth has not yet met, but already admired, Phoebe Palmer when Rev. Arthur

Augustus Rees attacks Palmer and woman's right to public ministry. Writing immediately to her mother, Booth laments that Palmer's defenders

> do not deal with the question at all to my satisfaction. They make so many uncalled-for *admissions* that I would almost as soon answer her *defenders* as her opponent. I send you by this post Mr. Rees' notable production. It was delivered in the form of an address to his congregation and repeated a second time by request to a crowded chapel, and then published! Would you believe that a congregation half composed of ladies could sit and hear such self-depreciatory rubbish? They really don't deserve to be taken up cudgels for![22]

Catherine Booth reacts so strongly to Rev. Rees's pamphlet because she has heard it all before. In 1854, a Congregationalist minister whom she admired, Rev. David Thomas, preached on woman's inferiority. Booth, only twenty-four and without great learning or experience, writes to Rev. Thomas a letter which touchingly reveals both her instinctive (and very Victorian) deference before authority figures and her irresistible (and very Victorian) need to speak out at all costs.

> DEAR SIR—You will doubtless be surprised at the receipt of this communication, and I assure you it is with great reluctance and a feeling of profound respect that I make it. Were it not for the high estimate I entertain for both your intellect and heart, I would spare the sacrifice it will cost me. . . .
>
> Permit me, my dear sir, to ask whether you have ever made the subject of woman's equality as a *being*, the matter of calm investigation and thought? . . .
>
> So far as Scriptural evidence is concerned, did I but possess ability to do justice to the subject, I dare take my stand on *it* against the world in defending her perfect equality. (117–18)

Remaining a parishioner of Rev. Thomas (he officiated at her wedding), Catherine becomes increasingly involved with another cleric whose views on women need amending. William Booth quips to his fiancée that "woman has a fibre more in her heart and a cell less in her brain" (117). When Catherine expresses to William her feelings on the Woman Question in 1855, she has no thought of entering the pulpit herself. Like Louise

Religion

Cheeves McCord and most opponents of woman's ministry and indeed most Victorians, Catherine Booth recognizes a hieratic universe ruled by the white male. How can woman exercise within that universe the talent which defines her identity and which comes from the Maker of the universe Himself?

I am ready to admit that in the majority of cases the training of woman has made her man's inferior, as under the degrading slavery of heathen lands she is inferior to her own sex in Christian countries; but that *naturally* she is in any respect except physical strength and courage, inferior to man I cannot see *cause* to believe, and I am sure no one can prove it from the *Word of God*, and it is on *this* foundation that professors of religion always try to establish it. . . . I would not alter woman's domestic position (when indeed it is scriptural) because God has plainly fixed it; *He* has told her to obey her husband, and therefore she ought to do so, if she profess to serve God; her husband's rule over her was part of the sentence for her disobedience, which would, by the by, have been no curse at all if he had ruled over her *before*, by dint of superiority—but God *ordained* her subjection as a punishment *for sin*, and *therefore* I submit; but I cannot believe that inferiority was the ground of it; if it had, it *must* have existed prior to the curse and thus have nullified it. . . .

It is worthy of remark that there are no less than *six* prophetesses mentioned in the Old Testament, one of whom was unquestionably *judge* as well as prophet. . . . Now God having *once* spoken *directly* by *woman*, and man having once recognized her divine commission, and obeyed it, on what ground is Omnipotence to be restricted, or woman's spiritual labours ignored? . . . Why should the swaddling bands of blind custom which in Wesley's days were so triumphantly broken, and with such glorious results thrown to the moles and bats, be again wrapped round the female disciples of the Lord, as if the natural, and in some cases, distressing timidity of woman's nature, were not sufficient barrier to her obeying the dictates of the Spirit, whenever that Spirit calls her to any public testimony for her Lord? . . . Will the plea of bashfulness or custom excuse her to *Him* who has put such honour upon *her*, as to deign to become her *Son*, in order to redeem her race; will these pleas excuse her to *Him* who last at the cross and first at the sepulchre was attended by women who so far forgot bashfulness as to testify their love for Him before a taunting rabble, and who so far overcame *custom* that when *all* (even fellow-disciples) forsook Him and fled, they remained faithful to the last and even then lingered "afar off" loath to lose sight of an object so precious? . . . Oh that many Marys may yet *tell* of His wonderful salvation.[23]

MRS. BOOTH IN THE DOME, BRIGHTON.

6. Mrs. Booth in the Dome, Brighton, 1868
The Life of Catherine Booth (by F. de L. Booth-Tucker), 1892

In its love and courage and humility, Catherine Booth's letter reflects the spirit of her life; the ending of the letter echoes the ending of Sarah Grimké's own letters on religion and women. "I am *thine* in love's own bonds." Catherine's 1859 reply to Rev. Rees, her momentous decision in 1860 to enter the pulpit herself, and her subsequent triumphs are more than enough to persuade William. As General of the fast-growing Salvation Army he will soon say, "the best men in my Army are the women."[24] Unlike so many males whose praise for woman diverges from their practice toward her, General Booth achieves in his army true equality of the sexes. By 1875, forty-one of the ninety-one officers are women, and the percentage continues at least that high throughout Booth's life. No other Victorian religious organization can boast such equality; probably no Christian force since Methodism affects religious and social life so much. As shaper of William Booth's ideas, as "mother of the Salvation Army," and as its premier preacher [see Illustration 6], Catherine Booth becomes one of the most influential women of the century.

But what of women who yearn to preach and never gain a pulpit? Literature allows the sharing in and even the coopting of ministerial functions. When hymn writing, for example, becomes a major enterprise of Victorian women, hymns change in kind and in liturgical function. Unlike earlier religious songs which were largely adaptations of the psalms, the myriad hymns which pour from Victorian pens express individual beliefs and hopes. In turn, the hymn encroaches upon the sermon in Protestant liturgy, as more than one minister realized: Rev. Joel Hawes used to announce caustically after a hymn that "divine service would now recommence."[25]

The other literary form through which women preach is fiction. Elizabeth Barrett Browning, George Eliot, Elizabeth Gaskell, Harriet Beecher Stowe, Susan Warner (plus Hawthorne and many others) present women who speak to rapt listeners and speak about woman's right to speak. The literary work which deals with this issue most directly is "A Woman's Pulpit" (1870) by Elizabeth Stuart Phelps.[26] Her father, an Andover divine, and her mother, a popular writer, christened their daughter Mary Graves Phelps, but she took as nom de plume her mother's name and made "Elizabeth Stuart Phelps" internationally known. In 1868 she wrote one of the century's best-selling novels, *Gates*

Ajar. Literature gave to Phelps the pulpit which Andover denied. She attacked male hegemony in ministry and exegesis, and she preached the power of the female heart and the domestic quality of heaven.

The very theme of "A Woman's Pulpit" is thus the dilemma that underlay the fiction of many women. Phelps's opening sentence—"I fell to regretting today, for the first time in my life, that I am an old maid"(11)—serves several functions. Besides connecting the story with the Victorian discussion of spinsterhood, Phelps establishes immediately that the narrator's life has remained limited, despite the promise which the retrospectively-told story may seem to hold out. Thus, a tone of loss qualifies and complicates the humor and wit to come. Phelps also establishes quickly the bond of unmarried women by dramatizing the close, if at times caustic, tie between the narrator (J.W. Bangs) and her maid, Mädchen. What then unfolds is the story of the narrator's move to a small ministerless town, her success there, and her final return to private life. In the process of telling the story, Phelps raises virtually every question of the pulpit (and indeed the woman) controversy—male condescension to female delicacy; woman's anxiety at public performance; "the coming woman"; the plight of the male clergy who recognize their increasing physical and social debility; and the final bonds which draw woman back into the private sphere, to nurse rather than to lead.

HERCULES, FEBRUARY 28, 18—.
SECRETARY OF THE NEW VEALSHIRE HOME MISSIONARY SOCIETY.

REVEREND AND DEAR SIR:—I am desirous of occupying one of your vacant posts of ministerial service: place and time entirely at your disposal. I am not a college graduate, nor have I yet applied for license to preach. I am, however, I believe, the possessor of a fair education, and of some slight experience in usefulness of a kind akin to that which I seek under your auspices, as well as of an interest in the neglected portions of New England, which *ought* to warrant me success in an attempt to serve their religious welfare.

For confirmation of these statements I will refer you, if you like, to the Rev. Dr. Dagon of Dagonsville, and to Professor Tacitus of Sparta.

An answer at your earliest convenience, informing me if you are disposed to accept my services, and giving me details of terms and times, will oblige,

Yours respectfully,
J.W. BANGS.

J.W. BANGS, ESQ.

MY DEAR SIR:—Your lack of collegiate education is an objection to your filling one of our stations, but not an insurmountable one. I like your letter, and am inclined to think favorably of the question of accepting your services. I should probably send you among the Gray Hills, and in March. We pay six dollars a week and "found" [room and board]. Will this be satisfactory? Let me hear from you again.

Truly yours,
Z.Z. ZANGROW,
Sect. N.V.H.M.S.

P.S. I have been too busy as yet to pursue your recommendations, but have no doubt that they are satisfactory.

HERCULES, MARCH 9, 18—.
REV. DR. ZANGROW.

DEAR SIR:—Yours of the 5th is at hand. Terms are satisfactory. I neglected to mention in my last that I am a woman.

Yours truly,
JERUSHA W. BANGS.

HARMONY, N.V., MARCH 9, 18—.
JERUSHA W. BANGS.

DEAR MADAM:—You have played me an admirable joke. Regret that I have no time to return it.

Yours very sincerely,
Z.Z. ZANGROW, *Sect.*

HERCULES, MARCH 11th.
DEAR SIR:—I was never more in earnest in my life.

Yours,
J.W. BANGS.

HARMONY, MARCH 14th.
DEAR MADAM:—I am sorry to hear it.

Yours,
Z.Z. ZANGROW.

HERCULES, MARCH 15, 18—.
REV. DR. ZANGROW.

MY DEAR SIR:—After begging your pardon for encroaching again upon your time and patience, permit me to inquire if you are not conscious of some slight—we will call it by its mildest possible cognomen—inconsistency in your recent correspondence with me? By your own showing, I am individually and concretely qualified for the business in question; I am generally and abstractly beyond

Religion   185

its serious recognition. As an educated American Christian, I am capable, by the word that goeth forth out of my mouth, of saving the Vealshire Mountain soul. As an educated American Christian woman, I am remanded by the piano and the crochet-needle to the Hercules parlor soul.

You will—or you would, if it fell to your lot—send me under the feminine truce flag of "teacher" into Virginia to speak on Sabbath mornings to a promiscuous audience of a thousand negroes: you forbid me to manage a score of White-Mountaineers. Mr. Spurgeon's famous lady parishioner may preach to a "Sabbath-school class" of seven hundred men: you would deny her the scanty hearing of your mission pulpits.

My dear sir, to crack a hard argument, you have, in the words of Sir William [Hamilton] the logical, "mistaken the associations of thought for the connections of existence." If you will appoint me a brief meeting at your own convenience in your own office in Harmony, I shall not only be very much in debt to your courtesy, but I shall convince you that you ought to send me into New Vealshire.

Meantime I am
Sincerely yours,
J.W. Bangs.

· ·

A telegram from the secretary, however, generously allowed me three days "to pack." If I had been less kindly entreated at his hands, I should have had nothing to pack but my wounded dignity. I *always* travel in a bag. Did he expect me to preach out a Saratoga trunkful of flounces? I explosively demanded of Mädchen?

"He is a man," said Mädchen, soothingly," and he has n't behaved in the least like one. Don't be hard upon him."

I relented so far as to pack a lace collar and an extra paper of hairpins. Mädchen suggested my best bonnet. I am sorry to say that I locked her out of the room.

· ·

I arrived there on Saturday night, at the end of the day, a ten miles' stage-ride, and a final patch of crooked railway, in a snow-storm. . . . "Step right round here, ma'am!"

"Right round here," brought us up against an old buggy sleigh, and an old horse with patient ears. "Hold on a spell," said Mr. Dobbins, "I'll put ye in."

Now Mr. Dobbins was not, as I have intimated, a large man. Whether he were actually a dwarf, or whether he only got so far and stopped, I never satisfactorily discovered. But at all events, I could have "put" Mr. Dobbins into anything twice as comfortably as I could support the reversal of the process; to say nothing of the fact that the ascent of a sleigh is not at most a superhuman undertaking. However, not wishing to wound his feelings, I submitted to the situation, and Mr. Dobbins handed me in and tucked me up, with consummate gallantry. I mention this circumstance, not because I was prepared for, or expected, or demanded, in my ministerial capacity, any peculiar deference to my sex, but because it is indicative of the treatment which, throughout my ministerial experience, I received.

"Comfortable?" asked Mr. Dobbins after a pause, as we turned our faces eastward, towards a lonely landscape of billowy gray and white, and in the jaws of the storm; "'cause there's four miles and three quarters of this. Tough for a lady."

I assured him that I was quite comfortable, and that if the weather were tough for a lady, I was too.

. . . .

[The next evening]

Mr. Dobbins, it should be noted, met me at the church door, and conducted me, with much respect, up the pulpit stairs. When he left me, I removed my hat and intrenched my beating heart behind a hymn-book.

It will be understood that, while I was not unpractised in Sabbath-school teaching, mission prayer-meeting exhortation, "remarks" at sewing-schools, and other like avenues of religious influence, of the kind considered suitable for my sex, I had never engaged in anything which could be denominated public speech; and that, when the clear clang of the bell hushed suddenly, and the pause on the faces of my audience—there may have been forty of them—warned me that my hour had come, I was in no wise more ready to meet it than any Miss A, B, or C, who would be content to employ life in making sofa-pillows, but would be quite safe from putting it to the *outré* purpose of making sermons.

So I got through my introductory exercises with a grim desperation, and made haste to my sermon. Once with the manuscript in my hands, I drew breath. Once having looked my audience fairly in the eye, I was prepared to conquer or be conquered by it. There should be no half-way work between us. So I held up my head and did my best.

The criticism of that sermon would be, I suspect, a choice morning's work for any professor of homiletics in the country. Its divisions were numerous and startling; its introduction occurred just where I thought it would sound best, and its conclusion was adjusted to the clock. I reasoned of righteousness and judgment to come, in learned phrase. Theology and metaphysics, exegesis and zoölogy, poetry and botany, were impressed liberally into its pages. I quoted Sir William Hamilton, Strauss, Aristotle, in liberal allowance. I toyed with the names of Schleiermacher and Copernicus. I played battledoor and shuttlecock with "views" of Hegel and Hobbes. As nearly as I can recollect, that sermon was a hash of literature in five syllables, with a seasoning of astronomy and Adam.

I had the satisfaction of knowing, when I read as modestly, reverently, and as much like an unanointed churchmember as I knew how, a biblical benediction, and sat down again on the pulpit cushions, that if I had not preached the Gospel, I had at least subdued the church-going population of Storm.

Certain rough-looking fellows, upon whom I had had my eye since they came in,—there were several of them, grimy and glum, with keen eyes; men who read Tom Paine, you would say, and had come in "to see the fun,"—while I must admit that they neither wept nor prayed, left the house in a respectful, stupid way that was encouraging.

"You gin it to us!" said Mr. Dobbins, enthusiastically. "Folks is all upsot about ye. That there was an eloquent discourse, marm. Why, they don't see but ye know jest as much as if ye was n't a woman!"

. . . .

Among my other parochial discoveries, I learned one day, to my exceeding surprise, that Samphiry [Bangs's landlady and Mary Ann's mother]—who had been reticent on her family affairs—was the widow of one of my predecessors. She had married him when she was young and pretty, and he was young and ambitious,— "Fond of his book, my dear," she said, as if she had been talking of some dead child, "but slow in speech, like Aaron of old. And three hundred and fifty dollars was tight living for a family like ours. And his heart ran out, and his people, and maybe his sermons, too. So the salary kept a-dropping off, twenty-five dollars at a time, and he could n't take a newspaper, besides selling the library mostly for doctor's bills. And so he grew old and sick and took to farming here, without the salary, and baptized babies and prayed with sick folks free and willing, and never bore anybody a grudge. So he died year before last, and half the valley turned out to bury him. But that did n't help it any, and I know you'd never guess me to be a minister's widow, as well as you do, my dear. I'm all washed out and flattened in. And I can't educate my children, one of them. If you'll believe it, I don't know enough to tell when they talk bad grammar half the time, and I'd about as lieves they'd eat with their knives as not. If they get anything to eat, it's all I've got heart to care. I've got an aunt down in Massachusetts, but it's such a piece of work to get there. So I suppose we shall live and die here, and I don't know but it's just as well."

What a life it was! I felt so young, so crude, so blessed and bewildered beside it, that I gave out that night, at evening prayers, and asked Samphiry to "lead" for herself and me. But I felt no older, no more finished, no less blessed or bewildered, when she had done so.

I should not neglect to mention that I conducted several funerals while I was in Storm. I did not know how, but I knew how to be sorry, which seemed to answer the same purpose; at least they sought me out for the object from far and near. On one occasion I was visited by a distant neighbor, with the request that I would bury his wife. I happened to know that the dead woman had been once a member of the Methodist church in East Storm, whose pastor was alive, active, and a man.

"Would it not be more suitable," I therefore suggested, "at least more agreeable to the feelings of Brother Hand, if you were to ask him to conduct either the whole or a part of the service?"

"Waal, ye see, marm," urged the widower, "the cops was partikelar sot on hevin' you, and as long as I promised her afore she drawed her last that you should conduct the business, I think we'd better perceed without any reference to Brother Hand. I've been thinking of it over, and I come to the conclusion that he could n't take offence *on so slight an occasion!*"

I had ministered "on trial" to the people of Storm, undisturbed by Rev. Dr. Zangrow, who, I suspect, was in private communication of some sort with Mr. Dobbins, for a month,—a month of pouting, spring weather, and long, lazy walks for thinking, and brisk, bright ones for doing; of growing quite fond of salt-pork and barley bread; of calling on old, bedridden women, and hunting up neglected girls, and keeping one eye on my Tom Paine friends; of preaching and practising, of hoping and doubting, of struggling and succeeding, of finding my heart and hands and head as full as life could hold; of feeling that there was a place for me in the earnest world, and that I was in my place; of feeling thankful every day and hour that my womanhood and my work had hit and fitted; of a great many other things which I have agreed not to mention here,—when one night the stage brought me a letter which ran:—

HERCULES, APRIL 28, 18—.

MY DEAR:—I have the measles.

MADCHEN.

Did ever a woman try to do anything, that some of the children did not have the measles?

I felt that fate was stronger than I. I bowed my head submissively, and packed my valise shockingly. Some of the people came in a little knot that night to say good by. The women cried and the men shook hands hard. It was very pleasant and very heartbreaking. I felt a dismal foreboding that, once in the clutches of Hercules and Mädchen, I should never see their dull, dear faces again. I left my sorrow and my Jeremy Taylor for Happen, and my rubber-boots for Samphiry. I tucked the lace collar and the spare paper of hairpins into Mary Ann's upper drawer. I begged Mr. Dobbins's acceptance of Barnes on Matthew, with the request that he would start a Sunday school.

In the gray of the early morning the patient horse trotted me over, with lightened valise and heavy heart, to the crazy station. When I turned my head for a farewell look at my parish, the awful hills were crossed with Happen's red-hot bars, and Mary Ann, with her mouth open, stood in her mother's crumbling door.

Elizabeth Stuart Phelps.

(11–22)

The retreat of Phelps's heroine is not only odd (why does she retreat, why does she not simply nurse Mädchen back to health and then return to her pulpit?); it is both unrepresentative and symptomatic of woman's response to the pulpit controversy after 1870. The retreat is unrepresentative because women definitely continue to demand ministry. In one year, 1876, in one religious weekly, the *Advance*, no fewer than twenty-five articles and letters appeared on women preaching. The abundance of controversialists in America and Britain is matched by the variety of positions. Many denominational publications, such as the *Congregational Quarterly*, printed articles both pro and con; responding to claims that Protestantism liberated womankind, Catholic periodicals called the feminist controversy a reaction against Protestant repressiveness and a return to Medieval activism for women; *New Englander* offered a compromise which pleased no one—women may preach when men invite their utterance.[27] During the last quarter of the nineteenth century, some denominations became increasingly restrictive, but overall the number of women in the ministry continued to grow steadily.

The heroine's retreat in "A Woman's Pulpit" is, nonetheless, a symptomatic gesture in the sense that after 1870 most women who want to preach do not achieve ordination. The mission fields and the Mission Societies, the various purity and temperance and suffrage crusades, all allow women in America and increasingly in Britain to address "promiscuous" assemblies. Retaining her traditional role as moral sanctifier, woman expands her sphere to include more and more of those sanctifying offices which had traditionally been reserved for the male clergy. The ministering angel was becoming the angelic minister.

III

Woman's right to ministry is part of the larger Victorian debate over the efficacy of religion itself. Increasingly women go beyond specific doctrines and texts and question the impact of the whole Christian tradition. In 1883, for example, one of America's foremost divines, Rev. Morgan Dix of Trinity Church, New York, gives a series of Lenten Sermons which reaffirm traditional attitudes toward woman's nature and life. Rev. Dix suddenly finds himself taken up, sermon for sermon, by one of America's foremost feminists, Lillie Devereux Blake. As an admirer of "Of Queens' Gardens," Rev. Dix bases his argument for woman's debt to Christianity upon a very orthodox definition of woman.

> The test and measure of a Christian woman is, whether, and to what extent, she is qualified to help, order, comfort, and adorn her home. . . . Go to some church, at evening, where they sing the "Magnificat," and listen. . . . If you be true women, you can also say to God:
> "MY SOUL DOTH MAGNIFY THE LORD: AND MY SPIRIT HATH REJOICED IN GOD MY SAVIOUR.
> "FOR HE HATH REGARDED THE LOWLINESS OF HIS HANDMAIDEN.
> "FOR HE THAT IS MIGHTY HATH MAGNIFIED ME: AND HOLY IS HIS NAME. . . ."
> Remember: woman owes to Christianity whatever of power and honor she enjoys.

Not surprisingly, Blake disagrees. Without "for one moment . . . [suggesting] that I have aught to say of disrespect to what is purest and best in Christianity," Blake asks, what does the worthy man consider should be their greatest pleasure? To adorn their minds with knowledge? To earn an honest livelihood? To make the path of life easier for others of their sex? Oh, no, none of these. They must go to church and listen to the singing to the Magnificat! They must not even sing themselves, but listen to the singing of this chant, intoned by a chorus of male voices. . . . Ah, my friends, there is a grander hymn even than the Magnificat, as there is 'a word that is dearer than mother, home, or heaven, and that word is liberty.'[28]

The controversy over religion's impact involves both the Old and the New Testaments. How downtrodden were Old Testament women? Carlos White in *Ecce Femina* (1870) speaks for many Victorians who see scripture establishing the same communality of conjugal interest which James Mill posited in his "Article on Government" (I.2). "Throughout the Bible, the husband is regarded as the head and protector of the family, and there is no provision for separate interests."[29] White then describes Old Testament life.

> The management of public affairs was in the hands of men. Miriam [Exod. 15] led the women in singing and dancing; but she was not satisfied with this pre-eminence. She seemed to have the modern idea of *woman's rights*, as she tried to form a conspiracy against Moses, for which she was smitten with leprosy. [Num. 12]. This was not a very propitious beginning for the cause which has now become an important movement. (185)

Replies to such orthodox interpretations of Old Testament life come from two sides. Those who see Jewish women sorely repressed point to discriminatory practices (like exclusion from the priesthood and the Torah) and to traditional attitudes (expressed in the male prayer—"praised be God that He has not made me a woman"). Lillie Blake, in turn, speaks for those who find that the Old Testament encourages and rewards female achievement in diverse spheres.

> We are told, in the first place, in verse 11 [of Prov. 31], that "the heart of her husband doth safely trust in her;" showing that this perfect woman, described as a model for all time, was not a silly, dependent weakling, but a woman, with all womanly grace and beauty doubtless, but also strong and self-reliant, so that husband and children could safely rely upon her in every emergency.

"She considereth a field, and buyeth it: with the fruit of her hands she planteth a vineyard." . . .

No mention is made of her asking her husband whether she should buy the property or not, or meekly signing her name to a paper after he had bought it without consulting her, and very likely with her money. . . .

"She stretcheth out her hand to the poor; yea, she reacheth forth her hands to the needy."

A perfect woman indeed, foremost in all good words and work! . . .

And now we come to verse 23, to which I desire especially to call your attention:

"Her husband is known in the gates, when he sitteth among the elders of the land."

You will perceive that he is known as "her husband," pointed out doubtless as the husband of this grand woman. Evidently he did not amount to very much himself, and was only known as her husband. . . .

The closing verses are all devoted to further praise of this most perfect woman, described as a model for her sex, and, one would think, for the utter discomfiture of Dr. Dix and all others who would pretend to condemn women to a restricted and dependent life, and find a warrant for their dictations in this good book. . . .

"Give her of the fruit of her hands; and let her own works praise her in the gates."

Now this "praise in the gates" was the greatest publicity a person could have in those days when newspapers were unknown; we specially commend this verse to the consideration of this worthy divine, who was so shocked that a woman's name should be publicly known, and printed in full like a man's. (83–87)

However they define woman in the Old Testament, Victorians face the inevitable question: has she been elevated or degraded by Christianity? Those who see woman elevated offer both iconoclastic and quietist arguments. Lillie Blake and others argue that Martin Luther's iconoclastic stand against authority involved more than individual interpretation of Scripture. "And when Martin Luther took a nun in honorable marriage he struck the first blow for woman's final emancipation from the monastic thralldom of the medieval period" (24). Another iconoclastic hero is Jesus Christ himself. "Christ came to break *every* yoke." This position is sufficiently traditional that the speaker here is archconservative Carlos White (187), but

Christians who agree about Jesus as iconoclast often disagreed about Jesus' attitude toward women. Compare White:

> if he had found woman abused as much as some say she is, he would have set the example by choosing them to preach, or in some way would have condemned the existing customs. . . . (187)

and Josephine Butler:

> I appeal to the open Book and to the intelligence of every candid student of Gospel history for justification of my assertion that in all important instances of His dealings with women His dismissal of each case was accompanied by a distinct act of *Liberation*.[30]

The subversive potential of Christ's example is demonstrated by the devout wife of a Birmingham minister, Elizabeth Gaskell. In her novel *Ruth* (1853), the fallen woman's spiritual guide, Rev. Benson, must face the community's spokesman, righteous Mr. Bradshaw.

> "Come, come, Mr. Benson, let us have no more of this morbid way of talking. The world has decided how such women are to be treated. . . ."
> "I take my stand with Christ against the world," said Mr. Benson.[31]

Bolstered by her Unitarian commitment to activism, Elizabeth Gaskell recognizes that Christ's defiance of the clerical establishment and His affirmation of individual dignity constitutes a precedent for contemporary treatment of women—and for contemporary women themselves. After *Ruth*, some of Gaskell's "friends" never speak to her again.

More widely held than the iconoclast position is the quietist view that woman has received from Christianity all the elevation she needs. Often this view is buttressed by historical analyses (W.E.H. Lecky's is probably the most prestigious) which survey various non-Christian cultures—early pagan, Hebrew, Greek, Roman, Teuton, Moslem, Hindu—and find them all wanting.[32] The chivalric woman-worship of the Middle Ages provides a particularly appealing model for Victorians nostalgic for all things medieval. Historical nostalgia also heightens the attractiveness of another quietist model, the Virgin Mary. Although Protestant response to the Catholic dogma of the Immaculate Conception is overwhelmingly negative, the Anglo-American attitude toward Mary herself is generally positive. In *The Scarlet Letter* (1850), Hester Prynne, standing on the scaffold before righteous puritan eyes, evokes from Hawthorne the speculation that "had there been a Papist among the crowd of Puritans, he might have seen in this beautiful woman, so picturesque in her attire and mien, and with the infant at her bosom, an object to remind him of the image of Divine Maternity." The narrator of *The Blithedale Romance* (1853) admits, "I have always envied the Catholics their faith in that sweet, sacred Virgin Mother who stands between them and the Diety."[33]

Such feelings became more widespread in the 1860s. The *London Review* noted that Anna Jameson and other art historians have awakened "artistic interest" in Mary "even in the most protestant of English minds"; *Blackwood's* spoke fondly of "Mary of Galilee, of many a painter's imagination, and of many a reverential and tender thought"; even the severe *Athenaeum* admitted that "there is enough in the Evangelists to make Mary an object of respect."[34] Books which appeared in the 1860s also reflected an increased interest in Mary. Raphael Melia's defense of Catholic attitudes toward Mary, *The Woman Blessed by All Generations* (1868), received gentle reviews; Margaret Oliphant, ever in touch with the culture, entitled her domestic novel of 1867 *Madonna Mary*; even a 1635 *Life of the Blessed Virgin* was reprinted with the new title *The Female Glory* (1869).[35] Understanding the peculiar nature of Mary's glory is basic to understanding the Woman Question.

The increase of woman-worship during the Victorian period brings Mary inevitably into prominence. Since her virtues reside less in herself than in her maternal role, a culture which idolized Motherhood eulogizes Mary's innate spirituality, passivity, devotion. John Henry Newman's sermon on "The Feast of the Annunciation of the Blessed Virgin Mary, the Reverence Due Her" (1832)[36] expresses the traditional view eloquently. "In her the curse pronounced on Eve was changed to a blessing. Eve was doomed to bear children in sorrow; but now this very dispensation . . . was made the means by which salvation came into the world" (129). Mary's (and thus woman's) elevation in Christianity does not raise her high enough to occasion a prideful fall, however. The selfless service which Newman praises in terms of Christian humility constitutes the ideal also for Victorian lives essentially secular. Compare his words "the silent duties of every day . . . are blest to the sufficient sanctification of thousands, whom the world knows not of" (136) and George Eliot's final words in *Middlemarch*: "That things are not so ill with you and me as they might have been, is half owing to the number who lived faithfully a hidden life, and rest in unvisited tombs."[37]

This self-effacing, Mary-like ideal remains a female standard for the rest of the era, but increasingly after mid-century Victorians question the efficacy of female spirituality. Why has the morally superior half of the race been so unsuccessful in transforming the world into her image and likeness? A few Victorians answer this question by denying its premise. Anne Dryden in *Can Woman Regenerate Society* (1844) said skeptically, "I have not yet seen this [female spirituality] so clearly demonstrated, as I would like to believe it to be. . . . If she thinks of Heaven because she is unhappy upon earth, supposing her mere weariness of existence here to be a sure passport elsewhere, the idea does not involve that of spirituality."[38] Dryden goes on to attribute supposedly "innate, female" traits to cultural conditioning; and some Victorians after mid-century perpetuated her behaviorist argument. But the overwhelming majority in Britain and America ask not whether woman can regenerate society, but what has thwarted her innate powers thus far. Three causes are singled out. One is inadequate education; speaking for many Victorians, Rev. Moncure Conway modifies Newman's Mary-ideal by bolstering woman's innate powers with schooling and technology. This turning to man for help is just what a second group of Victorians blames woman's long ineffectuality upon. Eliza W. Farnham pushes woman-worship to its logical conclusion—that women rely upon their superiority and become literally the sovereigns of society. A third group blames woman's subjection upon Christianity itself. Elizabeth Cady Stanton insists that nineteen hundred years of bondage must end before female effectuality can begin.

Moncure Conway, "The American Minister in England," is a southern divine who lives abroad, writes prolifically on many subjects, and eventually helps officiate at the funeral of his long-time friend, Elizabeth Cady Stanton.[39] In "The Madonna of Montbazon" (1883), Conway presents a Virgin more public than Newman's in her prominence, yet as traditional as Newman's in her elevation and limitations. The power of Woman remains maternal; her weaknesses warrant both her reliance upon male technology and her insistence upon more education. By defining the ideal union of female and male powers as the partnership of maternity and science, Conway anticipates by a quarter-century the fullest formulation of this ideal—and indeed the last great profession of Victorian woman-worship—in Henry Adams' "The Virgin and the Dynamo."

From the distance of a league I first saw Montbazon. With that perspective the remnant of the castle appeared as a square pedestal supporting a gigantic image. Approaching nearer, the castle was seen to be entirely covered with vines, mosses, flowers, leaving hardly visible its apertures and turrets, from which archers once rained death on besiegers. Above the high walls so sweetly foliated, stood the image,—the largest bronze statue in Europe,— the Madonna of Montbazon . . . with her child.

On the close view there was something rather amusing about the image. The head was encircled by what seemed a strange kind of halo, made of darting rays of light. But examination proved these to be the diverging points of a lightning-rod. The rod ran up the Madonna's back and branched out into a circlet of points. It seemed rather droll that the pious people should have thought it necessary to protect their protectress, to shield the Queen of Heaven from the lightnings of Heaven. . . .

From the dawn of history until now, every reign of savagery and barbarism has disappeared under the soft siege of the Mother and her Babe. I do not mean that it was under the gentle influence and persuasion of woman, but through the inevitable necessities of maternity and of the home. Women also have been war-like. . . . But experience steadily modified and mastered that passion. It was found that so the home could not be built, and the babe reared. . . . The Madonna of Montbazon rightly holds under foot the barbaric fortress, whose ruin meant the security of the babe she holds. One or the other had to be sacrificed, the babe or the battlement. Yet as a type of woman she no less needs that crown of science which Franklin wove for her head. For until the mother is so crowned she and her child cannot be protected from the storms of elemental nature which beat upon their heads, nor from the paralyzing dogmas related to those elements. . . .

Superstitions survive longest in women, because they beset the most delicate nerves, and they appeal to sentiment. For untold ages submission has been the badge of woman by reason of her physical weakness; ages of masculine supremacy have drilled her into the habit of unquestioning sufferance. . . . So are she and her child still struck by lightnings from the ancient heavens,—weakened, lowered, impoverished in mind and heart, by perversions of their power.

So, at least, it has been for a long time; but I trust a new day is dawning. The Madonna's protecting crown seemed to signal the clearer day. It is something when a Catholic priesthood and peasantry recognize facts sufficiently to admit that their gods require scientific protection. . . . As mastery of the lightning took its place even above the Madonna's sovereignty, so has chloroform taken its place above Eve's penalty. The old spell begins to lift. It will lift more and more till the power of woman—the finest power in the world—is set free.

. . . Nothing can be more serious than the moral situation of to-day, with its religious interregnum, wherein the passions of men are as keen as ever, their opportunities multiplied, their restraints reduced to a minimum. But I believe that again the ancient traditions of the world will be justified, that the seed of the woman shall bruise the serpent's head. It is plain that human society must hereafter depend upon friendliness between man and man, upon obligations of honour, upon sentiment, sympathy, and the love of peace; it must depend on these because the old hopes and fears are gone; and it is difficult to see where the new resources are to be found except in that sex with which those qualities are constitutional. No doubt there are unwomanly women as there are unmanly men; but the exceptions do but confirm the rule that with women are preëminently associated the moral and spiritual qualities which alone can make life worth living. By such elements, which have their completest culture in the home, the very heart and brain of woman have been organized. She is a result of their evolution. Where ancient theology expressed this fact in a physical way, seeing in the Madonna and her babe literal incarnations of the divine, reason sees a spiritual truth. The seed of the woman is the moral genius of woman, that which she implants in the heart and mind of childhood, and diffuses throughout the social world of which she is the centre. . . . under the new conditions her influence must be largely increased.

And how is that increase to be secured? Not merely by giving her a vote, though that would be just and right. Still more, as I think, by increasing her resources of knowledge and culture, whereby she may grow with the growing world, and adapt her influence and strength to every new phase of the world's unfolding thought and power as it arrives. Because our predecessors did not recognize this we have come upon a serious peril,—that is, a separation between the masculine and the feminine characters. There is nothing more painful and more dangerous than to find young men outgrowing their mothers intellectually, and coming to look down upon their sisters. . . . The time arrives in many a man's life when too late he realizes that the old feeling he had when his mother was his holy Madonna belonged to the depths of his being, and he would be glad to give up much of his learning and all of his pride to bring it back again. But it ought not to have been lost, and it will not be lost when parents realize that unless daughters grow in knowledge sons cannot grow in morality. Only by an equal culture can the high human powers commingle harmoniously, mutually restraining and guiding each other.

. . . And so ends my parable of the Madonna crowned by science, treading down all hardness and barren force, and my parable of the babe she bears, with whom is the hope of the world. (309–13, 319–21)

Conway and most who await a new spiritual era agree finally with tradition that woman, despite her moral superiority, always is and must always be subordinate to man. Some Victorians, however, carry the doctrine of woman-worship to its logical—if apocalyptic—conclusion. If morality is the prime concern of a Christian society, then woman should be the prime force in that society. Apocalyptic feminists answer Anne Dryden's skeptical question, "Can Woman Regenerate Society?" with a resounding YES. Woman must not remain hidden in a shrine like Newman's Virgin or remain bound to male technology like Conway's Madonna. Woman must be active in her superiority because history has reached an apocalyptic moment. The reign of force is ending, the reign of spirit beginning; female love supersedes male power. The most succinctly eloquent statement of this position is probably Henry James, Sr.'s "The Woman Thou Gavest Me" (1870),[40] but the major expression of apocalyptic feminism is Eliza W. Farnham's *Woman and Her Era* (1864). Why Farnham's book lacked contemporary impact is complicated. Its great length and its stylistic and technical density, plus her own death soon after publication, are factors. What cannot be credited is the claim that "no one was ready for a doctrine of female superiority."[41] *Woman and Her Era*, and indeed the idea of apocalyptic feminism, are part of that "feminization" of culture which became prominent in Victorian America after Margaret Fuller and which England had been discussing since Lady Morgan's *Woman and Her Master* (1840).[42] (The tradition goes back at least to Agrippa von Nettesheim's *Female Pre-Eminence, or,*

The Dignity and Excellency of that Sex, Above the Male in 1670.) America
with its messianic mission led the cry for woman's era, but
British interest pro and con appears strongly in the 1860s. "The
Feminine Element in 'The Modern Spirit'" (1867) defines contemporary "tendencies to extol the female type of mind . . . not
only above religious dogma, but even above the intellectual side
of faith," and Eliza Lynn Linton expresses orthodoxy's hostility
to "the sect . . . [which believes] the feminine is the highest, the
divine element in humanity. Manhood represents pride, glut-
tony, selfishness, hate, wrath. . . ."[43]

Predating *Woman and Her Era* by twenty-five years and enduring into the twentieth century, commitment to the reign of
woman grows from millennialist and perfectionist impulses in
the 1840s and 1850s. Individual responsibility for remedying
the world's ills means that morally superior individuals—women
—must be particularly active. Lydia Maria Child, Catharine
Beecher, Lydia Huntley Sigourney, William Lloyd Garrison,
Nathaniel Hawthorne, Thomas Wentworth Higginson, Theodore Parker, the Grimkés, plus Swedenborgians, early Comteans, and many others, all maintain that society would improve
morally as woman prompted man to accept her standards. Sarah
Josepha Hale is unequivocal:

> The moral power in which [women] excel, is yet to rule the world.
> The empire of physical strength, in which lay man's superiority, is
> waxing old, wearing out . . . the reign of brute force is now over,
> and that of intellect and feeling is at hand.[44]

Hale, like Beecher and others, will not campaign actively for
woman's dominance. Farnham and those who do find encouragement from two sources—a particular aspect of the Virgin Mary's
character and an increased Victorian concern with androgyny.

Mary is credited by many Christians with a definite, if
limited, capacity for action. "The Mother of Jesus," said the
popular historian Charles Merivale in 1866, "is the type and
pattern of them [holy women] all—the type of true female
purity, loving, trusting, accepting, realizing. She receives her
faith, but she makes it her own."[45] By giving birth to the
Messiah, Mary crushes the serpent's head *and* atones for Eve's
fall. "[Woman]is the inheritor of new, unheard-of, and wondrous
blessings,—blessings which come to her *through* that blessed
Maid, Wife, Mother . . . the Virgin Mary."[46] Mary's power
makes many Protestants uneasy, however. The *Athenaeum* warns

in 1867 that "Roman publications begin to call the Virgin the *Co-redemptress*."[47] Seeing Mary as coredeemer can make her—though Catholicism would vehemently disagree—the equal of Jesus and thus, in fact, a God. To become like God was Eve's aspiration. And, according to anxious Victorians, it is the aspiration of any "new woman" who seeks to leave her place of traditional obscurity and usurp more active roles as "cominister" in the pulpit or "coauthority" in the home. To Farnham and others, however, this active potential in the Mary-ideal is appealing—especially appealing because an idea debated since patristic times becomes increasingly prominent after the mid-century: divine androgyny.

Though Catholicism and many Protestant denominations denounce any suggestion of equality between Jesus and Mary as coredeemers, some Christian sects frankly embrace the equation of God and woman. Mary Baker Eddy calls God "Father-Mother" and Swedenborgians see the entire universe divided between "male" and "female" forces. Among more orthodox Christians there is a definite tendency in the 1850s and 1860s to emphasize the feminine quality of Christ's nature and to soften the traditional harshness of God the Father. Divine love and sacrifice and patience take precedence over wrath and righteousness and implacability. "Trust in God; She will protect you!" is a Victorian utterance, but spiritual androgyny had interested Protestant preachers since the mid-eighteenth century.[48] Sermons which used the bride-groom image to describe the soul's relation to God were requiring male parishioners to consider themselves female. Considering *God* female is what the mid-nineteenth century found increasingly satisfying. The next step for some Christians was a female Messiah. Shakers and other millennialists believe that Jesus at the second coming will be female. Mother Ann Lee of the Shakers, Jemima Wilkinson, and later Mary Baker Eddy consider themselves that second Jesus.

Not all Victorians who support woman's active role in reform consider woman *superior* to man, of course. As Margaret Fuller could look forward to woman's era without believing in female superiority, women (and men) at the Ninth National Women's Rights Convention in 1858 give a respectful hearing but not unanimous agreement to Farnham's

> theory of woman's superiority . . . [her] long speech . . . was received with apparent satisfaction by the audience, though several on the platform dissented from the claim of superiority, thinking it

would be a sufficient triumph over the tyrannies of the past, if popular thought could be educated to the idea of the equality of the sexes.[49]

In the 1870s, perfectionism declines in America and Britain, but belief in woman's era does not. In fact, the major postwar shift in attitude toward woman's role is precisely in the direction advocated by Farnham, and before her by Margaret Fuller. True Woman remains the basic ideal but expands her sphere outside the home in order to purify the world corrupted by men. Both the Temperance and the Purity [Volume II, Chapter 3] crusades premise that man must be raised to woman's standards and that a new age of love must replace the old violence and use. In anthropology, Bachofen (1861) and Morgan (1877) foster and reflect the period's increasing concern with woman's role by studying (however chauvinistically) the nature and duration of matriarchy in human evolution. Although the "new" sociology of Lester Ward contains more sexual stereotyping than his most liberated passages indicate, Ward in 1886 expressly calls woman the primary sex and defines the coming age as one of her "redemption."[50] Women writers contemporary with Ward, as Elaine Showalter notes, "glorified and idealized the womanly values of chastity and maternal love, and believed that those values must be forced upon a degenerate male society."[51]

In the context of a half-century commitment to woman's era, *Woman and Her Era* becomes a more intelligible and a more representative effort. Farnham, like Louise Cheeves McCord, insists upon consistency. "[If] preachers, physicians, politicians, editors, and authors proclaim woman's superiority and assign to her the moral health of the society, then these Authority Figures must yield to her authority" (II, 449). Farnham does *not* argue for sexual equality. She accepts the traditional division of traits—woman as less sensual and materialistic, more spiritual and intuitive—and refuses to battle man for the lower world of Force. "He is to command the lower external, to which he belongs, for her physical sustenance, comfort and service" (II, 36). Farnham's defense of woman's right to rule raises virtually every issue of the day: brain weight, evolution, comparative physiology, prostitution, voluntary motherhood, divine androgyny.

Farnham, like George Drysdale and Antoinette Brown Blackwell, founds her argument upon physiology. Using evolutionary biology in volume I to "prove" the superior sophistication

of woman's body [Volume II, Chapter 2], Farnham can conclude that moral supremacy derives "inevitably" from physical;
Volume II then goes on to explain both why woman has not yet
inherited the earth and what the dawning of her era will bring.

I begin with this syllogism:
Life is exalted in proportion to its Organic and Functional
Complexity;
Woman's Organism is more Complex and her totality of Func-
tion larger than those of any other being inhabiting our earth;
Therefore her position in the scale of Life is the most ex-
alted—the Sovereign one. (I, 26)

Why does this Sovereign not yet rule the planet? The self-love of
the masculine era has meant exploitation in both the private and
the public realms—both the sexual subjection which wives share
with prostitutes and the political subjection which all women
share with the proletariat.

Man is the degrader of the Love-relations; Woman their ele-
vator. This aphoristic statement is equally supported by the primary truths of the respective natures, and by the facts through
which they have been demonstrated, from the beginning of human
history. It is man who seeks the material relation; who plans and
compasses it, decently or otherwise; who lays diabolical plots
thereto, and executes them without shame or remorse. . . .
The spontaneous attractions of the feminine on the side of
sense, are in connection with its maternal office. . . . The matured
young female who has never known it, thinks of *it* as the summit
and crown of her love—not as man does, of the *relations* which
introduce her to it. What is an end, ardently desired by him, is only
a means to her, and quite overlooked in view of the end. Sense is
consummation to him—but only maternity is consummation to
her.
. . . According to her divine nature, a true woman sees
chastity as a spiritual quality primarily, and secondarily as the
result of outward facts. She feels that chastity is of the soul first,
and may be there, pure and strong, when the body has suffered
the most revolting violation. . . . when she becomes conscious
that it is so—that her nature does indeed transcend and include
man's, exceeding it both for good and evil, she can no longer
actually accept his standards. No matter what her personal or
social position—no matter what the acknowledged or the urged
claims upon her; the old conventional responsibilities, the false
moral ones, the misinterpreted natural ones, drop beneath her

feet, and there descends upon her a new and brighter tissue of obligations. . . . with her fine insight and acknowledged capacities for spiritual leadership, she but touches with the fire from the altar of her own soul, the soul of her sister who is yet in bondage, and there is henceforth understanding, companionship, sympathy and co-operation between them. They have a common cause and work together, in Love—not Self-Love. They have not to conquer themselves first, in order to be virtuous, but, already armed and panoplied in the natural goodness which is of their diviner consititution, their conquest begins for Good, not for self, which has been thus far almost the only conquest we have seen on this planet.

. . . Let them not be skeptical or indifferent to a state whose pains and penalties are so grievous and humiliating, and also so commonly the lot of their sex, that every other form of protest sinks into insignificance before this growing army of Protestant Women who are filling the civilized lands. Let man look to them and consider.

. . . We see and cannot choose but see, how slender is the actual relation between man's organic nature and the institutions in which he has clothed himself. . . . Thus there is not in existence, nor has there ever been, a Church which has had its origin in any intelligent understanding of the human being. . . .

In like manner there is no Government, nor has there ever been, which got itself constituted by virtue of a clear understanding of what is needful for the physical, social, intellectual, and spiritual well-being of its subjects: nor was there ever a Government which, in its administration, made even a remote approach to any such system of treatment. So no social order ever existed which was founded upon a just perception of the natural claims and rights of those whom it distributed and co-ordinated in labor and business, or society; the motive in all past or existing systems having been self-love. . . . This relation, in which the strongest and ablest party does not foster—according to the divine; but exploits—according to the diabolic spirit—the feeble and unable party, produces a state whose inseparable body of evils deserve not from us the noble name of Civilization, and certainly will never be honored by it, among the generations of even the near future. . . . Self-redemption is effected by the few who persistently struggle upward to the better lot; while the second, and incomparably the larger body, are precipitated, by their feeble, impotent protest, into either utter ruin, the ruin of drunkenness, crime, or prostitution, becoming thus captains in that great army which Society everywhere musters into its service, the "Dangerous Classes," or they stop, groping and maundering helplessly, on the middle ground of poverty, ignorance, and destitution of all that can sweeten and brighten life, and thus join themselves to that gigantic army, equally present in all high civic states, known as the "Perishing Classes." (II, 75, 107, 99, 100, 101, 92; I, 19; II, 432–33)

The Dangerous Class, the Perishing Class, and the Army of Protestant Women will triumph, not because of their numerical majority, but because of maternity's inevitable superiority. Farnham's argument for Motherhood Regnant is particularly complex and symptomatic of the period because she does not limit motherhood to the childbearing years. "The post-maternal period, that of Universal Motherhood, is preeminently the feminine one. Womanhood cannot be known till it is studied or lived beyond these portals, which have heretofore been closed, to shut it, in coldness and darkness, out from the shining circle of human sympathies . . . the years which make him [man] more masculine, must make her more feminine, (spiritual)" (II, 389). What is finally born out of Maternal Love is both the mother herself ("the awakened mother will demand all that is the right of maternity—not for her sake, but for its sake" [II, 399]) and her ultimate progeny, the perfect society of woman's era.

Let us glance at some of the leading features it will develop as the Era of Woman advances.

The nobler Organic Life of Woman, coming into the scale of Forces above instead of below, must tend to refine and purify every system it impinges upon. Sense, and the pleasures of Sense, must take on a finer character through her ascendency, and fall from the rank of leaders to their harmonious ultimate one of servants.

Her more affectional nature must replace, in the world of motive and action, (as springing from human relations), force with persuasion; iron will, that lacerates while it coerces, with the gentle rule of love, that develops and beautifies while it attracts.

Her more spiritual Intellect will win down to earth Truth and her heaven of peace, in place of the discord and controversy which Man maintains in his efforts to find and prove her. Many of the most vital moral Truths, which contain the very essence of human welfare, are self-evident to Woman. . . . Thus the master-Truth, perhaps, of the human career, and one so self-evident that any mind at once good, intelligent, and intuitive, even to a moderate degree, is shamed by the attempt to prove it, is that contained in the affirmation of the right of every soul to the completest development it is capable of attaining. Yet every Government that Man has founded since he came on the earth, has utterly ignored it. . . .

. . . For this affirmation, admitted, carries in the train of its consequences freedom to all—which is the atmosphere of growth —a consequent surrender of Self-Love by the powerful few, and unwavering faithfulness to the Idea of Democracy, which is its direct, legitimate outcome, to be practically striven *for*—not *against*, by those who can accept it.*

I said Woman had been enthroned and crowned sovereign in the kingdom of Use. Not yet, however, is this actually done. Throne is vacant, and crown empty, till Nature's grand designs get a little farther unfolded. . . .

If we take into the account, in looking at the future of Woman, the broad and substantial basis of recognition for her laid down in Gall's discoveries and the writings of his followers; the great American movement for the securing of her natural rights; which, in a less popular but not less pronounced form, has extended to England; the legislation for her which that country has been constrained to discuss, when not to make; the French movement, of which the most prominent signs visible across the Atlantic . . . when we consider the general breaking up of the old crust of form and thought which has contained Woman, the freedom, in study and action, which she has practically gained within the last quarter of a century, and specially within the last decade—the pen so largely and ably assumed by her—professional positions taken and most creditably and successfully held, under the combined disadvantages of the opposition of Men, Women and Schools, the skepticism of society, and inferior pay for the same service—the moral freedom, so widely achieved, to do anything she is able to do; the increasing respect for her in any position she is moved to take; seeing all this, one sees that the ERA OF WOMAN, so long postponed, the dream of the ages, has at length opened. (II, 388–89, 399, 445–47, 358, 410, 446–47)

A small but growing minority agree that woman owes her present status to religion—and lament that status as deplorable.

*I would not be understood as desiring that even political Freedom, the most external form of this inestimable blessing, should, on any given year or day become the possession of all human beings. Nature has wisely made it impossible. For Freedom is not simple release from external power or control. If it were, it might safely be given to all at any time when the gift was possible. This, however, is but one element of it, of which *fitness to receive and turn such release to the noblest account in the life,* is another and *higher.*

On both sides of the Atlantic important figures in the 1850s accused Christianity of repression and discrimination. The popular American preacher Theodore Parker refuses to distinguish Christian from non-Christian treatment of women. "[That woman] is practically regarded as man's inferior . . . not a free spiritual individuality like him . . . appears . . . in the 're-vealed religion' of Jews and Christians, as well as in that of Brahmans and Mahometans."[52] In England, John Henry Newman found his antithesis in his brilliant, if less famous, brother, Francis William. These brothers differ about virtually everything. Becoming steadily more agnostic and anticlerical as John moves toward Catholicism, Frank challenges assumptions sacred to his older brother and to most Christians. "We are told that Christianity is the great influence which has raised *woman-kind:*—this does not appear to be true." Frank came to abhor what he called "the disgusting admiration and invocation of Mary's perpetual virginity."[53]

Francis Newman is a major influence upon the most effective of Christianity's female critics, Elizabeth Cady Stanton. Stanton helps lead the growing minority which shocks the 1870s and 1880s with criticisms of Christian influence. On both sides of the Atlantic, Robert G. Ingersoll, for example, draws vast crowds and criticism by accusing religion of sexual bias.[54] Stanton's lifelong difficulties with religion derived less from Scripture than from male exegeses and discriminatory customs. Addressing women of every caste in America and Britain, Stanton says about religion what she said about suffrage—that nothing warranted tyranny. With the downtrodden wives of polygynous Mormons, she exhibits "no Phariseeism, no shudders of Puritanic horror, no standing afar off; but a simple, loving, fraternal clasp of hands with these struggling women, and an earnest work with them—not to ameliorate but to abolish the whole system of woman's subjection to man in both polygamy and monogamy." With the nunlike daughters of an English curate, Stanton asks questions until the young women begin questioning themselves.

> When one of the daughters, pointing to the cover on the altar, remarked with pride, "Sister and I worked that," she asked designingly, "Did you place it on the altar?"
> "Oh no," she replied, "no woman is allowed to enter this enclosure."

"Why?" asked Elizabeth, well knowing the answer.

"It is too sacred."

"But," Elizabeth remonstrated, "men go there; and it is said that women are purer, more delicate, refined, and naturally religious than they are."

"Yes, but women are not allowed," repeated the curate's daughter.

"Shall I explain the reason to you?" continued Elizabeth. "It is because the Church believes that woman brought sin into the world, that she was the cause of man's fall from holiness, that she was cursed of God, and has ever since been in collusion with the devil. Hence, the Church has considered her unfit to sing in the choir or enter the Holy of Holies."

And the curate's daughter, looking very thoughtful said, "I never supposed these old customs had such significance."

"Yes," concluded Elizabeth, driving her point home, "every old custom, every fashion, every point of etiquette is based on some principle, and women ignorantly submit to many degrading customs, because they do not understand their origin."[55]

Stanton's Protestant belief in individual interpretation and her feminist distrust of male exegesis led eventually to *The Woman's Bible* (1895–98). But her most succinctly wide-ranging attack upon religion comes earlier. Distilled from a series of talks which begin in 1871 and include a London "sermon" in 1882, "Has Christianity Benefited Woman?" (1885)[56] stands as one of feminism's most powerful essays.

THE assertion that woman owes all the advantages of her present position to the Christian church, has been repeated so often, that it is accepted as an established truth by those who would be unwilling to admit that all the injustice and degradation she has suffered might be logically traced to the same source. A consideration of woman's position before Christianity, under Christianity, and at the present time, shows that she is not indebted to any form of religion for one step of progress, or one new liberty; on the contrary, it has been through the perversion of her religious sentiments that she has been so long held in a condition of slavery. All religions thus far have taught the headship and superiority of man, the inferiority and subordination of woman. . . . History shows, too, that the moral degradation of woman is due more to theological superstitions than to all other influences together. It is not to any form of religion that we are to look for woman's advancement, but to material civilization, to commerce, science, art, invention, to the discovery of the art of printing, and the general dissemination of knowledge. Buckle, in his "History of Civilization," calls attention to the fact that when woman became valuable in a commercial sense, in proportion as she secured material elevation and wealth through her property rights, she began to be treated with a deference and respect that the Christian church never accorded. In ancient Egypt, at the most brilliant period of its history, woman sat upon the throne and directed the civilization of the country. In the marriage relation she was supreme in all things—a rule that, according to Wilkinson, was productive of lasting fidelity. As priestess she performed the most holy offices of religion, and to her is traced the foundation of Egyptian literature, the sacred songs of Isis, said by Plato to be ten thousand years old. Colleges for women were founded there twelve hundred years before Christ, and the medical profession was in the hands of women. It is a sad commentary on the Christianity of England and America, to find professors in medical colleges of the nineteenth century less liberal than those in the earliest civilizations. . . .

With regard to intellectual growth and elevation, we have the same causes alike for man and woman. What either acquired was in opposition to the church, which sedulously tried to keep all learning within itself. Man, seeking after knowledge, was opposed by the church; woman, by both church and man. Educated men in our own day, who have outgrown many of the popular theological superstitions, do not share with the women of their households the freedom they themselves enjoy. Hence, it is not unusual to find the wives of clergymen far more bigoted than their husbands. . . .

By the dishonoring of womanhood on the ground of original sin, by the dishonoring of all relations with her as carnal and unclean, the whole sex touched a depth of moral degradation that it had never known before. Rescued in a measure from the miseries of polygamy, woman was plunged into the more degrading and unnatural condition of celibacy. Out of this grew the terrible persecutions of witchcraft, which raged for centuries, women being its chief victims. They were hunted down by the clergy, tortured, burned, drowned, dragged into the courts, tried, and condemned, for crimes that never existed but in the minds of religious devotees. The clergy sustained witchcraft as Bible doctrine, far into the eighteenth century, until the spirit of rationalism laughed the whole thing to scorn and gave mankind a more cheerful view of life. The reformation brought no new hope to woman. The great head of the movement, while declaring the right of individual conscience and judgment above church authority, as if to warn woman that she had no share in this liberty, was wont to say, "No gown worse becomes a woman than that she should be wise." Here is the key-note to the Protestant pulpit for three centuries, and it grates harshly on our ears to-day. The Catholic Church, in its holy sisterhoods, so honored and revered, and in its worship of the Virgin Mary, Mother of Jesus, has preserved some recognition of the feminine element in its religion; but from Protestantism it is wholly eliminated. Religions like the Jewish and Christian, which make God exclusively male and man supreme, consign woman logically to the subordinate position assigned her in Mohammedism. History has perpetuated this tradition, and her subjection has existed as an invariable element in Christian civilization. It could not be otherwise, with the Godhead represented as a trinity of males. . . .

The present position of woman in the spirit of our creeds and codes is far behind the civilization of the age, and unworthy the representative women of this day. And now, as ever, the strongest adverse influence to her elevation comes from the church, judging from its Biblical expositions, the attitude of the clergy, and the insignificant status the woman holds in the various sectarian organizations. For nearly forty years there has been an organized movement in England and America to liberalize the laws in relation to woman, to secure a more profitable place in the world of work, to open the colleges for higher education, and the schools of medicine, law, and theology, and to give woman an equal voice in the government and religion of the country. These demands, one by one, are slowly being conceded by the secular branch of the government, while the sectarian influence has been uniformly in the opposite direction. Appeals before legislative assemblies, constitutional conventions, and the highest courts have been respectfully heard and decided, while propositions for the consideration even of some honors to women in the church have uniformly been received with sneers and denunciations by leading denominations, who quote Scripture freely to maintain their position.

. . . In imitation of the high churches in England, we have some in this country in which boys from twelve to fifteen supply the place of women in the choir, that the sacred altars may not be defiled by the inferior sex—an early Christian idea. The discourses of clergymen, when they enlarge on the condition of woman read more like canons in the fifth century than sermons in the nineteenth, addressed to those who are their peers in religious thought and scientific attainment. The Rev. Morgan Dix's Lenten lectures last spring, and Bishop Littlejohn's last triennial sermon, are fair specimens. The latter recommends that all the liberal legislation of the past forty years for woman should be reversed, while the former is the chief obstacle in the way of woman's admission to Columbia College. And these fairly represent the sentiments of the vast majority, who never refer to the movement for woman's enfranchisement but with ridicule and contempt—sentiments that they insidiously infuse into all classes of women under their influence. None of the leading theological seminaries will admit women who are preparing for the ministry, and none of the leading denominations will ordain them when prepared. . . . And yet women are the chief supporters of the church to-day. They make the surplices and gowns, get up the fairs and donation-parties, and are the untiring beggars for its benefit. They supply its enthusiasm, and are continually making large bequests to its treasury; and their reward is still the echo of the old canon law of woman's subjection, from pulpit to pulpit throughout Christendom. Though England and America are the two nations in which the Christian religion is dominant, and can boast the highest type of womanhood, and the greatest number in every department of art, science, and literature, yet even here women have been compelled to clear their own way for every step in progress. Not one wrong has been righted until women themselves made organized resistance against it. In the face of every form of opposition they are throwing off the disabilities of the old common law, which Lord Brougham said long ago "was in relation to woman the opprobrium of the age and Christianity." And not until they make an organized resistance against the withering influence of the canon law, will they rid themselves of the moral disabilities growing out of the theologies of our times. When I was standing near the last resting-place of the Rev. Charles Kingsley not long ago, his warning words for woman, in a letter to John Stuart Mill, seemed lik a voice from the clouds, saying with new inspiration and power, "This will never be a good world for woman until the last remnant of the canon law is civilized off the face of the earth." (389, 389–90, 393, 396–97, 398, 398–99)

Notes

For long quotations, references are given first to pages from which quotation has been made; inclusive page numbers for the entire article are given in square brackets.

Chapter 1

[1]Basic books on American laws affecting women during the nineteenth century include Nelson Manfred Blake, *The Road to Reno: A History of Divorce in the United States* (New York: Macmillan, 1962); Eleanor Flexner, *Century of Struggle: The Woman's Rights Movement in the United States* (New York: Atheneum, 1972); George E. Howard, *A History of Matrimonial Institutions*, 3 vols. (Chicago: Univ. of Chicago Press, 1904); Leo Kanowitz, *Women and the Law: The Unfinished Revolution* (Albuquerque: Univ. of New Mexico Press, 1973).

On English laws, see R.H. Graveson and F.R. Crane, eds., *A Century of Family Law, 1857–1957* (London: Sweet and Maxwell, 1957); O.R. McGregor, *Divorce in England* (London: Heinemann, 1957); Erna Reiss, *Rights and Duties of Englishwomen: A Study in Law and Public Opinion* (Manchester: Sherratt and Hughes, 1934); Ray Strachey, *The Cause: A Short History of the Women's Movement in Great Britain* (London: G. Bell, 1928). In *Suffer and Be Still*, ed. Martha Vicinus (Bloomington: Indiana Univ. Press, 1972), Sections VI and VII of S. Barbara Kanner's bibliographical essay are especially helpful.

Some comparative studies are Richard J. Evans, *The Feminists: Women's Emancipation Movements in Europe, America, and Australasia, 1840–1920* (New York: Barnes and Noble, 1978); William O'Neill, *The Woman Movement: Feminism in the United States and England* (Chicago: Quadrangle, 1969); Albie Sachs and Joan Hoff Wilson,

212

Sexism and the Law: A Study of Male Beliefs and Legal Bias in Britain and the United States (London: Robertson, 1978). See also the bibliographic entries for factory legislation [Ch. 3, n. 18 & 27] and the Contagious Diseases Acts [Ch. 3, n. 71].

[2]Caroline H. Dall, *Woman's Rights under the Law* (Boston, 1861), p. viii. The lecture was incorporated into her important 1867 book, *The College, the Market, and the Court*. For an excellent account of what happened when women went beyond writing criticism and actually attempted to enter the legal profession, consult D. Kelly Weisberg, "Barred from the Bar: Women and Legal Education in the United States, 1870-1890," *Journal of Legal Education*, 28 (1977), 485-507.

[3]Barbara Leigh Smith Bodichon, *A Brief Summary in Plain Language of the Most Important Laws Concerning Women* (1854; rpt. London, 1869), p. 23.

[4]Bodichon, p. 21.

[5]William Blackstone, *Commentaries on the Laws of England* (London, 1765), I, xv. The legal fiction of marital unity suggests a simple situation; the legal reality was much more complex. In *Woman as Force in History* (New York: Macmillan, 1946), Mary R. Beard criticizes Stanton, Dall, and other American feminists for placing too much emphasis on Blackstone and for disregarding the rights women actually enjoyed under custom and equity. Much more detailed study of cases and court records is needed to distinguish polemics from practice.

[6]Dall, p. 34.

[7][J.W. Kaye], "The Non-Existence of Women," *North British Review*, 23 (1855), 558-59 [536-62].

[8][Margaret Oliphant], "The Laws Concerning Women," *Blackwood's*, 76 (1856), 379-82 [379-87].

[9]Ida H. Harper, *The Life and Work of Susan B. Anthony* (Indianapolis, 1898), I, 200-205.

[10]For biographical details on Norton's life, see Alice Acland, *Caroline Norton* (London: Constable, 1949) and Jane Grey Perkins, *The Life of Mrs. Norton* (New York: Holt, 1909). For an anthology of her work, see *Selected Writings of Caroline Norton*, ed. James O. Hoge and Jane Marcus (Delmar, N.Y.: Scholar's Facsimiles and Reprints, 1978). For background on the legal status of children, see Ivy Pinchbeck and Margaret Hewitt, *Children in English Society* (London: Routledge, 1973), esp. Vol. II, Ch. 13.

[11]*Hansard*, 14 February 1838, cc. 1114-23, and 30 July 1838, cc. 772-91.

[12][J.M. Kemble], "Custody of Infants Bill," *British and Foreign Quarterly Review*, 7 (1838), 280-81, 323, 330-31, 358 [269-411]. John Killham provides a good analysis of Kemble's article in *Tennyson and "The Princess": Reflections of an Age* (London: Athlone, 1958), pp. 149-69.

[13]Caroline Norton, *A Plain Letter to the Lord Chancellor on the Infant Custody Bill* (London, 1839), pp. 11, 94-95, 107-8.

[14]"The Infant Custody Bill," *Law Review Magazine*, 21 (1839), 145; [Nathaniel Ogle], "The Custody of Infants' Bill," *Fraser's*, 19 (1839), 214.

[15]Harriet Martineau, *A History of the Thirty Year's Peace* (London, 1878), IV, 10.

[16]Some of the best research on women's legal history has been done about New York, including Norma Basch's "Invisible Women: The Legal Fiction of Marital Unity in Nineteenth-Century America," *Feminist Studies*, 5 (1979), 346-66; and Peggy Rabkin's "The Origins of Law Reform: The Social Significance of the Nineteenth-Century Codification Movement and Its Contribution to the Passage of the Early Married Women's Property Acts," *Buffalo Law Review*, 24 (1975), 683-760.

Notes   213

[17]Strachey, p. 72.

[18]The petition is reprinted in Cornelia Cornwallis' fine essay "The Property of Married Women," *Westminster Review*, 66 (1856), 331–60; see also her "Capabilities and Disabilities of Women," *Westminster Review*, 67 (1857), 42–72.

[19]Sir Richard Bethall, *Hansard*, 14 May 1857, c. 275; quoted in Lee Holcombe's excellent article "Victorian Wives and Property: Reform of the Married Women's Property Law, 1857–1882," in *A Widening Sphere*, ed. Martha Vicinus (Bloomington: Indiana Univ. Press, 1977), pp. 3–28.

[20]Caroline Norton, *A Letter to the Queen on Lord Chancellor Cranworth's Marriage and Divorce Bill* (London, 1855), pp. 98–99, 84–85, 82, 152–53.

[21]Wendell Phillips, Address to the Tenth National Woman's Rights Convention, May 10, 1860, rpt. *History of Woman Suffrage*, ed. Elizabeth Cady Stanton, Susan B. Anthony, Matilda Joslyn Gage (New York, 1881), I, 707. Linton defines her position in *Household Words*: "Rights and Wrongs of Women," and "One of Our Legal Fictions," 9 (1854), 158–61 and 257–60; "Marriage Gaolers," 13 (1856), 583–85.

[22]"The Working of the New Divorce Bill," *Englishwoman's Journal*, 1 (1858), 340. Sally Mitchell's provocative new book, *The Fallen Angel: Chastity, Class and Women's Reading, 1835–1880* (Bowling Green, O.: Bowling Green Univ. Popular Press, 1981), is relevant here. Mitchell shows how the literary images of unchaste women are affected by the concepts of woman as property and woman as channel for transmitting property. In the section about the penny weekly magazines of the 1870s, Mitchell concludes that the heroines admired by working women demonstrated a greater sense of individuality and choice than their middle-class counterparts—partly as a result of the Matrimonial Causes Act of 1857. The working woman was less dependent on her husband because she knew that she could retain control of her earnings if he deserted her.

[23]Lord St. Leonards, *Hansard*, 25 May 1857, c. 800; quoted in Holcombe, p. 12.

[24][Frances Power Cobbe], "Criminals, Idiots, Women and Minors: Is the Classification Sound?" *Fraser's*, 78 (1868), 778–90 [777–94].

[25]Holcombe, p. 27. To discover whether judges enforced the new laws, more investigation of case law is needed. Basch's study of New York shows that judges, jurists, and legislators continued to uphold the common-law doctrine of marital unity long after the property acts were passed.

[26]The essay is printed in John Stuart Mill and Harriet Taylor Mill, *Essays on Sex Equality*, ed. Alice S. Rossi (Chicago: Univ. of Chicago Press, 1970), pp. 67–84.

[27]For the Owen-Robinson and Blackwell-Stone marriage documents, see *History of Woman Suffrage*, I, 294–95, 260–61. Mill's repudiation of the marriage contract is reprinted in *The Letters of John Stuart Mill*, ed. H.R.S. Elliott (London: Longmans, 1910), I, 158–59.

[28]The following are helpful here: Louis J. Kern, *An Ordered Love: Sex Roles and Sexuality in Victorian Utopias* (Chapel Hill: Univ. of North Carolina Press, 1980); Raymond L. Muncy, *Sex and Marriage in Utopian Communities* (Bloomington: Indiana Univ. Press, 1973); and Taylor Stoehr, *Free Love in America: A Documentary History* (New York: AMS Press, 1979). Carol Weisbrod and Pamela Sheingorn analyze the law's attempt to regulate one kind of experimental marriage—polygamy—and its effect on the women's movement in "*Reynolds v. United States*: Nineteenth Century Forms of Marriage and the Status of Women," *Connecticut Law Review*, 10 (1978), 828–58.

[29]The Royal Commission on Divorce reported that an absolute divorce would cost at least £700–800 in 1850, but in many cases the expenses were

considerably higher. In 150 years, only four cases were recorded of a wife obtaining an absolute divorce by private act of Parliament. Neither *divorce a mensa* nor *divorce a vinculo* was common. According to John D. Baird ("Divorce and Matrimonial Causes: An Aspect of *Hard Times*," *Victorian Studies*, 20 [1977], 400–12), an average of 4.4 divorce acts was passed annually from 1841 to 1845, while judicial separations averaged 9 per year between 1845 and 1850. See also Margaret K. Woodhouse, "The Marriage and Divorce Bill of 1857," *American Journal of Legal History*, 3 (1959), 260–75.

³⁰Taylor's unpublished essay on divorce is in *Essays on Sex Equality*, pp. 84–87.

³¹Lord Cranworth, *Hansard*, 25 May 1857, c. 813. Keith Thomas gives a modern perspective on the double standard in "The Double Standard," *Journal of the History of Ideas*, 20 (1959), 195–215. On the social and literary significance of adultery, see Tony Tanner's *Adultery in the Novel: Contract and Transgression* (Baltimore: Johns Hopkins Univ. Press, 1979).

³²T.D. Woolsey, "Divorce—Part IV," *New Englander*, 27 (1868), 44. His influential series appeared in five parts during 1867–68.

³³In addition to Blake and Howard, the reader interested in American attitudes toward divorce might consult James Harwood Barnett, *Divorce and the American Divorce Novel, 1858–1937* (Philadelphia: Univ. of Pennsylvania Press, 1939); and William L. O'Neill, "Divorce as a Moral Issue," in *Remember the Ladies*, ed. Carol R.V. George (Syracuse: Syracuse Univ. Press, 1975), 127–44, and *Divorce in the Progressive Era* (New Haven: Yale Univ. Press, 1967).

³⁴Their disagreement was carried on in the editorial pages of the *Tribune* during March and April of 1860. It is reprinted in Greeley's *Recollections of a Busy Life* (New York, 1868), pp. 571–617.

³⁵Quoted in Blake, p. 88.

³⁶*History of Woman Suffrage*, I, 716–35. The controversy receives further comment in Blake, Ch. 5; Alma Lutz, *Created Equal: A Biography of Elizabeth Cady Stanton* (New York: John Day, 1940), pp. 111–18; and Elizabeth Cady Stanton, *Eighty Years and More* (London, 1898), pp. 215–25.

³⁷"To Susan B. Anthony," June 27, 1870, *Elizabeth Cady Stanton as Revealed in Her Letters, Diary and Reminiscences*, ed. Theodore Stanton and Harriet Stanton Blanch (New York: Harper, 1922), II, 127. Two of Stanton's speeches from this period, "Speech to the McFarland-Richardson Protest Meeting" (May, 1869) and "Home Life" (c. 1875) are included in Elizabeth Cady Stanton and Susan B. Anthony, *Correspondence, Writings, Speeches*, ed. Ellen Carol DuBois (New York: Schocken, 1981).

³⁸Quoted in Blake, p. 106.

³⁹These are the figures provided by Carroll D. Wright's important 1891 government report. See Blake, Ch. 10.

⁴⁰Laura Bullard, "What Justifies Marriage?" *Revolution*, 6 (August 18, 1870), 104.

⁴¹"An Appeal Against Female Suffrage," *Nineteenth Century*, 25 (1889), 781–88; see also the reply of M.G. Fawcett and M.M. Dilke in 26 (1889), 86–103.

⁴²Flexner, p. 295.

⁴³Some American historians, including William O'Neill and Carroll Smith Rosenberg, have found the effects of the franchise negligible and the campaign irrelevant to most women's lives; see *Everyone Was Brave: The Rise and Fall of Feminism in America* (New York: Quadrangle, 1969) and "The New Woman and the New History," *Feminist Studies*, 3 (1975), 185–98. Two recent studies stress the radical nature of suffrage in its nineteenth-century context. In *At Odds:*

Women and the Family in America from the Revolution to the Present (New York: Oxford, 1980), Carl Degler maintains that the Victorians saw suffrage as an attack on the family. In *Feminism and Suffrage: The Emergence of an Independent Women's Movement in America, 1848-1869* (Ithaca, N.Y.: Cornell Univ. Press, 1978), Ellen DuBois studies suffrage as a social movement, "the first independent movement of women for their own liberation."

44Early and still useful sources for suffragism in England include Helen Blackburn, *Women's Suffrage: A Record of the Women's Suffrage Movement in the British Isles* (1902; rpt. New York: Source Book Press, 1978); Millicent Garrett Fawcett, *Women's Suffrage: A Short History of a Great Movement* (1912; rpt. New York: Source Book Press, 1970); and Strachey. Good twentieth-century studies are Roger Fulford, *Votes for Women* (London: Faber & Faber, 1957); Brian Harrison, *Separate Spheres: The Opposition to Women's Suffrage in Britain* (New York: Holmes & Meier, 1978); and Constance Rover, *Women's Suffrage and Party Politics in Britain, 1866-1914* (Toronto: Univ. of Toronto Press, 1967). By studying the experiences of working-class women, Jill Liddington and Jill Norris challenge the idea that suffrage was a middle-class movement; see *One Hand Tied Behind Us: The Rise of the Woman's Suffrage Movement* (London: Virago Press, 1978). The role of women writers in the suffrage movement has been ably chronicled by Elaine Showalter in Ch. 8 of *A Literature of Their Own* (Princeton: Princeton Univ. Press (1977).

45The petition and the comments from the 1866 *Law Times* are reprinted in Blackburn's *Women's Suffrage*, pp. 54 and 58.

46See, for example, Barbara Bodichon, *Reasons for the Enfranchisement of Women* and *Objections to the Enfranchisement of Women* (London, 1866); Lydia Becker, "Female Suffrage," *Contemporary Review*, 4 (1867), 307-16; F.P. Cobbe, *Why Women Desire the Franchise* (London, 1869); and Helen Taylor, "The Claims of Women to the Franchise," *Westminster Review*, 87 (1867), 63-69.

47John Stuart Mill et al., *Hansard*, 20 May 1867, cc. 817-45. The Court of Dahomey, which Laing cited in his reply to Mill, was notorious for using women warriors and for encouraging human sacrifice. Sir Richard Burton had recently described the warriors' activities as evidence of women's bloodthirsty instincts in *A Mission to Gelele, King of Dahome* (London, 1864).

Although the *Illustrated London News* announced that Mill had given the best modern address on the Woman Question, most of the other papers were negative. Emily Faithfull reprinted their responses in "Admission of Women to the Electoral Franchise," *Victoria Magazine*, 9 (1867), 236-70. Although the magazine was not a strong supporter of suffrage, it is an excellent source of information on meetings, press responses, and public opinion. *London Review* chided Mill for being studious and inexperienced with women. *Saturday Review* railed against "the unfitness and impropriety of allowing women an active share in public affairs." Invoking a conventional argument, the *Times* used one disability to sustain another: because common law prevented women from accepting the responsibilities of citizenship, such as jury service, they were not entitled to claim its rights. While these journals urged married women to rely on the "natural affection" of their husbands, Margaret Oliphant spoke plaintively for single women who felt insulted by Mill's proposal: "He has made us out to be something less than woman, something almost man" ("The Great Unrepresented," *Blackwood's*, 100 [1866], 371). In 1869 *The Subjection of Women* would provoke much greater fury because of its criticism of the sexual tyranny in marriage.

48"To Priscilla McLaren," December 12, 1868, *Later Letters of J.S. Mill*, ed.

Francis E. Mineka and Dwight N. Lindley (Toronto: Univ. of Toronto Press, 1972), XVI, 1521.

⁴⁹Millicent Garrett Fawcett, *What I Remember* (1925; rpt. Westport, Conn.: Hyperion Press, 1976), p. 64.

⁵⁰Evelyn Pugh, "John Stuart Mill, Harriet Taylor, and Women's Rights in America," *Canadian Journal of History*, 13 (1978), 428–29.

⁵¹Rover, pp. 22–52.

⁵²In *Sexism and the Law*, Sachs and Wilson discuss the Manchester voters in relation to "an issue with which British judges were to wrestle for six decades, namely whether or not a woman could in law be recognized as a person" (p. 22).

⁵³For recent work on women abolitionists, see Blanche Glassman Hersh, *The Slavery of Sex: Feminist Abolitionists in America* (Urbana: Univ. of Illinois Press, 1978).

⁵⁴Quoted by DuBois, *Feminism and Suffrage*, p. 61. She gives a detailed account of Stanton and Anthony's involvement in the Fourteenth and Fifteenth Amendments.

⁵⁵See, for example, Victoria Woodhull's Memorial and Petition to the Judiciary Committee of the House of Representatives, December 19, 1870, and January 11, 1871; rpt. in *History of Woman Suffrage*, II, 443–48.

⁵⁶Harper, *The Life and Work of Susan B. Anthony*, II, 977, 981–84, 986–87, 989 [977–92]. On her arrest and trial, see Harper, I, 409–48; *History of Woman Suffrage*, II, 630–715; and Sachs and Wilson, pp. 85–94.

⁵⁷Rover, pp. 118–20; Strachey, pp. 177–78; and Josephine Kamm, *Rapiers and Battleaxes* (London: George Allen, 1966), p. 137. For Gladstone's speech, see *Hansard*, 10 June 1884, cc. 1962–63.

⁵⁸Emmeline Pankhurst, *My Own Story* (New York: Hearst, 1914), pp. 16–17.

Chapter 2

¹Primary and secondary documents on Victorian sexuality are so numerous that we can make no attempt to list even a fraction of them here. Primary texts are copiously cited in John S. and Robin M. Haller's *The Physician and Sexuality in Victorian America* (Urbana: Univ. of Illinois Press, 1974) and in G.J. Barker-Benfield's *Horrors of the Half-Known Life* (New York: Harper, 1976). Secondary studies before 1976, including the important essays in *Clio's Consciousness Raised*, ed. Mary S. Hartman and Lois Banner (New York: Harper, 1974) and by Carroll Smith-Rosenberg and Charles E. Rosenberg, are reviewed by Martha H. Verbrugge in "Women and Medicine in Nineteenth-Century America," *Signs*, 1 (1976), 957–72. Nancy F. Cott provides an extensive bibliography of works through 1977 in her excellent "Passionlessness: An Interpretation of Victorian Sexual Ideology, 1790–1850," *Signs*, 4 (1978), 219–36. For other important recent work, see F. Barry Smith, "Sexuality in Britain, 1800–1900" in *A Widening Sphere*, ed. Martha Vicinus (Bloomington: Indiana Univ. Press, 1977); Vern L. Bullough and Bonnie Bullough, *Sin, Sickness, & Sanity* (New York: Garland, 1977); Lorna Duffin, "The Conspicuous Consumptive: Woman as Invalid" in *The Nineteenth-Century Woman*, ed. Sara Delamont and Duffin (New York: Barnes & Noble, 1978); Barbara Caine, "Woman's 'Natural' State: Marriage and the 19th Century Feminists," *Hecate*, 3 (1977), 84–102; Fraser Harrison, *The Dark Angel* (New York: Universe 1978); Deborah Gorham, "The 'Maiden Tribute of Modern Babylon' Re-Examined: Child Prostitution and the Idea of Childhood in Late-

Victorian England," *Victorian Studies*, 21 (1978), 353–79; Judith M. Hughes, "Self-Suppression & Attachment: Mid-Victorian Emotional Life," *Massachusetts Review*, 19 (1978), 541–55; Barbara Ehrenreich and Deirdre English, *For Her Own Good* (Garden City, N.Y.: Anchor, 1978); Elizabeth Fee, "Psychology, Sexuality, and Social Control in Victorian England," *Social Science Quarterly*, 58 (1978), 632–46; D'Ann Campbell, "Women's Life in Utopia: The Shaker Experiment in Sexual Equality Reappraised—1810 to 1860," *New England Quarterly*, 51 (1978), 23–38; William G. Shade, "A Mental Passion: Female Sexuality in Victorian America," *International Journal of Women's Studies* 1 (1978): 13–29; Susan Sleeth Mosedale, "Science Corrupted: Victorian Biologists Consider 'The Woman Question," *Journal of Historical Biology* 11 (1978): 1–55. Elaine Showalter "Victorian Women and Insanity," *Victorian Studies*, 23 (1980), 157–81; Carl N. Degler, "Women's Sexuality in 19th Century America" in his *At Odds* (New York: Oxford Univ. Press, 1980), pp. 249–78.

²Parvin's defense of moderation and the quotation appear in Barker-Benfield (p. 113), whose discussion of "spermatic economy" is the best available.

³Dr. William Acton, *The Functions and Disorders of the Reproductive Organs* (London, 1857); references will be incorporated into the text.

⁴Steven Marcus, *The Other Victorians* (New York: Basic Books, 1964), p. 26.

⁵Besides Barker-Benfield, the Hallers, and the Bulloughs, recent work on masturbation which provides both references to Victorian texts and analyses of Victorian practices are: René Spitz, "Authority and Masturbation," *Psychoanalytic Quarterly*, 21 (1952), 490–527; E.H. Hare, "Masturbatory Insanity: The History of an Idea," *Journal of Mental Science*, 108 (1962), 1–25; Robert H. MacDonald, "The Frightful Consequences of Onanism," *Journal of the History of Ideas*, 28 (1967), 423–31; Gerhart S. Schwartz, "Devices to Prevent Masturbation," *Medical Aspects of Human Sexuality*, 7 (1973), 141–53; Ronald G. Walters, *Primers for Prudery* (Englewood Cliffs, N.J.: Prentice-Hall, 1974); Mary S. Hartman, "Child Abuse and Self-Abuse: Two Victorian Cases," *History of Childhood Quarterly*, 2 (1974), 221–48. For arguments for partial or complete marital continence, see: Dr. John Cowan, *The Science of a New Life* (New York, 1878); Mrs. E.B. Duffey, *The Relations of the Sexes* (New York, 1876); Dr. Augustus K. Gardner, *Conjugal Sins* (New York, 1870) and *Our Children* (Hartford, Conn., 1872). For the Purity Crusaders, see David J. Pivar, *Purity Crusade* (Westport, Conn.: Greenwood, 1973) and Edward J. Bristow's *Vice and Vigilance: Purity Movements in Britain Since 1700* (Dublin: Gill and Macmillan, 1977).

⁶Drysdale's book was titled *Physical, Sexual, and Natural Religion* on its appearance in 1854. With the third edition (London, 1860) came a new fourth section, "Social Science," and the new title *The Elements of Social Science*; references will be incorporated into the text. Very little study has been devoted to this most undervalued of major Victorian works. Dr. Charles R. Drysdale's "Introduction" to the 1905 posthumous edition of *Elements* gives the only contemporary account that we have of his brother; Margaret Sanger's glowing "The Vision of George Drysdale," *Birth Control Review*, 7 (1923), 177–79, 198–201, 210, 225–27, 258–61, draws upon information provided by Drysdale's sister-in-law, Dr. Alice Vickery Drysdale. Other contemporary responses to so radical a book are inevitably few and fierce. Charles Bradlaugh's "defense" of the *Elements* (*Jesus, Shelley, and Malthus; or Pious Poverty and Heterodox Happiness* [London, 1861]) was answered by Charles R. Mackay's scathing chapter in *Life of Charles Bradlaugh, M.P.* (London, 1888), pp. 228–46. Among what were no doubt many hostile pamphlets are Joseph

Barker's *A Review of "The Elements of Social Science"* [*by George Drysdale*] (London, 1863) and Peter Agate's *Sexual Economy as Taught by Charles Bradlaugh* (London, n.d.). We have found only two reviews of the *Elements*: the *Examiner* piece cited by Sanger and a *British Journal of Homeopathy* essay for 1860; Peter Fryer (*The Birth Controllers* [London: Secker and Warburg, 1965]) notes two other contemporary responses, by George Jacob Holyoake and George Standring (p. 297). Among major Victorians, only three confess familiarity with *Elements*. Havelock Ellis' debt to Drysdale is fully documented in *My Life* (Boston: Houghton Mifflin, 1939), pp. 114, 132, 163. For the ambivalent response of Bertrand Russell's father, Lord Amberley, see Fryer (pp. 123–31). We are indebted to Mr. Mark McLaughlin for discovery of a comparable ambivalence on the part of J.S. Mill. To Bradlaugh's claim that he had endorsed the *Elements*, Mill replied in 1870, "I have most certainly never on any occasion whatever, in public or private, expressed any approbation of the book entitled *Elements of Social Science*" (*The Later Letters of John Stuart Mill, 1849–1873*, ed. Francis E. Mineka and Dwight N. Lindley [Toronto: Univ. of Toronto Press, 1972], XVII, 1768). A year before, however, Mill had written to Gustave D'Eichtal that "sans avoir lu tout le livre [*Elements*], j'en pris un pen connaissance à l'epoque de sa première publication: J'y trouvai d'excellentes choses, avec quelques autres qui ne me plaissaient pas. Je crois l'auteur, au reste, un homme éclairé, et tres zélé pour la plupart des bonnes causes" [Without having read the whole book, I took note of it at the time of its initial publication: I found in it some excellent things, along with others which did not please me. I believe the author is, all in all, an enlightened man, and is for the most part zealous on behalf of good causes.] (*John Stuart Mill: Correspondance Inédite avec Gustave D'Eichtal*, ed. Eugène D'Eichtal [Paris, 1898], p. 217). Most important among the few recent discussions of Drysdale are Norman E. Himes's *Medical History of Contraception* (New York: Gamut, 1963), pp. 233–38; J.A. and Olive Banks's *Feminism and Family Planning in Victorian England* (New York: Schocken, 1964), pp. 116–21; Fryer, pp. 110–12, 123, 160, 166, 297–98; Lloyd Fernando's "The Radical Ideology of the New Woman," *Southern Review*, 2 (1966–67), 206–22; and Rosanna Ledbetter's *A History of the Malthusian League* (Columbus: Ohio State Univ. Press, 1976), pp. 9–17, 26–28, 32–33.

[7]Acton's sales are indicated by the fact that *Functions* went through fourteen Victorian editions in English (six in Britain, eight in America), the last being in 1895, a full twenty years after Acton's death. *Elements* went through thirty-five editions of 88,000 copies in English by 1905, plus numerous continental translations and abridgments. Although *Elements* had inevitably less public visibility than *Functions*, its influence, particularly among the British and continental proletariat and intelligentsia, was considerable. Acton and Mackay would not have attacked so fiercely an uninfluential opponent.

[8]Taylor Stoehr's *Free Love in America* (New York: AMS, 1979) summarizes previous scholarship and analyzes all aspects of the free love movement. For Victoria Woodhull in particular, see Johanna Johnston's *Mrs. Satan* (New York: Putnam's, 1967) and M.M. Marberry's *Vicky: A Biography of Victoria C. Woodhull* (New York: Funk & Wagnalls, 1967).

[9]Dr. George H. Napheys, *The Physical Life of Woman* (Philadelphia, 1869); quotations are taken from the "rewritten, enlarged, and revised" Philadelphia edition of 1876, pp. 96, 99.

[10]Orson S. Fowler, *Creative and Sexual Science* (Philadelphia, 1875), p. 680; later references will be incorporated into the text. For more on Fowler's belief in

Notes   219

sexual equality, and for his popularity and that of other family members, see Madeleine B. Stern's *Heads and Headlines: The Phrenological Fowlers* (Norman: Univ. of Oklahoma Press, 1971).

11Hooker and Stanton are quoted by Linda Gordon in *Clio's Consciousness Raised*, p. 56.

12Gordon S. Haight, *George Eliot: A Biography* (New York: Oxford Univ. Press, 1968), p. 205.

13J.A. Banks (*Prosperity and Parenthood* [London: Routledge & Kegan Paul, 1954]) emphasizes the husband and economic pressures. For historians stressing woman's role, see Daniel Scott Smith's "Family Limitation, Sexual Control, and Domestic Feminism in Victorian America" in *Clio's Consciousness Raised*, pp. 119–36; Patricia Branca's *Silent Sisterhood* (London: Croom Helm, 1975); and Linda Gordon's *Woman's Body, Woman's Right* (New York: Grossman, 1976). For other recent works on birth control besides Ledbetter and Fryer, see Michael A. La Sorte's "Nineteenth Century Family Planning Practices," *Journal of Psychohistory*, 4 (1976), 163–83; Vern L. Bullough's "Women: Birth Control, Prostitution, and the Fox," *Transaction Conference Group Society of Administrative History*, 6 (1976), 20–31; James Reed's *From Private Vice to Public Virtue* (New York: Basic Books, 1978); Angus McLaren's *Birth Control in Nineteenth-Century England* (London: Croom Helm, 1978). For works specifically on abortion, see R. Sauer's "Infanticide and Abortion in Nineteenth-Century Britain" *Population Studies*, 32 (1978), 80–93; Patricia Knight's "Women and Abortion in Victorian and Edwardian England" and Angus McLaren's "Woman's Work and the Regulation of Family Size: The Question of Abortion in 19th Century England," *History Workshop*, 4 (1977), 57–68 and 70–81; and Degler's "Abortion: Women's Last Resort" in *At Odds*, pp. 227–48.

14Ann Douglas Wood, *Clio's Consciousness Raised*, p. 4.

15Jean Jacques Rousseau, *Emile* (1762; London: Dent, 1911), p. 324; J.H. Kellogg, *Ladies' Guide in Health and Disease* (Des Moines, 1883, rpt. Battle Creek, Mich., 1910), p. 371.

16For conflicting views of Mitchell, see Wood, and Regina Morantz in *Clio's Consciousness Raised*, pp. 38–53.

17Marc H. Hollender, "Conversion Hysteria: A Post-Freudian Reinterpretation of 19th Century Psychosocial Data," *Archives of General Psychiatry*, 26 (1972), 314 [311–14]. The position of opisthotonos is reached when the back is bowed so far that only the heels and the back of the head are touching the bed.

18For the growth of and attacks upon medicine, see William G. Rothstein's *American Physicians in the Nineteenth Century* (Baltimore: Johns Hopkins Univ. Press, 1972), pp. 125–97.

19Mary S. Hartman, *Victorian Murderesses* (New York: Schocken, 1977), p. 233.

20Cott and Hughes are particularly strong in their arguments about the advantages to women of sexual restriction.

21For the brain-weight controversy, see the Hallers, pp. 47–68; also *Madness and Morals*, ed. Vieda Skultans (London: Routledge and Kegan Paul, 1975), and Susan Phinney Conrad's *Perish the Thought* (New York: Oxford Univ. Press, 1976), pp. 15–44.

22J.V.C. Smith, *The Ways of Women in their Physical, Moral and Intellectual Relations* (Hartford, Conn., 1875), pp. 342–46.

23Eliza W. Farnham, *Woman and Her Era* (New York, 1864), I, 26.

²⁴J. McGrigor Allan, "On the Differences in the Minds of Men and Women," *Journal, Royal Anthropological Society of London*, 7 (1869), ccx [cciv-ccxix].

²⁵Lydia Ernestine Becker, "On the Study of Science by Women," *Contemporary Review*, 10 (1869), 388 [386-404]. For recent work on what Victorian science said about woman's learning capacity, see Flavia Alaya's "Victorian Science and the 'Genius' of Woman," *Journal of the History of Ideas*, 38 (1977), 261-80. Michele L. Aldrich reviews work on the Victorian period in "Women in Science," *Signs*, 4 (1978), 126-35.

²⁶As an introduction to the enormous literature on women and medicine, see Mary Roth Walsh's *"Doctors Wanted, No Women Need Apply"* (New Haven: Yale Univ. Press 1977); Sandra L. Chaff's *Women in Medicine: A Bibliography of the Literature on Women Physicians* (Metuchen, N.J.: Scarecrow, 1977); and Dorothy Rosenthal Mandelbaum's "Women in Medicine," *Signs*, 4 (1978), 136-45. For recent work besides Ehrenreich and English, see Jean Donnison's "Medical Women and Lady Midwives: A Case Study in Medical and Feminist Politics," *Women's Studies*, 3 (1976), 229-50, and *Midwives and Medical Men* (London: Heinemann, 1977); Ann Roberts' "Mothers and Babies: The Wet-nurse and Her Employer in Mid-Nineteenth Century England," *Women's Studies*, 3 (1976), 279-94; Richard W. Wertz and Dorothy C. Wertz's *Lying In* (New York: Free Press, 1977); Janet Bogdan's "Care or Cure? Childbirth Practices in Nineteenth Century America," *Feminist Studies*, 4 (1978), 92-99; Mary Roth Walsh's "Images of Women Doctors in Popular Fiction: A Comparison of the 19th and 20th Centuries," *Journal of American Culture*, 1 (1978), 276-84; Steven J. Peitzman's "The Quiet Life of a Philadelphia Medical Woman: Mary Willits (1855-1902)," *Journal of the American Medical Woman's Association*, 34 (1979), 443-57.

²⁷Mary A.E. Wager, "Women as Physicians," *Galaxy*, 6 (1868), 775 [774-89]. For Blackwell's event-filled life, her many publications on women in medicine, and her numerous biographers, see Dorothy Clarke Wilson's *Lone Woman: The Story of Elizabeth Blackwell, the First Woman Doctor* (Boston: Little, Brown, 1970).

²⁸For Mary Gove Nichols, see Helen Beal Woodward's chapter "Brown Bread, Cold Water and Sex: Mary Gove Nichols" in *The Bold Women* (New York: Farrar, Straus, 1953) and John B. Blake's "Mary Gove Nichols, Prophetess of Health," *Proceedings of the American Philosophical Society*, 106 (1962), 219-34. For Emma Willard, see Alma Lutz's *Emma Willard: Pioneer Educator of American Women* (Boston: Beacon, 1964). For Harriot Hunt, her own *Glances and Glimpses* (Boston, 1856; rpt. New York: Source Book, 1970), and Wood in *Clio's Consciousness Raised*, pp. 44-47; for Paulina Wright Davis, see Alma Lutz's *Created Equal* (New York: Day, 1940) and Rheta Childe Dorr's *Susan B. Anthony* (New York: AMS, 1970).

²⁹The best overall history of women in science remains H.J. Mozans' *Woman in Science* (New York: Appleton, 1913; rpt. Cambridge: MIT Press, 1974). For discussions of Victorian woman's troubles in science and with science education, see Thomas Woody's *A History of Woman's Education in the United States* (New York: Science Press, 1929); Edna Yost's *American Women of Science* (Philadelphia: Lippincott, 1943); Lloyd G. Stephenson's "Science Down the Drain," *Bulletin of the History of Medicine*, 29 (1955), 1-26; Barbara Welter's "Anti-Intellectualism and the American Woman, 1800-1860," *Mid-America*, 48 (1966), 258-70, rpt. in *Dimity Convictions* (Athens: Ohio Univ. Press, 1976), pp. 77-82; J.H. Wilson's "Dancing Dogs of the Colonial Period: Women Scientists," *Early American Literature*, 7 (1972/3), 225-35; Margaret Rossiter's "Women Scientists in America before 1920," *American Scientist*, 62 (1974), 312-23; Sally Gregory Kohlstedt's

Notes

"In from the Periphery: American Women in Science, 1830-1880," *Signs*, 4 (1978), 81-96; Stephanie Morris' "The Franklin Institute: Women and Technology," *Signs*, 4 (1978), 173-74; and Aldrich.

30Mary Somerville, *Personal Reflections of Mary Somerville* (Boston, 1874), p. 88. For other adverse reactions to Somerville's scientific studies, see pp. 27-29, 37, 87. For recent work on Somerville, see A.W. Richeson's "Mary Somerville," *Scripta Mathematica*, 8 (1941), 5-13; George Basalla's "Mary Somerville: A Neglected Popularizer of Science," *New Scientist*, 17 (1963), 531-33; Elizabeth C. Patterson's "Mary Somerville," *The British Journal for the History of Science*, 4 (1968-69), 311-39, and "The Case of Mary Somerville: An Aspect of Nineteenth-Century Science," *Proceedings of the American Philosophical Society*, 118 (1974), 269-75; Bruce Toth and Emily Toth's "Mary Who?" *The Johns Hopkins Magazine*, 29 (1978), 25-29. For America's closest analogue to Mary Somerville, the astronomer Maria Mitchell, see Eve Merriam's chapter in *Growing Up Female in America* (Garden City, N.Y.: Doubleday, 1971), pp. 75-90, and Sally Gregory Kohlstedt's "Maria Mitchell: The Advancement of Women in Science," *New Scientist*, 51 (1978), 39-63. Mitchell discusses with pride and enthusiasm her 1858 meeting with Somerville in Florence (*Maria Mitchell: Life, Letters, & Journals*, ed. Phebe Mitchell Kendall [Boston, 1896], pp. 159-65).

31"Mrs. Somerville," *Saturday Review*, 37 (1874), 53 [53-55]. For other Victorian responses to Somerville's death and to her posthumously published autobiography, see "Editor's Table," *Godey's Ladies' Book*, 88 (1874), 377-78; "Contemporary Literature," *British Quarterly Review*, 59 (1874), 226-28; "Mary Somerville," *Chamber's Journal*, 11 (1874), 33-36; "Recent Literature," *Atlantic Monthly*, 33 (1874), 494-96; "Literature of the Day," *Lippincott's Magazine*, 13 (1874), 518-20; "History and Biography," *Westminster Review*, 101 (1874), 575-77.

32Mary W. Hale, "Comparative Intellectual Character of the Sexes," *Godey's Ladies' Book*, 20 (1840), 273-75.

33Quoted by Patterson from unpublished Somerville papers ("The Case. . . ," p. 274). The Mary Shelley quotation is from *The Letters of Mary W. Shelley*, ed. Frederick L. Jones (Norman: Univ. of Oklahoma Press, 1944), II, 98; the George Eliot quotation is from "Woman in France: Madame de Sable," *Westminster Review*, 62, (1854), 448-73, rpt. in *Essays of George Eliot*, ed. Thomas Pinney (New York: Columbia Univ. Press, 1963), pp. 56 [52-81].

34Mary Somerville, "Letter to Josephine Butler" in *Woman's Work and Woman's Culture*, ed. Butler (London, 1869), pp. 138-40.

35Hawthorne says in *The Scarlet Letter* that "every successive mother [for a series of six or seven generations] has transmitted to her [female] child a fainter bloom, a more delicate and briefer beauty, and a slighter physical frame . . . than her own" (Ch. 2). Martineau's criticism of the health of American women (*Society in America* [New York, 1837], II, 58, 260-67) was echoed repeatedly before Beecher took up the cry (*Letters to the People on Health and Happiness* [New York, 1855]), a cry which her sister repeated in the 1860s (Harriet Beecher Stowe, "Bodily Religion: A Sermon on Good Health," *Atlantic Monthly*, 18 [1866], 85-93). For Catharine Beecher's many writings on health, see Kathryn Kish Sklar's *Catharine Beecher* (New Haven: Yale Univ. Press, 1973), pp. 204-15. Worries about the health of British women surfaced at least as early as 1846 in the anonymous *The English Nation* (London, 1846), pp. 133-34. One of the most comprehensive of the British studies concerned itself with the health of both American and English women: "American Women: Their Health and Education," *Westminster Review*, 102 (1874), 456-99. For recent work on the Victorian health controversy, see

Barker-Benfield, the Hallers, Smith-Rosenberg and Rosenberg, plus William B. Walker's "The Health Reform Movement in the United States, 1830-1870" (Ph.D. dissertation, Johns Hopkins, 1955), Barbara Cross's *The Educated Woman in America* (New York: Teacher's College Press, 1965), pp. 1, 6-13, 51-101; John R. Bett's "Mind and Body in Early American Thought," *Journal of American History*, 54 (1968), 787-805; Page Smith's *Daughters of the Promised Land* (Boston: Little, Brown, 1970), pp. 131-40; Sheila Ryan Johansson's "Sex and Death in Victorian England" in *A Widening Sphere*, pp. 163-81; Ronald Numbers' *Prophetess of Health: A Study of Ellen G. White* (New York: Harper & Row, 1976); Helene E. Roberts' "The Exquisite Slave: The Role of Clothes in the Making of the Victorian Woman," *Signs*, 2 (1977), 554-69; and Bruce Haley's *The Healthy Body and Victorian Culture* (Cambridge, Mass.: Harvard Univ. Press, 1978).

[36]"Recent Literature," *Atlantic Monthly*, 32 (1873), 739 [737-56].

[37]Dr. Augustus K. Gardner, "Physical Decline of American Women," *The Knickerbocker*, 55 (1860), 37-52.

[38]Edward H. Clarke, M.D., *Sex in Education* (Boston, 1873); references will be incorporated into the text. "Editor's Literary Record," *Harper's*, 49 (1874), 287 [287-88]. A complete bibliography of the Clarke controversy has never been compiled. We have catalogued at least thirty-four items between 1874 and 1882. For modern work on this controversy and on Victorian attitudes toward menstruation generally, see Butt, the Bulloughs, and Willystine Goodsell's *The Education of Women* (New York: Macmillan, 1923); Dorothy McGuigan's *A Dangerous Experiment* (Ann Arbor: Center for Continuing Education of Women, 1970), pp. 53-58; Elaine and English Showalter's "Victorian Women and Menstruation" in *Suffer and Be Still*, ed. Martha Vicinus (Bloomington: Indiana Univ. Press, 1972), pp. 38-44; Joan N. Burstyn's "Education and Sex: The Medical Case Against Higher Education for Women in England, 1870-1900," *Proceedings of the American Philological Society*, 117 (1973), 79-89; Janice Law Trecker's "Sex, Science and Education," *American Quarterly*, 26 (1974), 352-66; Janice Delaney's *The Curse* (New York: Dutton, 1976).

[39]Henry Maudsley, "Sex in Mind and in Education," *Fortnightly* 21 (1874), 478 [466-83]; Maudsley's argument appeared in book form in 1884 (*Sex in Mind and in Education* [Syracuse, 1884]); Nathan Allan supported Clarke in his *The Education of Girls, as Connected with Their Growth and Physical Development* (Boston, 1879). Huxley's counterposition is quoted by Cyril Bibby in *T.H. Huxley: Scientist, Humanist, and Educator* (London: Watts, 1959), p. 35.

[40]Mary Putnam Jacobi, "Mental Action and Physical Health" in Howe (see below); Elizabeth Garrett Anderson, "Sex in Mind and Education: A Reply," *Fortnightly*, 21 (1874), 582-94. *Blackwood's* then replied to Clarke, Maudsley, and Anderson in "Sex in Mind and Education: A Commentary," 115 (1874), 736-49. See also *Sex and Education*, ed. Julia Ward Howe, (Boston, 1874); *The Education of American Girls*, ed. Anna C. Brackett (New York, 1874; rpt. 1879); George F. and Anna M. Comfort's *Woman's Education and Woman's Health* (Syracuse, N.Y., 1874); Antoinette Brown Blackwell's "Sex and Work" in *The Sexes Throughout Nature* (New York, 1875), pp. 149-218; Sarah Stevenson's *The Physiology of Woman, Embracing Girlhood, Maturity, and Mature Age* (Chicago, 1880); Marion Harland's *Eve's Daughters* (New York, 1881); Josephine Pollard's *Co education* (New York, 1883).

[41]Mrs. E.B. Duffey, *No Sex in Education* (Philadelphia, 1874); references will be incorporated into the text.

[42]William B. Greene, *Critical Comments Upon Certain Passages in the Introductory Portion of Dr. Edward H. Clarke's Book on "Sex in Education"* (Boston, 1874), p. 10.

Notes   223

⁴³Edward H. Clarke, *The Building of a Brain* (Boston, 1874). This book also was widely reviewed, but much less intensely, because Clarke's claims and proposals were considerably moderated.

⁴⁴For recent work which provides bibliography and good analysis of Victorian woman considered developmentally, see Dr. Earl W. Count, "The Evolution of the Race Idea in Modern Western Culture during the Period of the Pre-Darwinian Nineteenth Century," *Transactions*, New York Academy of Science, 2nd series, 8 (1946), 139–65; George W. Stocking, Jr.'s *Race, Culture, and Evolution* (New York: Free Press, 1968); Joan N. Burstyn's "Brain and Intellect: Science Applied to a Social Issue 1860-1875," *Actes du XIIe Congrès International d'Histoire des Sciences* IX (Paris, 1971), pp. 13–16; Julia Schwendinger and Herman Schwendinger's "Sociology's Founding Fathers: Sexists to a Man," *Journal of Marriage and the Family*, 33 (1971), 783–99; John S. Haller, Jr.'s *Outcasts from Evolution* (Urbana: Univ. of Illinois Press, 1971); Jill Conway's "Stereotypes of Femininity in a Theory of Sexual Evolution," *Suffer and Be Still*, pp. 140–54; Elizabeth Fee's "The Sexual Politics of Victorian Social Anthropology," *Clio's Consciousness Raised*, pp. 86–102; Rosalind Rosenberg's "In Search of Woman's Nature, 1850-1920," *Feminist Studies*, 3 (1975), 141–54; Evelyn Reed's *Woman's Evolution: From Matriarchal Clan to Patriarchal Family* (New York: Pathfinder, 1975); Karen Trenfield's "On the Role of Biology in Feminist Ideology," *Hecate*, 3 (1977), 41–56; Flavia Alaya; Lorna Duffin's "Prisoners of Progress: Women and Evolution" in *The Nineteenth-Century Woman*, pp. 57–91.

⁴⁵W.K. Brooks, "The Condition of Women from a Zoological Point of View," *Popular Science Monthly* 15 (1879), 145–55, 347–56; Patrick Geddes and J. Arthur Thompson, *The Evolution of Sex* (London, 1889).

⁴⁶See M.A. Hardaker's "Science and the Woman Question," *Popular Science Monthly*, 20 (1881–82), 577–84, and Mrs. A.M.G.'s "The Intellectuality of Woman," *International Review*, 13 (1882), 123–36.

⁴⁷Vogt is quoted by the Hallers, p. 51.

⁴⁸As early as 1826 William Thompson calls woman "slave" in his title and throughout the *Appeal* (pp. 39, 55-58). See also Lucretia Mott, *Slavery and 'The Woman Question'* (Haverford, Penn., 1840); "Table Talk," *Putnam's*, 5 (1870), 124; "The Mission of Woman," *Southern Review*, 9 (1871), 923–42. The Walker quotation appears on p. 147 of his *Women* (London, 1840). For modern studies of woman as slave and of white slavery generally, see Guion G. Johnson's *Ante-Bellum North Carolina* (Chapel Hill: Univ. of North Carolina Press, 1937), pp. 242–43; Charles Terrot's *The Maiden Tribute: A Study of the White Slave Traffic in the Nineteenth-Century* (London: Muller, 1959); Donald Meyer's *The Positive Thinkers* (Garden City, N.Y.: Doubleday, 1965), pp. 52–53; Conrad, pp. 101–4; Ellen Moers' *Literary Women* (Garden City, N.Y.: Doubleday, 1976), pp. 14–18, 83–88, et passim.

⁴⁹Margaret Fuller, *Woman in the Nineteenth Century* (1845; rpt. New York: Norton, 1971), pp. 31, 37.

⁵⁰Sarah Grimké, *Letters on the Equality of the Sexes, and the Condition of Woman* (Boston, 1838); references will be incorporated into the text.

⁵¹Catharine E. Beecher, *An Essay on Slavery and Abolitionism* (Philadelphia, 1837), p. 6.

⁵²A.E. Grimké, *Letters to Catharine E. Beecher* (Boston, 1838), p. 13. For perspectives on this exchange, see Gerda Lerner's *The Grimké Sisters from South Carolina* (Boston: Houghton Mifflin, 1967), pp. 184–87, and Sklar, pp. 132–37.

⁵³Louise Cheeves McCord, "British Philanthropy and American Slavery," *Debow's Review*, 14 (1853), 275 [258–80]; later references will be incorporated into

the text. McCord is replying to the 1852 *North British Review* article "'American Slavery and Uncle Tom's Cabin.' An Affectionate and Christian address of the women of England to their sisters, the women of the United States of America" (pp. 127–40). McCord attacks Harriet Beecher Stowe in "Uncle Tom's Cabin," *Southern Quarterly Review*, 7 (1853), 81–120. For what little work there is on McCord, see Jessie Melville Fraser's *Louise C. McCord* (Columbia: Univ. of South Carolina Press, 1920); Margaret F. Thorp's *Female Persuasion: Six Strong-Minded Women* (New Haven: Yale Univ. Press, 1949), pp. 179–215; also *Notable American Women* (Cambridge, Mass.: Harvard Univ. Press, 1971), II, 450–52; Conrad, pp.189–95.

⁵⁴"The Mission of Woman," p. 941.

⁵⁵Thomas Henry Huxley, "Emancipation—Black and White" in his *Lay Sermons, Addresses and Reviews* (London, 1870), pp. 20–26.

⁵⁶Quoted by James M. McPherson in "Abolitionists, Woman Suffrage, and the Negro, 1865–1869," *Mid-America*, 47 (1965); 44, 46 [40–47]. For other studies of the mixed and at times not so mixed feelings of women toward black and immigrant men, see Benjamin Quarles' "Frederick Douglass and the Woman's Rights Movement," *Journal of Negro History*, 25 (1940), 35–44; Mary Massey's chapter "Women and Negroes" in *Bonnet Brigades* (New York: Knopf, 1966), pp. 271, 272, 279, 286; Walters, pp. 98–104; Conrad, pp. 101ff.

⁵⁷Ludwig Büchner, "The Brain of Women," *New Review*, 9 (1893), 176 [166–76], quoted by The Hallers in *Physician*, p. 53.

⁵⁸"The Intellectuality of Woman," pp. 126–27.

⁵⁹Farnham quotes these lines in *Woman and Her Era* (New York, 1864), II, 425.

⁶⁰*Common Sense About Women* (Boston, 1881) contains both the *Women's Journal* articles and Higginson's brilliant "Women and the Alphabet," which originally appeared under the title "Ought Women to Learn the Alphabet" in the February, 1859 number of *Atlantic Monthly* (pp. 139–50). It was then issued as a tract (1870, 1871, 1875), and appeared in its final form as *Women and the Alphabet* (Boston, 1881). Tilden G. Edelstein's *Strange Enthusiasm: A Life of Thomas Wentworth Higginson* (New Haven: Yale Univ. Press, 1968) discusses Higginson's views on both women and blacks. For the comparable turning away from Negroes, and the even more sentimental view of women of Robert G. Ingersoll, see his "True Liberty and Man, Woman, and Child" (1877) in *The Works of Robert G. Ingersoll* (New York: The Ingersoll League, 1929), I, 329–98, and "Preface to Helen H. Gardner's 'Men, Women and Gods,'" (1885) in *Works*, 12, 39–44.

⁶¹Antoinette Brown Blackwell, *The Sexes Throughout Nature* (New York, 1875), pp. 124–25; later references will be incorporated into the text.

Chapter 3

¹Sarah Stickney Ellis, *The Women of England* (New York, 1839), p. 51.

²Harriet Martineau, *Society in America* (London, 1837), III, 148–51.

³The classic studies of the impact of industrialization on Victorian women's work correct this picture. See Ivy Pinchbeck, *Women Workers and the Industrial Revolution, 1750–1850* (1930; rpt. New York: A.M. Kelley, 1969) and Wanda Fraiken Neff, *Victorian Working Women: An Historical and Literary Study of Women in British Industries and Professions, 1832–1850* (New York: Columbia Univ. Press, 1929). Victorian perceptions are called still further into question by recent social historians; see esp. Louise Tilly and Joan Scott, *Women, Work and Family* (New York: Holt, Rinehart and Winston, 1978).

4See Margaret Hewitt, *Wives and Mothers in Victorian Industry* (London: Rockliff, 1958); and Tilly and Scott.

5Martineau, *Society in America*, III, 147.

6[J.W. Kaye] "The 'Non-Existence' of Women," *North British Review*, 23 (1855), 559.

7See esp. Carlyle's *Past and Present* (1843).

8Anna Jameson, *The Communion of Labour* (London, 1856).

9Bessie Rayner Parkes, *Essays on Women's Work* (London, 1865), p. 216.

10Frances Trollope, *Michael Armstrong: The Factory Boy* (1840); Charlotte Elizabeth Tonna, *Helen Fleetwood* (1841); Elizabeth Gaskell, *Mary Barton* (1848), *Ruth* (1853), *North and South* (1855); Benjamin Disraeli, *Sybil, or The Two Nations* (1845); Charles Kingsley, *Yeast* (1848), *Alton Locke* (1850); Charles Dickens, *Hard Times* (1855), but see also his depictions of urban poverty in a number of earlier novels, from *Oliver Twist* (1837–38) through *Bleak House* (1852–53), and in later novels, through *Our Mutual Friend* (1864–65); Friedrich Engels, *Condition of the Working Class in England in 1844* (1845; first English translation, 1885). The single book of most importance both for the middle-class consciousness of working-class conditions and for the middle-class belief in work as a social and moral solution to the unrest was probably Thomas Carlyle's *Past and Present* (1843).

11Thomas Hood, "The Song of the Shirt," *Punch*, 5 (1843), 260.

12See, for example, Anna Blunden, *The Song of the Shirt* (exhib. 1854, engraved for the *Illustrated London News*), G.F. Watts, *The Seamstress* (ca. 1849–50, unfinished), and the cartoons in *Punch*, 17 (1849), 240–41, and 18 (1850), 15. Further portrayals of the plight of the seamstress are in Elizabeth Gaskell's novels *Mary Barton* and *Ruth*, Charles Kingsley's *Alton Locke*, Dickens' *Nicholas Nickleby* (1838–39), *David Copperfield* (1849–50), *Little Dorrit* (1855–57), and *Our Mutual Friend*; and Charlotte Elizabeth Tonna's *The Wrongs of Women* (1844). On Victorian views of the seamstress and on actual conditions, see Neff, pp. 115–50; for a fuller discussion of the paintings, particularly, see T.J. Edelstein, "They Sang 'The Song of the Shirt': The Visual Iconography of the Seamstress," *Victorian Studies*, 23 (1980), 183–210.

13*Punch*, 15 (1848), 78. For examples of Victorian depictions of the governess in art and fiction, see also Richard Redgrave's painting *The Poor Teacher* (1843), Lady Blessington's novel *The Governess* (1839), W.M. Thackeray's Becky Sharp in *Vanity Fair* (1847), Charlotte Brontë's *Jane Eyre* (1847), and Anne Brontë's *Agnes Grey* (1847). For governesses in *Punch*, see Alison Adburgham, *A Punch History of Manners and Modes, 1841–1940* (London, 1961); on the governess as literary heroine, Patricia Thomson, *The Victorian Heroine: A Changing Ideal, 1837–1873* (London: Oxford Univ. Press, 1956), pp. 37–56. M. Jeanne Peterson describes actual conditions in "The Victorian Governess: Status Incongruence in Family and Society," in *Suffer and Be Still: Women in the Victorian Age*, ed. Martha Vicinus (Bloomington: Indiana Univ. Press, 1973), pp. 3–19.

14Charlotte Brontë, "To Emily J. Brontë," June 8, 1839, *The Brontës: Life and Letters*, ed. Clement Shorter (New York: Charles Scribner's Sons, 1908), I, 158–59.

15[Elizabeth Rigby, Lady Eastlake], "*Vanity Fair* and *Jane Eyre*," *Quarterly Review*, 84 (1848), 153–85.

16Elizabeth Sewell, *Principles of Education* (London, 1865), II, 208–9.

17Theresa McBride gives an account of the real importance of domestic service as an occupation for Victorian women in *The Modernization of Household Service in England and France, 1820–1920* (New York: Holmes and Meier, 1976). See also David Katzman, *Seven Days a Week: Women and Domestic Service in Industrializing America* (New York: Oxford Univ. Press, 1978). Ellen DuBois has a good discussion of middle-class American attitudes toward factory workers as opposed to governesses and needlewomen in her description of Anthony's campaign to organize women typesetters in 1868; see *Feminism and Suffrage: The Emergence of an Independent Women's Movement in America, 1848-1869* (Ithaca, N.Y.: Cornell Univ. Press, 1978), pp. 136-37.

[18]See Nancy F. Cott, *The Bonds of Womanhood: "Woman's Sphere" in New England, 1780-1835* (New Haven: Yale Univ. Press, 1977), Ch. 1; W. Elliot Brownlee and Mary Brownlee, *Women in the American Economy: A Documentary History, 1675-1929* (New Haven: Yale Univ. Press, 1976) provides a short discussion plus some examples from the American debate. On the factory experience of American women in the early nineteenth century, see also the contemporary journals *Lowell Offering* and *Voice of Industry*; Harriet Robinson, *Loom and Spindle, or Life Among Early Mill Girls* (New York, 1898); Helen L. Sumner, *History of Women in Industry in the United States*, the U.S. Senate Report on the Condition of Woman and Child Wage-Earners in the United States (Washington,D.C.: Government Printing Office, 1910), Vol. IX; and Thomas Dublin, *Women at Work: The Transformation of Work and Community in Lowell, Massachusetts, 1826-1860* (New York: Columbia Univ. Press, 1979). For the history of the English protection debates, see B.L. Hutchins and A. Harrison, *A History of Factory Legislation* (1903; 3rd ed., rpt. New York: A.M. Kelley, 1966).

[19]*Hansard*, 15 March 1844, cc. 1088-89, 1091-96, 1099-1100.

[20]Charlotte Elizabeth Tonna, *The Wrongs of Women* (New York, 1844), pp. 132, 135. On Tonna see Monica Correa Fryckstedt, "Charlotte Elizabeth Tonna: A Forgotten Evangelical Writer," *Studia Neophilologica*, 52 (1980), 79-102.

[21]*Hansard*, 3 May 1844, c. 611.

[22]Parkes, pp. 236-37.

[23]Roebuck, *Autobiography and Letters*, ed. R.E. Leader (London, 1897), p. 117.

[24]*Hansard*, 3 May 1844, cc. 615, 617-18.

[25]*Hansard*, 15 March 1844, cc. 1119-1122.

[26]Anna Jameson, "Condition of the Women and the Female Children," *Athenaeum*, March 18, 1843, pp. 257-58; rpt. as "Woman's Mission and Woman's Position," in *Memoirs and Essays on Art, Literature and Social Morals* (London, 1846).

[27]The feminist opposition to protective laws in the last quarter of the century was especially strong in the English women's trade union movement; it brought the women's unions into direct conflict with the men's unions. This conflict can be traced in the pages of *The Women's Union Journal: The Organ of the Women's Protective and Provident League* (begun in 1876). Brownlee and Brownlee give documents expressing the positions of the women's unions in America both at this time and earlier in the century. For histories of the women's trade union movements and their connection with the Woman Question, see Barbara Drake, *Women and Trade Unions* (London: G. Allen and Unwin, 1920); Harry Goldman, *Emma Paterson: She Led Women into a Man's World* (London: Lawrence and Wishart, 1974); John Andrew and W.D.P. Bliss, *History of Women in Trade Unions*, U.S. Senate Report on the Condition of Woman and Child Wage-Earners in the United States (Washington, D.C.: Government Printing Office, 1911), Vol. X; Nancy Schrom Dye, *As Equals and As Sisters: Feminism, the Labor Movement, and the Women's Trade Union League of New York* (Columbia: Univ. of Missouri Press, 1980);

and two recent dissertations, Teresa Olcott Cohea, "Feminism and the Women's Trade Union Movement, 1874 to 1914" (Univ. of Leicester), and Robin M. Jacoby, "A Case Study of Feminism and Class Consciousness: The British and American Women's Trade Union Leagues, 1890-1925" (Harvard Univ., 1977), part of which appears as "The Women's Trade Union League and American Feminism" in *Feminist Studies*, 3 (1975), 126-40.

28See "Papers Relating to the Sanitary State of the People of England (June, 1858)," in John Simon, *Public Health Reports*, ed. for the Sanitary Institute by Edward Seaton (London, 1887), I, 469-70. The extensive debate on infant mortality and working mothers can be followed in part in the *Transactions of the National Association for the Promotion of Social Science* (TNAPSS), beginning in 1860.

29See Hewitt. Patricia Branca, *Silent Sisterhood: Middle Class Women in the Victorian Home* (London: Croom Helm, 1978), pp. 95-113, argues that wet-nursing declined in the middle class also as women chose the greater convenience of hand- or bottle-feeding. Though this created risks to infant health, reflected in the renewed emphasis on the benefits of nursing in prescriptive literature, the question of middle-class women's responsibility for infant mortality was not an extensive public controversy like that over working-class women and their children—nor did it directly affect the rights and conditions of women's work.

30*Sixth Report of the Medical Officer of the Privy Council* (London, 1863), p. 459.

31William Stanley Jevons, "Married Women in Factories," *Contemporary Review*, 41 (1882), 37, 41, 45, 48 [37-53].

32Richard Whately Cooke Taylor, "The Employment of Mothers in Factories," *Fortnightly Review*, 23 (1875), 668, 678-79 [664-679]; "Employment of Mothers in Manufactures," *Transactions of the National Association for the Promotion of Social Sciences*, 1874 (London, 1875), pp. 576, 575 [569-85].

33Two recent studies of the lives of ordinary middle-class, and upper-middle-class or upper-class women, respectively, who did *not* work or push for external employment are Branca, *Silent Sisterhood*, and Lenore Davidoff, *The Best Circles: Women and Society in Victorian England* (Totowa, N.J.: Rowman and Littlefield, 1973). The basic Victorian survey of middle-class women's employment needs and opportunities and the arguments for increasing them is John Duguid Milne, *Industrial Employment of Women in the Middle and Lower Ranks* (1857; rev. ed., London, 1870). Though Milne's book was widely reviewed, Milne himself does not seem to have taken much further part in the public debate. See also Lee Holcombe's *Victorian Ladies at Work: Middle Class Women in England and Wales, 1850-1914* (Hamden, Conn.: Archon Books, 1973).

34See Cott, *The Bonds of Womanhood*, esp. Ch. 1.

35[Dora Greenwell], "Our Single Women," *North British Review*, Am. ed., 36 (1862), 25.

36Martineau, *Society in America*; Jameson, *Winter Studies and Summer Rambles in Canada* (1838).

37Dinah Mulock Craik, *A Woman's Thoughts About Women* (London, 1858), pp. 1-3. Figures on marital status and proportions of women to men in England are from the 1851 census.

38See A. James Hammerton, *Emigrant Gentlewomen: Genteel Poverty and Female Emigration, 1830-1914* (London: Croom Helm, 1979), and "Feminism and Female Emigration, 1861-1886," in *A Widening Sphere: Changing Roles of Victorian Women*, ed. Martha Vicinus (Bloomington: Indiana Univ. Press, 1977), pp. 52-71.

39W.R. Greg, "Why Are Women Redundant?" *National Review*, 14 (1862), 434–60; rpt. in *Literary and Social Judgments* (Boston, 1873), pp. 275–81, 299–300, 295–96, 301–2, 306–8, [274–308].

40Jameson, p. 17.

41Ibid., pp. 3, 22–23.

42See F.D. Maurice, ed., *Lectures to Ladies on Practical Subjects* (2nd ed., Cambridge, England, 1856) and Ruskin's "Of Queens' Gardens," *Sesame and Lilies* (London, 1865).

43Alfred, Lord Tennyson, *The Princess* (1847), VII. 259–60.

44Horace Mann, *Lectures on Various Subjects* (New York, 1859), pp. 70–73.

45Tennyson, *The Princess*, VII. 270.

46Henry Wadsworth Longfellow, "Santa Filomena," *Altantic Monthly*, 1 (1857), 22–23.

47Quoted in Edward Cook, *Life of Florence Nightingale* (London: Macmillan, 1913), I, 213.

48Ibid., I, 385.

49Ibid., I, 34.

50Mill, *The Subjection of Women* (1869; rpt. in *Essays on Sex Equality*, ed. Alice Rossi [Chicago: Univ. of Chicago Press, 1970]), p. 211. See Cook, I, 471.

51Nightingale, "Cassandra," first published in Ray Strachey, *"The Cause": A Short History of the Women's Movement in Great Britain* (1928; rpt. New York: Duffield, 1930, as *Struggle*), pp. 396, 398–99, 402, 406, 403–7, 413–14 [395–418].

52Cook, I, 97.

53"To Ottilie von Goethe," July 13, 1857, Letter 193, *Letters of Anna Jameson to Ottilie von Goethe*, ed. G.H. Needler (London: Oxford Univ. Press, 1939), p. 217.

54Hester Burton, *Barbara Bodichon* (London: J. Murray, 1949). For further information on the controversial aspects of Bodichon's life, see Gordon Haight, *George Eliot: A Biography* (New York: Oxford Univ. Press, 1968), *George Eliot and John Chapman* (New Haven: Yale Univ. Press, 1940), and Haight's edition of *The George Eliot Letters* (New Haven: Yale Univ. Press, 1954–78), I, liii–lv. See also Barbara Bodichon, *An American Diary, 1857–58*, ed. Joseph Reed (London: Routledge and Kegan Paul, 1972).

55"George Eliot to Sara Sophia Hennell," July 16, [1852], *Letters*, ed. Haight, II, 45.

56Haight, *George Eliot*, p. 205.

57"Mme. Eugène Bodichon to George Eliot," April 26, [1859], *Letters*, ed. Haight, III, 56.

58Clara Thomas, *Love and Work Enough: The Life of Anna Jameson* (Toronto: Univ. of Toronto Press, 1967), pp. 209–10.

59Bodichon, *Women and Work* (1856; American ed., New York, 1859), pp. 30, 27–29, 15, 35.

60Caroline Healey Dall, *Woman's Right to Labor* (1859 lecture; published Boston, 1860), p. 104.

On Victorian prostitution, see Peter Cominos, "Late Victorian Sexual Responsibility and the Social System," *International Review of Social History*, 8 (1863), 18–48, 216–50; E.M. Sigsworth and T.J. Wyke, "A Study of Victorian Prostitution and Venereal Disease," *Suffer and Be Still*, ed. Vicinus, pp. 77–99. Older books which explore prostitution in the context of Victorian sexuality include Steven Marcus, *The Other Victorians: A Study of Sexuality and Pornography in Mid-Nineteenth*

Century England (New York: Basic Books, 1966); and Ronald Pearsall, *The Worm in the Bud: The World of Victorian Sexuality* (New York: Macmillan, 1969). For criticism of Marcus' and Pearsall's work, see F. Barry Smith, "Sexuality in Britain, 1800–1900: Some Suggested Revisions," *Widening Sphere*, ed. Vicinus, pp. 182–98. Further discussions of Victorian sexuality can be found in Chapter 2 and Volume III, Chapter 4.

⁶¹So wrote William Acton, *Prostitution Considered in Its Moral, Social, and Sanitary Aspects* (1857; 2nd ed., London, 1870).

⁶² "The Vices of the Streets," *Meliora*, 1 (1859), 70–71, 74 [70–79].

⁶³On the late eighteenth-century shift of emphasis, among moralists, ministers, and prescriptive writers, from woman's carnal nature to her superior spirituality, see Nancy F. Cott, "Passionlessness: An Interpretation of Victorian Sexual Ideology, 1790–1850," *Signs*, 4 (1978), 219–36.

⁶⁴Henry Mayhew, quoted by [W.R. Greg], "Prostitution," *Westminster Review*, 53 (1850), 462–63.

⁶⁵Acton, *Prostitution*; A.J.B. Parent-Duchatelet, *De la prostitution dans la ville de Paris* (Paris, 1836).

⁶⁶[Greg], "Prostitution," pp. 450–52, 454–55, 471, 504 [448–506].

⁶⁷G.F. Watts, *Found Drowned* (1848–50), Augustus Egg, *Past and Present No. 3* (1858), D.G. Rossetti, *Found* (unfinished, begun 1854). Millais' *Ophelia* (1851–52) is iconographically similar, although the drowned Ophelia is supposedly innocent of the improprieties Hamlet imputes to her. (Hood's poem alludes to Ophelia in an epigraph.) Fictional portraits of the fallen woman as victim in this period include Elizabeth Gaskell's *Ruth* and Elizabeth Barrett Browning's *Aurora Leigh;* for further discussion see Volume III, Chapter 4. On the visual and literary iconography, see Helene E. Roberts, "Marriage, Redundancy or Sin: The Painter's View of Woman in the First Twenty-Five Years of Victoria's Reign," *Suffer and Be Still*, ed. Vicinus, pp. 45–76; Susan Ball Bandelein, "'Allegorizing On One's Own Hook': Works Before 1863" in *Dante Gabriel Rossetti and the Double Work of Art*, ed. Maryan Wynn Ainsworth (New Haven: Yale Univ. Art Gallery, 1976), pp. 37–51; Linda Nochlin, "Lost and Found: Once More the Fallen Woman," *Art Bulletin*, 60 (1978), 139–53; T.J. Edelstein, "Reply with Rejoinder to Nochlin," *Art Bulletin*, 61 (1979), 509–10; and Nina Auerbach, "The Rise of the Fallen Woman," *Nineteenth Century Fiction*, 35 (1980), 29–52.

⁶⁸Sallie Mitchell makes this point in her "The Forgotten Woman of the Period: Penny Weekly Family Magazines of the 1840s and 1850s," in *Widening Sphere*, ed. Vicinus, pp. 29–51.

⁶⁹William W. Sanger, *The History of Prostitution: Its Causes, and Effects Throughout the World* (New York, 1858).

⁷⁰Acton, *Prostitution*, p. 49.

⁷¹The debate within the medical profession during the 1850s can be followed in such journals as *Lancet, Medical Times and Gazette*, and *British and Foreign Medico-Chirurgical Review*. Among the earliest public protests over the new acts were articles by Harriet Martineau in the *Daily News* for September 4, 10, and 23, 1862. For a clear account of the repeal campaign in Britain, see J.L. and B. Hammond, *James Stansfield, a Victorian Champion of Sex Equality* (London: Longmans, Green, 1932). For the opposition in America, see David Pivar, *Purity Crusade: Sexual Morality and Social Control, 1868–1900* (Westport, Conn.: Greenwood Press, 1973). On the actual effects of the Contagious Diseases Acts on working-class women and prostitutes in naval and garrison towns in Britain, see Judith R. Walkowitz,

Prostitution and Victorian Society: Women, Class and the State (Cambridge, England: Cambridge Univ. Press, 1980).

[72]Dall, *Woman's Right to Labor*, pp. 4–5, 32–33, 50, 8–9, 104–5.

[73]John Morley, "A Short Letter to Some Ladies," *Fortnightly*, 13 (1870), 373–75 [372–76].

[74]"Dirt-Pies," *Saturday Review*, 29 (1870), 277–78; Elphinstone, quoted in Benjamin Scott, *A State Iniquity* (London, 1890), p. 143.

[75]*Charles Kingsley: His Letters and Memories of His Life*, ed. Fannie Kingsley (London, 1891), II, 246–50.

[76]Josephine Butler, ed., *Woman's Work and Woman's Culture* (London, 1869), pp. lvi–lvii.

[77]Butler, "The Constitution Violated" (1871), rpt. in *Josephine Butler: An Autobiographical Memoir*, ed. G.W. and L.A. Johnson (London: Simpkin, Marshall, Hamilton, Kent, 1909), pp. 119–24.

[78]Butler, from "Address at Croyden" (July 3, 1871) and "Address at Bradford" (November 11, 1874), quoted in Scott, *A State Iniquity*, pp. 113–14, 187, 191–92.

Chapter 4

[1]For the substantial and fast-growing body of work on women and Victorian religion, three bibliographies give good coverage through 1975. Dorothy Bass's *American Women in Church and Society, 1607–1920: A Bibliography* (New York: The Auburn Program at Theological Seminary, 1973); Clare B. Fischer's *Women: A Theological Perspective* (Berkeley, Calif.: Graduate Theological Union, 1974); and Anne Barstow Driver's "Religion: Review Essay," *Signs*, 2 (1976), 434–42. Important work produced since 1975 will be cited in the relevant sections of this chapter.

[2]Olive J. Brose, for example, does not even mention the women controversies in *Church and Parliament* (Palo Alto, Calif.: Stanford Univ. Press, 1959); nor does Desmond Bowen in *The Idea of the Victorian Church* (Montreal: McGill Univ. Press, 1968). In turn, many histories of religion pass over the Victorian period entirely, including D.S. Bailey's *The Man-Woman Relation in Christian Thought* (London: Longmans, 1959).

[3]For an excellent brief history of women and the Bible, see "Something Remains to Dare," Barbara Welter's introduction to *The Original Feminist Attack on the Bible* (New York: Arno, 1974), pp. v–xxxiv Margaret Fuller, Antoinette Brown, and Mary Baker Eddy receive special emphasis in Gayle Kimball's "A Counter-Ideology" in *Women and Religion*, ed. Judith Plaskow and Joan Arnold (Missoula, Mont.: Scholar's Press, 1974), pp. 177–87. For recent work on women in the Old and New Testaments, see Phyllis Bird's "Images of Women in the Old Testament," Bernard P. Prusak's "Woman: Seductive Siren and Source of Sin?" Constance F. Parvey's 'The Theology and Leadership of Women in the New Testament," and Rosemary Reuther's "Misogynism and Virginal Feminism in the Fathers of the Church," in *Religion and Sexism*, ed. Reuther (New York: Simon & Schuster, 1974), pp. 41–88, 89–116, 117–49, 150–83; Dorothy D. Burlage's "Judaeo-Christian Influences on Female Sexuality" in *Sexist Religion and Women in the Church*, ed. Alice L. Hageman (New York: Association Press, 1974), pp. 93–116; Wayne A. Meeks's "The Image of the Androgyne: Some Use of a Symbol in Earliest Christianity," *History of Religions*, 13 (1974), 165–208; Winsome Munro's "Patriarchy and Charismatic Community in 'Paul'" in *Women and Religion*, pp. 189–98; Jo Ann McNamara's "Sexual Equality and the Cult of

Virginity in Early Christian Thought," *Feminist Studies*, 3 (1976), 145–58; Elaine H. Pagels' "What Became of God the Mother? Conflicting Images of God in Early Christianity," *Signs*, 2 (1976), 293–303; Hamilton Hess's "Changing Forms of Ministry in the Early Church" in *Sexism and Church Law*, ed. James A. Coriden (New York: Paulist Press, 1977), pp. 43–57; Elizabeth Schüssler Fiorenza's "Word, Spirit and Power: Women in Early Christian Communities" and Rosemary Reuther's "Mothers of the Church: Ascetic Women in the Late Patristic Age" in *Women of Spirit*, ed. Reuther and Eleanor McLaughlin (New York: Simon & Schuster, 1979), pp. 29–70 and 71–98; Denise Lardner Carmody's chapter on "Judaism" in her *Women & World Religions* (Nashville: Abingdon, 1979), pp. 92–112; Jo Ann McNamara, "Wives and Widows in Early Christian Thought," *International Journal of Women's Studies* 2 (1979): 575–92.

⁴William Landels, *Woman's Sphere and Work Considered in the Light of Scriptures* (London, 1869), pp. 10, 27; later references will be incorporated into the text. Olive Anderson in her excellent "Women Preachers in Mid-Victorian Britain: Some Reflections on Feminism, Popular Religion, and Social Change" (*The Historian*, 12 [1969], 467–84) argues that the general softening of strictures against women preaching is reflected in the much milder stance which Landels took eleven years later in his *Woman: Her Position and Power* (London, 1870).

⁵Sarah Josepha Hale, *Woman's Record* (New York, 1853; third edition, revised and enlarged, 1870), pp. xxxvi, xxxvi–xxxvii, xxxvii, xxxvi, xxxvii; later references will be incorporated into the text. Considering how influential and complicated Hale was, very little work has been done on her. See Sidney Ditzion's *Marriage, Morals, and Sex in America* (New York: Bookman, 1953), pp. 244–46; Helen Beal Woodward's chapter in *The Bold Women* (New York: Farrar, Straus, 1953), pp. 181–200; Glenda Gates Riley's "The Subtle Subversion: Changes in the Traditionalist Image of the American Woman," *The Historian*, 32 (1970), 210–27; and Susan Phinney Conrad's *Perish the Thought* (New York: Oxford Univ. Press, 1976), pp. 38–44 et passim.

⁶Tertullian is quoted by Reuther in "Misogynism. . . ," pp. 157. For Calvin, see his *Commentary Upon The Book of Genesis* (Edinburgh, 1898), I p. 152. Though woman's status in the Reformation is debated, some aspects of her situation show definite improvement. See Jane Dempsey Douglass' "Women and the Continental Reformation" in *Religion and Sexism*, pp. 292–318.

⁷William H. Holcombe, *The Sexes, Here and Hereafter* (Philadelphia, 1869), p. 68.

⁸Charles Kingsley, "The Tree of Knowledge" (1874) in *Sanitary and Social Lectures and Essays* (London, 1880), IX, 170–71.

⁹Sarah Grimké, *Letters on the Equality of the Sexes and the Condition of Woman* (Boston, 1838), pp. 6, 6–7, 7.

¹⁰Eliza W. Farnham, *Woman and Her Era*, 2 vols. (New York, 1864), I, 137–38, 138, 139, 140; later references will be incorporated into the text. For Charlotte Brontë's Promethean vision of Eve, see *Shirley*.

¹¹Charles G. Finney, "Letters from Prof. Finney to Miss A.E. of Vermont . . . No. 4," *Oberlin Evangelist*, 7 (1845), 68. Moody allowed women to preach at his revivals.

¹²Besides R. Pierce Beaver's standard work, *All Loves Excelling* (Grand Rapids, Mich.: Eerdmans, 1968), and Elaine Magalis' study of Methodist women (*Conduct Becoming to a Woman: Bolted Doors and Bourgeoning Missions* [New York: United Methodist Church, 1973]), see Alice L. Hageman's "Women and Missions: The Cost of Liberation" in *Sexist Religion*, pp. 167–93; Barbara Corrado Pope's "Angels in the Devil's Workshop: Women in Nineteenth-Century England and France"

in *Becoming Visible: Women in European History*, ed. Renate Bridenthal and Claudia Koonz (Boston: Houghton Mifflin, 1977), pp. 296-324; Anne M. Boylan's "Evangelical Womanhood in the Nineteenth Century: The Role of Women in Sunday Schools," *Feminist Studies*, 4 (1978), 62-80; Mary Ewens' o.p. *The Role of the Nun in Nineteenth-century America* (New York: Arno, 1979); Barbara Welter's "She Hath Done What She Could: Protestant Women's Missionary Careers in Nineteenth-Century America" and Mary J. Oates's "Organized Voluntarism: The Catholic Sisters in Massachusetts" in *Women in American Religion*, ed. Janet Wilson James (Philadelphia: Univ. of Pennsylvania Press, 1980), pp. 111-25 and 141-69; and Rosemary Skinner Keller's "Lay Women in the Protestant Tradition," in *Women & Religion in America*, ed. Rosemary Radford Ruether and Keller (San Francisco: Harper & Row, 1981), vol. I, pp. 242-93.

¹³Annie C.F. Cunningham, "Woman's Work in the American Church," *Catholic Presbyterian*, 9 (1883), 362 [359-64].

¹⁴Elizabeth Strutt, *The Feminine Soul* (London, 1857), p. 96.

¹⁵The question, and Miss Langley's answer, appear in Rev. Henry C. Potter's *Sisterhoods and Deaconesses at Home and Abroad* (New York, 1873), pp. 57, 69.

¹⁶The Pastoral Letter, and the Whittier and Chapman replies, appear in *History of Woman Suffrage*, ed. Elizabeth Cady Stanton, Susan B. Anthony, Matilda Joslyn Gage (Rochester, N.Y., 1881), I, 81-82, 84, 82-83. For recent work on women and preaching, see Janis Calvo's "Quaker Women Ministers in Nineteenth Century America," *Quaker History*, 63 (1974), 75-93; Nelle Morton's "Preaching the Word" and Letty M. Russell's "Women and Ministry" in *Sexist Religion*, pp. 29-46 and 47-62; Beverly Wildung Harrison's "The Early Feminists and the Clergy: A Case Study in the Dynamics of Secularism," *Review and Expositor*, 72 (1975), 41-52; Donald W. Dayton and Lucile Sider Dayton's "Evangelical Feminism," *Post American*, 3 (1974), 7-10; "The Holiness Churches: A Significant Ethical Tradition," *Christian Century*, 92 (1975), 197-201; "'Your Daughters Shall Prophesy': Feminism in the Holiness Movement," *Methodist History*, 14 (1976), 67-92; Harry Leon McBeth's "The Role of Women in Southern Baptist History" and Helen Emery Falls's "Baptist Women in Missions Support in the Nineteenth Century," *Baptist Historical Heritage*, 12 (1977), 3-25 and 26-36; William T. Noll's "Women as Clergy and Laity in the Nineteenth-Century Methodist Protestant Church," *Methodist History*, 15 (1977), 107-21; Janet Harbison Penfield's "Women in the Presbyterian Church—An Historical Overview," *Journal of Presbyterian History*, 55 (1977), 107-23; Victoria Booth Demarest's *Sex and Spirit* (St. Petersburg, Fla.: Valkyrie, 1977), pp. 19-70; Lois A. Boyd's "Shall Women Speak? Confrontation in The Church 1876" *Journal of Presbyterian History* 56 (1978): 279-94; Elaine C. Huber's "'A Woman Must Not Speak': Quaker Women in the English Left Wing" and Virginia Lieson Brereton and Christa Ressmeyer Klein's "American Women in Ministry: A History of Protestant Beginning Points" in *Women of Spirit*, pp. 153-82 and 301-32; Barbara Brown Zikmund's "The Struggle for the Right to Preach" in *Women & Religion in America*, vol. I, pp. 193-241.

¹⁷Sarah Grimké, pp. 18-19, 20-21.

¹⁸Lucretia Mott, *History of Woman Suffrage*, I, 70-73.

¹⁹Rev. Luther Lee, "Woman's Right to Preach the Gospel" in *Five Sermons and a Tract by Luther Lee*, ed. with an intro. by Donald W. Dayton (Chicago: Holrad House, 1975), p. 90. For a Victorian argument against seeing Phoebe and other deaconesses as true ministers in the early church, see A. Spaeth's "Phoebe the Deaconess" in *The Lutheran Church Review*, 4 (1885), 210-22. Russell studies the concept of *diakonia* in "Women and Ministry."

Notes   233

[20]Phoebe Palmer, *Promise of the Father* (Boston, 1859). For recent work on Palmer, see Anne C. Loveland's "Domesticity and Religion in the Ante-Bellum Period: The Career of Phoebe Palmer," *The Historian*, 39 (1976/77), 455-71.

[21]Catherine Booth's *Female Ministry: or Women's Right to Preach the Gospel* appeared in pamphlet form in 1859 and in revised form in her *Papers on Practical Religion* (London, 1879).

[22]F. de L. Booth-Tucker, *The Life of Catherine Booth* (New York, 1892), I, p. 353; later references will be incorporated into the text.

[23]Harold Begbie, *The Life of General William Booth* (London: Macmillan, 1920), pp. 246, 247, 249.

[24]Richard Hugheson Collier, *The General Next to God* (London: Collins, 1965), p. 110.

[25]Ann Douglas, *The Feminization of American Culture* (New York: Knopf, 1977), p. 218. For a full-scale history of the hymn in America, see Susan S. Tamke's *Make a Joyful Noise Unto the Lord* (Athens: Ohio Univ. Press, 1978).

[26]Elizabeth Stuart Phelps, "A Woman's Pulpit," *Atlantic Monthly*, 26 (1870), 11-22; references will be incorporated into the text. Ann Douglas discusses Phelps in "Heaven Our Home: Consolation Literature in the Northern United States, 1830-1880," *American Quarterly*, 26 (1974), 496-515. See also Christine Stansell's "Elizabeth Stuart Phelps: A Study in Female Rebellion," *Massachusetts Review*, 13 (1972), 239-56.

[27]In *Congregational Quarterly* Rev. Charles W. Torrey's defense of woman's preaching ("Woman's Sphere in the Church," 9 [1867], 163-71) was answered by Rev. Stephen Knowlton's "The Silence of Women in the Churches" (9 [1867], 329-34). Seven years later the controversy flared again when the April number of *Congregational Quarterly* carried both the pro-woman essay of Rev. Harmon Loomis ("May a Woman Speak in a Promiscuous Religious Assembly," pp. 264-78) and a fierce negative statement by Augusta Moore ("May Women Speak in Meeting?" pp. 279-84). Loomis was then attacked in the October issue by the anonymous "Speaking or Babbling" (pp. 576-87). When D.R. Cady's negative vote was added in "The Biblical Position of Women" (12 [1870], 370-77), *Congregational Quarterly* over the seven years published twice as many negative as positive articles. For the Catholic view, see "Thoughts of the Women of the Times" and "How the Church Understands and Upholds the Rights of Women" in *Catholic World*, 14 (1872), 467-72 and 15 (1872), 78-91, 255-69, 366-80, 487-501. The equivocal *New Englander* position was advanced in "Woman's Voice in the Church" (36 [1877], 115-31). Other eminent Victorians who supported woman's ministry were Catharine and Henry Ward Beecher, Josephine Butler, Frances Power Cobb, Caroline Dall, Mary Baker Eddy, Phoebe A. Hanaford, Theodore Parker, Anna Howard Shaw, Calvin Stowe, and Frances E. Willard.

[28]Rev. Morgan Dix, *Lectures on the Calling of a Christian Woman and Her Training to Fulfill It* (New York, 1883; rpt. 1886), pp. 30, 58, 59, 59-60. Lillie Devereux Blake's replies appeared in *Woman's Place To-day* (New York, 1883), pp. 13, 49-50. For more on Blake, see *Champion of Women: The Life of Lille Devereux Blake* by Katharine Devereux Blake and Margaret Louise Wallace (New York: Revell, 1943).

[29]Carlos White, *Ecce Femina* (Boston, 1870), p. 182; later references will be incorporated into the text.

[30]Butler is quoted by F.D. Bacon in *Women in the Church* (London: Lutterworth, 1946), p. 75.

³¹Elizabeth Gaskell, *Ruth* (London, 1853; rpt. London: Dent, 1967), p. 347.

³²W.E.H. Lecky, "The Position of Women" in *History of European Morals* (London, 1859), II, 291–394. For other examples of this type of argument from history, see George W. Burnap's *The Sphere and Duties of Woman* (Baltimore, 1848), Charles Merivale's "Woman's Spiritual Claim," *Ladies' Repository,* 26 (1866), 677–80, and F.D. Maurice's *Social Morality* (Cambridge, England, 1869).

³³Nathaniel Hawthorne, *The Scarlet Letter* (Boston, 1850; rpt. Columbus: Ohio State Univ. Press, 1962), p. 56. The quotation from *The Blithedale Romance* appears on p. 139 of the Norton Edition (New York, 1958).

³⁴"The Virgin Mary," *London Review* 17 (1868), 211; [Margaret Oliphant] "Elizabeth and Mary," *Blackwood's,* 101 (1867), 389 [389–414]; "The Woman Blessed by All Generations," *Athenaeum,* 2120 (1868), 824 [823–24].

³⁵Rev. Raphael Melia, *The Woman Blessed by All Generations; or, Mary the Object of Veneration, Confidence and Imitation to All Christians* (London, 1868). Besides the *Athenaeum* review, see the *Spectator's* "Mariolatry for England," 41 (1868), 1077–78. Margaret Oliphant, *Madonna Mary* (London, 1867); for reviews which are pro and con about the Mary ideal, see "Madonna Mary," *Athenaeum,* 2039 (1866), 673–74 and "Madonna Mary," 22 *Saturday Review,* (1866), 651–52. As an indication of where the debate on Mary is today, see the differing views of Rosemary Reuther and Mary Daly in *New Woman/New Earth* (New York: Seabury, 1975) and *Gyn-Ecology* (Boston: Beacon, 1978).

³⁶John Henry Newman, "The Feast of the Annunciation of the Blessed Virgin Mary. The Reverence Due Her" was first delivered on March 25, 1832, and was published in the second volume of *Parochial Sermons* (London, 1835), pp. 127–36; specific references will be incorporated into the text. (Newman's view is complicated by the fact that Catholic worship of the Virgin is one of the factors which delayed his conversion.) For Newman's view of virginity, see Meriol Trevor's *Newman. The Pillar of the Cloud* (Garden City, N.Y.: Doubleday, 1962), pp. 88–96.

³⁷George Eliot, *Middlemarch* (Edinburgh, 1872; rpt. Boston: Houghton Mifflin, 1956), p. 613.

³⁸Anne Richlieu Dryden, *Can Women Regenerate Society?* (London, 1844), pp. 38, 182.

³⁹Moncure D. Conway preached "The Madonna of Montbazon" before the South Place Religious Society in 1833; it was published in *Moncure Daniel Conway, Addresses and Reprints, 1850-1907* (Boston: Houghton Mifflin, 1909), pp. 307–21; references will be incorporated into the text. For more on Conway, see his two-volume *Autobiography: Memories and Experiences* (Boston: Houghton Mifflin, 1904) and Mary Elizabeth Burtis' *Moncure Conway, 1832-1907* (New Brunswick, N.J.: Rutgers Univ. Press, 1952). For more on the relation between science and religion in nineteenth-century America, see Herbert Hovenkamp's *Science and Religion in America, 1800-1860* (Philadelphia: Univ. of Pennsylvania Press, 1980). For others who urged that more education was necessary if woman was to fulfill her traditional role, see "Women's Education," *Fraser's Magazine,* 79 (1869), 537–52; Felix Adler, "The Religious Conservativism of Women" in *Creed and Deed* (New York, 1877), 104–17. An interesting debate appeared in the April and May numbers of *Nineteenth Century* in 1880: Bertha Lathbury's "Agnosticism and Women" (pp. 619–27) was answered by J.H. Clapperton's "Agnosticism and Woman: A Reply" (pp. 840–44). That a demand for increased education was compatible with a belief in woman's innate moral superiority is proven by Sarah Josepha Hale's long insistence

on both propositions. For recent work on Victorian notions of woman's superiority, see Riley; Norman Mezvinsky's "An Idea of Female Superiority," *Midcontinent American Studies Journal*, 2 (1961), 17–26; and Barbara Welter's "The Cult of True Womanhood: 1820–1860," *American Quarterly*, 18 (1966), 151–74, rpt. in *Diminity Convictions* (Athens: Ohio Univ. Press, 1977), pp. 21–41.

[40]Henry James, Sr., "'The Woman Thou Gavest Me,'" 25 *Atlantic Monthly*, (1870), 66–72: James is particularly inclined to emphasize woman's traditional role as purifier because of his debt to Swedenborgianism. Numerous writers in America influenced by Swedenborg's *Arcana Coelestia* (London, 1749–56) saw the universe as bisexual and woman as a force of increasing power and beneficence. See Leo Miller's *Woman and the Divine Republic* (Buffalo, 1874).

[41]Ditzion, p. 240.

[42]Douglas, *Feminization of American Culture*; Barbara Welter, "The Feminization of American Religion: 1800–1860" in *Insights and Parallels*, ed. William L. O'Neill (Minneapolis: Burgess, 1973), pp. 305–31, reprinted in *Diminity Convictions*, pp. 83–102; Sidney Owenson, Lady Morgan, *Woman and Her Master* (London, 1840).

[43]"The Feminine Element in 'The Modern Spirit,'" *Spectator*, 40 (1867), 496 [495–96]; Eliza Lynn Linton, "Emancipated Women" in *Ourselves* (London, 1869), p. 46 [40–60]. See also "The British Mother Taking Alarm," *Saturday Review*, 32 (1871), 334–35.

[44]Quoted by Riley, p. 219.

[45]Merivale, p. 678.

[46]Rev. John W. Burgon's "Woman's Place" was delivered on February 12, 1871, and then published as a pamphlet (Oxford, 1871). The quotation is from p. 5.

[47]"The Woman Blessed. . . ," *Athenaeum*, p. 824.

[48]Constance Rover, *Love, Morals and the Feminists* (London: Routledge and Kegan Paul, 1970), p. 4; Margaret W. Masson, "The Typology of the Female as a Model for the Regenerate: Puritan Preaching 1690–1730," *Signs*, 2 (1976), 304–15.

[49]*History of Woman Suffrage*, I, 669.

[50]For Ward and other early sociologists, see Julia Schwendinger and Herman Schwendinger's "Sociology's Founding Fathers: Sexists to a Man," *Journal of Marriage and the Family*, 33 (1971), 783–99.

[51]Elaine Showalter, *A Literature of Their Own* (Princeton: Princeton Univ. Press, 1977), p. 30.

[52]Theodore Parker, *Autobiography, Poems and Prayers*, ed. Rufus Leighton (Boston: American Unitarian Association, 1911), p. 370.

[53]Francis William Newman, *Phases of Faith* (London, 1850), pp. 162, 165. For more on Frank, see Basil Willey's *More Nineteenth Century Studies* (London: Chatto & Windus, 1956), pp. 11–52.; for both brothers, see William Robbins' *The Newman Brothers* (Cambridge, Mass.: Harvard Univ. Press, 1966).

[54]Robert G. Ingersoll, "The Gods" (1872) in *The Works of Robert G. Ingersoll* (New York: The Ingersoll League, 1929), I, 7–90, and Preface to Dr. Edgar C. Beall's "The Brain and the Bible" (1881) in *Works*, XII, 27–35.

[55]Alma Lutz, *Created Equal* (New York: John Day, 1940), pp. 205, 257–58.

[56]Elizabeth Cady Standon, "Has Christianity Benefited Woman?" *North American Review*, 342 (1885), 89–97; specific references will be incorporated into the text.

Index

American Equal Rights Association, 47
American Woman Suffrage Association, 54
Anderson, Dr. Elizabeth Garrett, 85, 223n40
androgyny, 199, 200–01, 202
Angel in the House, xiv, 56, 91, 92, 117, 148, 192. *See also* woman, nature of
Angel out of the House, xv, 142–43, 148, 157
Anstey, Chisholm, 48–49
Anthony, Susan B., xiv, 233n16; on marriage, 164; laws, 8, 29, 37–38, 53; on suffrage, 47, 49, 50–54, 102; and Social Purity Reform, 158, 160; on marriage, 164
Anthony Amendment, 54
anthropology
    controversy over woman's developmental potential: Spencerian methodology, 89; three theories to "prove" woman's inferiority, 89–90; woman increasingly maternal, 90; her association with blacks and children, 91; woman as slave, 91–92
    Sarah Grimké's *Letters on the Equality of the Sexes* demands emancipation of women and blacks: indicts Christianity, 92–93; and laws, 93–94; McCord sees hierarchy with white male above white female and blacks, 95; Catharine Beecher vs. Angelina Grimké, 95; McCord attacks British double-standard, 96–97; defines True Womanhood, 97–98
    post-Civil War debate: "scientific" proofs of inferiority of white women and blacks, 98–99; Huxley, 98–102; feminists split over race, 102–03; Antoinette Brown Blackwell uses Spencerian biology to deny woman's developmental inferiority, 103–06; ends proving Spencerian conclusion that woman is maternal, 108; blacks ignored, 103, 108
    and religion, 165
    modern works on: Alaya, F., Conway, J., Duffin, L., Fee, E., Reed, E., Rosenberg, R., Schwendinger, J. and H., Stocking, G., Trenfield, K., 224n44; Haller, J. and R., 224n47, 225n57; Johnson, G., Meyer, D., Moers, E., Terrot, C., 224n48; Conrad, S., 224n48, 225nn53, 56; Lerner, G., Sklar, K., 224n52; Thorp, M., 225n53; Massey, M., McPherson, J., Walters, R., 225n56; Edelstein, T., 225n60
apocalyptic feminism, xv, 160; woman's superiority, 76; evolution toward woman's rule, 90, 103, 199–206; and Contagious Diseases Acts debates, 151, 160, 162–64. *See also* Christianity

Aristotle, 91
Arnold, Mrs. Matthew, 39
Ashley, Lord (Anthony Ashley Cooper, Seventh Earl of Shaftesbury), 121–24, 125, 127, 130, 141
Bachofen, 202
Barton, Clara, 142
Beall, Dr. Edgar C., 236n54
Becker, Lydia Earnestine, 41, 77, 221n25
Beecher, Catharine E., 81, 98, 200, 222n35, 234n27; *An Essay on Slavery and Abolition*, 95, 224n51
Beecher, Henry Ward, 234n27
Beecher, Lyman, 166
Bentham, Jeremy, 125
Bible
    used to defend paternal power, 10; to sustain double standard, 25; to argue for liberalized divorce laws, 28; to justify adultery as grounds for divorce, 28–29; and Butler, 160
    exegetical controversies: women exegetes, 167; story of creation—establishes woman's subordination, 167–68; establishes her equality and even superiority, 168–69; story of fall—Eve's responsibility for fall, 169–71; Adam's, 171–72; Eve as superior, 172–73; as heroic rebel, 174–75
    modern work on: Bass, D., Driver, A., Fischer, C., 231n1; Bailey, D., Bowen, D., Brose, O., 231n2; Arnold J., Bird, P., Burlage, D., Hageman, A., Parvey, C., Plaskow, J., Prusak, B., Welter, B., 231n3; Reuther, R., 231n3, 232nn3, 6; McNamara, J., 231n3, 232n4; Carmody, D., Coriden, J., Fiorenza, E., Hess, H., Kimball, G., Meeks, W., Munro, W., McLaughlin, E., Pagels, E., Anderson, O., 232n4; Conrad, S., Ditzion, S., Riley, G., Woodward, H., 232n5; Douglass, J., 233n6
Bickerdyke, "Mother," 142
birth control, 67–69, 72, 73, 82, 147
Blackstone, William, 4
Blackwell, Antoinette Brown: on divorce, 33–37; and science, 85; *The Sexes Throughout Nature*, 103–08, 223n40, 225n61; and religion, 176, 180, 202, 231n3. *See also* anthropology
Blackwell, Elizabeth, 77, 170, 221n27
Blackwell, Henry, 23
Blake, Lillie Devereaux, 167, 191, 192, 193, 234n28
Blessington, Lady, 226n13
Blunden, Anna, 226n12

Bodichon, Barbara: on laws affecting women, 3, 4; campaign for property reform, 13–15; suffrage petition, 40–41, 79; birth control, 72, 147; life, 147; on work for women, 140, 146–50
Booth, Catherine, 167, 175, 180, 181, 182, 183, 233n21
Booth, William, 181, 183
Boston Committee of Remonstrants, 39
Boucherett, Jessie, 147
Bowyer, Sir George, 46
Boyd, Robert, 75
Brackett, Anna C., 85, 233n40
Bradlaugh, Charles, 218n6, 219n6
British Association for the Advancement of Science, 79
Brontë, Anne, 226n13
Brontë, Charlotte, xi, 118–19, 226n13, 232n10
Brontë, Emily, 118
Brooks, William K., 89, 224n45
Brown, Rev. Antoinette, *see* Blackwell, Antoinette Brown
Brougham, Henry Peter, Baron, 9, 11, 210; Lord Brougham's Act (1859), 48–49
Browning, Elizabeth Barrett, 14, 146, 183, 230n67
Büchner, Ludwig, 102, 225n57
Buckland, Alexander, 79
Buckle, Henry Thomas, 209
Bullard, Laura, 39
Burgon, Rev. John W., 200, 236n46
Burnap, George W., 234n32
Butler, Josephine, 80–81, 160, 194, 222n34, 224n44, 234nn27, 30; and Contagious Diseases Acts, 161–64
Cady, D.R., 234n27
Cain and Abel, 172
Calvin, John, 83, 170, 232n6
Campbell, John, Baron, 25
Carey, Mathew, 117
Carlyle, Jane, 14
Carlyle, Thomas, 113, 141, 144
Chapman, John, 147
Chapman, Maria Weston, 178, 233n16
Chartism, 114, 121
chastity, 4, 23–24, 62, 65–67, 137, 147, 152–53
Chatelet, Marquise Émelie du, 78
Child, Lydia Maria, 102, 200
childbirth, 170, 172, 195, 198

church work (*continued*)
  Brereton, V., Calvo, J., Demarest, V., Falls, H., Harrison,
  B., Huber, E., Klein, C., Morton, N., McBeth, H., Noll, W.,
  Penfield, J., Zikmund, B., 233n16; Russell, L., 233n16, 19;
  Dayton, D. and L., 233n16, 19; Spaeth, A., 233n19;
  Loveland, A., 233n20; Booth-Tucker, F., 234n22; Begbie,
  H., 234n23; Collier, R., 234n24; Tamke, S., 234n25;
  Douglas, A., 234nn25, 26; Stansell, C., 234n26
Claflin, Tennessee, 71
Clapperton, J.H., 235n39
Clarke, Dr. Edward H., 57; *The Building of a Brain*, 89, 223n43;
  Sex in Education, see education
clitoridectomy, 73, 74
Cobbe, Frances Power, 17–21, 40–41, 234n27
Colenso, Bishop John William, 166
Comfort, George F. and Anna M., 223n40
Comstock, Anthony, xi
"Comstockery," 38
Comteans, 200
Contagious Diseases Acts, 156, 158, 164
continence, *see* sexuality
contraception, *see* birth control; sexuality
Conway, Rev. Moncure David, 196, 197, 199, 235n39
Cooper, Anthony Ashley, *see* Ashley, Lord (Seventh Earl of
  Shaftesbury)
Count, Dr. Earl W., 224n44
Cowan, Dr. John, 61, 218n5
Craig, Isa, 147
Craik, Dinah Mulock, 135
Cranworth, Robert Monsey Rolfe, Baron, 24–26
criminal conversation, 23–24
Cunningham, Annie C.F., 176, 233n13
Curie, Marie, 79
custody, *see* law
Custody of Infants Act (1886), 13
Dall, Caroline, 3, 4–5, 26, 150, 156–57, 234n27
Darwin, Charles, 78, 89, 91, 99, 103, 105
Davies, Emily, 40–41, 147
Davis, Paulina Wright, 78, 221n28
Deaconess Movement, 176, 177
Declaration of Independence, 102
Declaration of Sympathies, 180

Dickens, Charles, xiv, 114, 142, 226n12
Dinah Morris, 175
Disraeli, Benjamin, 47, 114
divorce, *see* law
Dix, Dorothea, 142
Dix, Rev. Morgan, 167, 191, 193, 210, 234n28
domestic service, 120, 126, 134, 137–38, 139, 159
double standard, 24–27, 215n31
Douglas, Frederick, 102
Dryden, Anne Richlieu, 196, 199, 235n38
Drysdale, Dr. Alice Vickery, 218n6
Drysdale, Dr. Charles R., 218n6
Drysdale, Dr. George, xiv, 57, 71, 202; *Elements of Social Science, see* sexuality
Duffey, Mrs. E.B., 61, 88, 218n5; *No Sex in Education*, 85, 225n41. *See also* education
Dunbar, Rev. Charles, 167
Eastlake, Lady, *see* Rigby, Elizabeth
economics, 60, 64, 65, 67–69, 88; metaphors applied to sexuality, 58, 218n2; wages, 109–10, 120, 122, 123–24, 125, 126, 130, 152, 155, 156–57, 158, 164; laissez-faire—"laws" of, 121, 124, 125, 131, 136, 138, 140; criticism of, 141
Eddy, Mary Baker, 167, 201, 231n3, 234n27
education
    woman's need for knowledge of bodily functions, 60–66
    scientific controversy over: woman's brain considered organically—quantitative and qualitative aspects, 75–76; considered functionally—capacity for abstract thought, 75–76; academic and professional achievements, 77–78; Mary Somerville—life, 78; reception, 78–79; agrees with Mary Shelley and George Eliot about woman's intellectual limitations, 79; letter to Butler, 80–81
    relation of health and education: woman's declining health, 81–82; Dr. Clarke's *Sex in Education*—menstruation limits educational potential, 82–84; race threatened, 84; reactions to Clarke—pro and con, 84–85; Mrs. Duffey attacks Clarke, 85–88; woman's subsequent achievements, 88–89
    middle class inadequate, 101, 129, 134–36, 144–46, 148–49, 189, 196, 197–99, 209–10
    exacerbates racial inequality, 101
    factory workers lacking, 124, 128–29
    desire for leads to fall, 171

education (*continued*)
    woman incapable of theology and logic, 176
    modern work on: Weisberg, D., 213n2; Conrad, S., Skultans,
        V., 220n21; Haller, J. and R., 220n21, 222n35; Alaya, F.,
        221n25; Aldrich, M., 221nn25, 29; Bogdan, J., Chaff, S.,
        Donnison, J., Ehrenreich, B., English, D., Mandelbaum,
        D., Peitzman, S., Roberts, A., Walsh, M., Wertz, R. and
        D., 221n26; Wilson, D., 221n27; Blake, J., Dorr, R., Lutz,
        A., Woodward, H., 221n28; Morris, S., Mozans, H., Ros-
        siter, M., Stephenson, L., Welter, B., Wilson, J., Woody,
        T., Yost, E., 221n29; Kohlstedt, S., 221n29, 222n30;
        Basalla, G., Kendall, P., Merriam, E., Richeson, A., Toth, B.
        and E., 222n30; Patterson, E., 222nn30, 33; Penney, T.,
        222n33; Barker-Benfield, J., Bett, J., Cross, B., Haley, B.,
        Johansson, S., Numbers, R., Roberts, H., Sklar, K., Smith,
        P., Walker, W., 222n35; Bullough, V. and B., Burstyn, J.,
        Butt, J., Delaney, J., Goodsell, W., McGuigan, D., Show-
        alter, E. and E., Trecker, J., Vicinus, M., 223n38; Allan, N.,
        Bibby, C., 223n39; Haller, J., 224n44
Egg, Augustus, 155
egalitarianism, between the sexes, xiv, xvi, 112; marital, 24–25,
        32, 35, 37; political, 50–53, 112, 140, 161–62; sexual, 64,
        65–67, 71–72; intellectual, 75–77, 82–88; religious, 165,
        168, 172, 179, 208–210
Eliot, George: and Bodichon, 72, 79, 147, 222n33; *Middlemarch,*
        146, 196, 235n37; *Daniel Deronda,* 146; *Adam Bede,* 147, 175,
        183
Ellis, Havelock, 219n6
Ellis, Sarah, xi, xiv, 109, 118
Elphinstone, James, 159
"Emancipation—Black and White," 99–102, 225n55
Emmet, Dr. T.A., 73
emigration, 135, 136, 139
Émile, 220n15
Engels, Friedrich, 114
Essays and Reviews, 166
evangelism, 102, 175–76
Eve, 174, 195, 198, 201, 232n10
evolution, 168, 198, 199–200, 202
exegesis, difficulties of, 165, 167, 172, 173, 180
'Ēzer, 165
factory work, women's, 115, 120–33, 134
Faithfull, Emily, 147, 167

Hale, Mary W., 222n32
Hale, Sarah Josepha, xv, 168, 169, 173, 174, 200, 232n5, 235n39
Hemans, Felicia, xiv
Hanaford, Phoebe A., 234n27
Hardacher, M.A., 224n46
Hare, E.H., 218n5
Harland, Marion, 85; 223n40
Hawes, Rev. Joel, 183
Hawthorne, Nathaniel, 81, 183, 195, 200, 222n35, 235n33
health, woman's, 80–81. *See also* education, scientific controversy
    over
Herschel, Caroline, 78, 79
Hester Prynne, 195
Higginson, Thomas Wentworth, 103, 108, 200; *Common Sense
    About Women*, 225n60
higher criticism, 165
Holcombe, William H., 170, 232n7
home, 192; ideal of—and women's work, 109–11, 113, 120, 123–
    24, 127, 128, 128–29, 133, 149, 151, 164; and protective
    legislation, 127, 133; work in home not recognized as work
    by Victorians, 111; middle-class activity centers on, 134,
    228n33
Holyoke, George Jacob, 219n6
Hood, Thomas: "The Song of the Shirt," 115–17, 150; "The
    Bridge of Sighs," 155
Hooker, Isabella Beecher, 72, 220n11
Howe, Julia Ward, 54, 85, 223n40
Hunt, Harriot, 77, 221n28
Huxley, Thomas Henry, 83, 84, 86, 223n39; "Emancipation—
    Black and White," 99–103, 225n55. *See also* anthropology
hysteria, 73
Immaculate Conception, 195
Infants and Child Custody Bill (1839), 8–13, 130
Ingersoll, Robert G., 103, 207, 225n60, 236n54
insanity, 82
Isis, 209
J.W. Bangs, 184
Jacobi, Dr. Mary Putnam, 85, 223n40
James, Henry (Sr.), 199, 235–36n40
Jameson, Anna, 14, 135, 146, 147, 148, 195; *The Communion of
    Labour*, 113, 140–41, 142, 144, 164; "Woman's Mission and
    Woman's Position," 127, 128–30, 137

Jevons, W.S., 131–32, 133
Jews, status of women, 192–93
Jewsbury, Geraldine, 14
Jex-Blake, Sophia, 79
Jowett, Benjamin, 144
Julian, G.W., 50
Kant, 83
Karslake, John Burgess, 44–45, 48
Kaye, J.W., 5–6, 112
Kellogg, J.H., 73, 220n15
Kemble, Fanny, 102
Kemble, John, 9–11
Kingsley, Charles, 114, 159, 170, 211, 226n12; "The Tree of
    Knowledge," 171, 232n8
Knight of Continence, 58
Knowlton, Rev. Stephen, 234n27
Ladies' Benevolent Association, 84
Laing, Samuel, 45–46
Landels, William, 168, 176, 232n4
Langley, Miss, 177, 233n15
Lathbury, Bertha, 235n39
law
    affecting single women, 41
    concept of coverture: defined, 4; criticized—by B. Bodichon, 4;
        by C. Dall, 4–5; by J.W. Kaye, 5–6; by S. Anthony, 53; de-
        fended—by M. Oliphant, 6–7; by J. Karslake, 45; under-
        mined by married women's property rights, 7, 14, 22
    separate legal interests of men and women, 6, 44, 53
    custody: in America, 8; in Great Britain—Caroline Norton's
        campaign, 8–12; controversy over, 9–10, 12; reform of,
        12–13
    married women's property laws: provisions of—under com-
        mon law, 13–14; settlement an alternative to, 14, 19–20;
        criticism of—as inconsistent with women's entry into the
        work force, 14; as unjust, 15–16, 18–19; as evidence of a
        warped concept of love, 20–21; defense of existing laws—
        as a way to maintain husband's authority and efficient
        household management, 17, 19; as necessary to protect
        marriage, 17; as consistent with man's responsibilities as
        bread-winner, 18; as sign of wife's submission to hus-
        band, 18; reform of, 17, 21–22
    separation and divorce in Great Britain: grounds and proce-

law (*continued*)
    dures for, 23–24; arguments for reform—contradiction
    between common law and equity jurisprudence, 23; cost
    and complexity of administration, 24; inconsistency and
    immorality of the double standard, 24–25; parliamentary
    response to, 26–27
separation and divorce in America: grounds for, 26–28; in-
    crease in frequency of, 38–39; reaction against, 38–39
separation and divorce in New York: grounds for, 27–28;
    defense of existing laws—as necessary to prevent im-
    morality, 28; as derived from Scripture, 28–29; as neces-
    sary to restrain egotism, 28; as consistent with parent-
    hood, the divine end of marriage, 29; arguments for
    liberalization—as sanctioned by Christ's teaching, 28; as
    necessary to alleviate human suffering, 28; as necessary
    to protect the individual right to happiness, 30, 36; as an
    acknowledgment of woman's power within the home, 31;
    in order to release woman from oppression and degrada-
    tion, 30–31, 35–37; to allow for new equality in marriage,
    32; to recognize woman's moral superiority, 33
civil and ecclesiastical compared, 93–94, 210, 211
modern work on: Blake, N., Crane, F., Evans, R., Flexner, E.,
    Graveson, R., Howard, G., Kanner, S., Kanowitz, L.,
    McGregor, O., O'Neill, W., Reiss, E., Sachs, A., Strachey,
    R., Wilson, J., 212n1; Beard, M., 213n5; Basch, B., Rabkin,
    P., 213n16; Holcombe, L., 214n19; Mitchell, S., 214n22;
    Weisbrod, C., Sheingorn, P., 214n28; Baird, J., Wood-
    house, M., 215n29; Tanner, T., 215n31; Barnett, J.,
    O'Neill, W., 215n33
See also protective legislation, Contagious Diseases Acts, suf-
    frage, New York Marriage Debate, Susan B. Anthony,
    John Stuart Mill, Caroline Norton, Elizabeth Cady Stan-
    ton, and under specific laws
Le Bon, Gustave, 90
Lecky, W.E.H., 194, 234n32
Lee, Mother Ann, 201
Lee, Rev. Luther, 180, 233n19
Lewes, George, 147
Lewis, Sarah, 13, 111, 113
Linton, Eliza Lynn, 16, 39, 88, 200, 236n43
Littlejohn, Bishop, 210
Logan, Olive, 99
Longfellow, Henry Wadsworth, 142–43

Maudsley, Dr. Henry, 84, 85, 223n39, 223n40
Maurice, F.D., 141, 142, 235n32
Mayhew, Henry, 117, 152–53, 155
medicine, attacked, 74. *See also* anthropology, education, sexuality
Melbourne, William Lamb, second Viscount, 24
Melia, Rev. Raphael, 195, 235n35
menstruation, *see* education, scientific controversy over
Merivale, Charles, 200, 235n32, 236n45
Methodism, 175
Mill, Harriet Taylor, *see* Taylor, Harriet
Mill, James, 192
Mill, John Stuart, xi, xiv, 104, 114, 159, 211; on marriage, 22, 23; on suffrage—support of petition, 40; argument to amend Reform Bill (1867), 41–48; speech to House of Commons, 41–44, 47, 79; on birth control, 67, 219n6; *Subjection of Women*, 104, 148; opposition to protective legislation, 125, 136; modern work on, 214n27, 217nn48, 50
Millais, J.E., 155
Miller, Leo, 236n40
Milne, J.D., 228n33
Milton, John, 150, 169, 170, 174
Minor v. Happersett, 54
Miriam, 192
Mitchell, Maria, 78, 222n30
Mitchell, S. Weir, 73, 220n16
Mohamud, 58
Monod, Adolphe, 168
Moodie, Dwight L., 176, 232n11
Moore, A., 234n27
Morgan, Lady (Sidney Owenson), 160, 199, 236n42
Morgan, Lewis Henry, 90, 202
Morley, John, 158–59
Mormons, 207
Moses, 175, 192
motherhood: limited rights of, 3, 8, 12–13; maternal love and custody laws, 11–12; self-sacrifice and divorce laws, 31, 33; ideal of, 59, 192, 195; as restrictive, 69; women's right to regulate, 70; anthropologically considered, 90, 108; interference of work with, 121, 122–24, 128, 130–33; work nobler than, 145; and science, 197–99; as redemptive, 202–06; universal, 205

Cott, N., 230n63; Roberts, H., Bandelein, S.B., Nochlin, L., Edelstein, T.J., Auerbach, N., 230n67; Hammond, J.L. and B., Pivar, D., Walkowitz, J., 230–31n71; Johnson, G.W. and L.A., 231n77

protective legislation: principle of, 7, 12, 15, 17, 120, 121; short-hours debate, 121–30; maternity and infant mortality debate, 121, 130–33

Purity Crusade, see Social Purity Reform

Quarles, Benjamin, 225n56

racism, 49, 95, 98, 99

Redgrave, Richard: *The Sempstress,* illustration 2; *The Poor Teacher,* 226n13

Rees, Rev. Arthur Augustus, 167, 180, 183

Reform Bill (1832), 40

Reform Bill (1867): feminists' attempt to amend—Bodichon's petition, 40–41; Mill's speech to the House of Commons, 41–44, 47; parliamentary debate, 44–47. *See also* Mill, John Stuart

Reform Bill (1884), 54–55

Reid, Marion, 40

religion: under fire, 165; textual difficulties, 165–66; controversies, 166–67. *See also* Bible, Christianity, church work

Rigby, Elizabeth (Lady Eastlake), 119

Robinson, H., 227n18

Robinson, Mary Jane, 23

Roebuck, J.A., 125, 126–27, 136, 140

Rose, Ernestine L., 35–37

Rossetti, Christina, 39

Rossetti, D.G., 155

Rousseau, Jean Jacques, 73, 220n15

Royal Commission on Divorce, 24

Royal Society of Great Britain, 78

Royer, Clemence Augustine, 78

Rubens, 87

Ruskin, John, 113, 141

Russell, Bertrand, 219n6

Rye, Maria, 147

St. Ambrose, 172

St. Leonards, Edward Sugden, Baron, 9, 10–11, 17

St. Paul, 61, 165, 167, 168, 169, 171–72, 175, 178, 179, 180

Saint-Simonians, 23

Salvation Army, 183

Warner, Susan, 183
Watts, G.F., 155, 226n12
Webster's Spelling Book, 102
Wesley, John, 175, 182
White, Carlos, 192, 193, 194, 234n29
White Slave Crusade, 102
Whittier, John Greenleaf, 177, 233n16
Wilberforce, William, 91, 97
Wilkerson, Jemima, 201
Willard, Emma, 77, 221n28
Willard, Frances E., 164, 175, 234n27
witchcraft, 209
Wollstonecraft, Mary, xiii, xv, 167
woman
    nature of: weakness needs court protection, 15; morally
        superior, 31, 33, 151, 158, 160, 162–64; instinctive, 32;
        selfless, 33, 39, 113, 196; sympathetic, 39; lacking judg-
        ment, 39; and suffrage, 39, 46, 48; angel/scientist, 78;
        domestic angel, 86, 182; sexless, 62, 75, 151; childish, 66,
        91; maternal, 89–90, 91, 101, 107–08; True Woman, 96–
        97, 97–98, 115, 125, 147; altered by work, 113, 123;
        physically fragile, 122; suited to factory work, 126–27;
        suited to domestic service, 137–38; unsuited for celibacy,
        137; suited to social service, 138, 140–42; complementary
        to man 140–41; emotional, 170, 171, 177, 197. *See also*
        Angel in the House, Angel out of the House, Christianity,
        sexuality
    as property, 20–21, 23, 37
    duties of: domestic, 42, 111, 123–24, 128–29, 130, 131, 134,
        140–42; public, 140–42, 144, 146, 150
    defined in terms of males, 61, 64–65, 86, 104
    anatomy of, 73
    era of, 202–06
Woman Question, the, 56, 89, 91, 104, 105, 109, 181, 195; as
    real question, xi, xii; as ongoing public debate, xi–xii, na-
    ture of participants in, xii, xiii; nature of subjects de-
    bated, xii; Anglo-American character of, xiii; relation of
    earlier and later phases of debate, xiii, xv–xvi; relation
    between public perceptions and reality, xiii–xiv; definition
    of feminist and anti-feminist positions in, xiv–xv
Woman's Bible, 167, 208
Woman's Christian Temperance Union, 164

work, women's *(continued)*
    effects on marriage and home, 120, 121, 122–24, 128–29,
    130–31, 132–33; and laissez-faire economics, 121, 125,
    131, 136, 138, 140; maternity and infant mortality, 121,
    122–23, 128, 130–33; Parliamentary Blue Books, 121,
    122–23, 124, 127, 128; prevents education, 124, 128–29
  domestic service, 120, 126, 134, 137–38, 139, 159
  agricultural labor, 126, 134
  writers, 134, 146, 183–91
  middle class: ladies not educated for, 129, 134, 136; statistics
    on, 134; and True Womanhood, 134–35; economic need,
    134–35; desire for work, 135, 144–46, 149; single woman
    problem—statistics on, 135, 136, 139, 149; emigration,
    135, 136, 139; high standard of living contributes to,
    135, 139; Greg on, 136–39; use of prostitutes contributes
    to, 139; arguments against—Greg, 136–39; arguments
    for—Jameson, 140–43; Nightingale, 143–46; Bodichon,
    147–50; "ladies of Langham Place," 147; Society for the
    Employment of Women, 147; compatability with mar-
    riage, 149
  nursing, 138, 142–43
  church: non-ministerial, 176–77; ministerial, 180, 183; literary,
    183–91
  modern work on: Weisberg, D., 213n2; Pinchbeck, I., 225n3;
    Neff, W., 225n3, 226n12; Tilly, L. and Scott, J., 225n3,
    226n4; Hewitt, M., 226n4, 228n29; Edelstein, T.J.,
    226n12; Peterson, M.J., Thomson, P., 226n13; McBride,
    T., 226n17; Katzman, D., 227n17; DuBois, E., 227n17;
    Sumner, H., Dublin, T., Hutchins, B.L. and Harrison, A.,
    227n18; Brownlee, W.E. and M., 227n18, 227n27; Fryck-
    stedt, M.C., 227n20; Cott, N.F., 227n18, 228n34; Drake,
    B., Goldman, H., Andrew, J. and Bliss, W.D.P., Dye, N.;
    Cohea, T.O., Jacoby, R.M., 227–28n27; Branca, P.,
    228n29, 33; Davidoff, L., 228n33; Holcombe, L., 228n33;
    Hammerton, A.J., 228n38; Cook, E.T., 229n47; Burton,
    H., Reed, J., 229n54; Haight, G., 229nn54, 55, 56, 57
  Zoroaster, 58